The Comprehensive Guide

To

Passing the New York Real Estate Sales Exam

Real Estate Review

Types of Property

There are two main types of property that are discussed in real estate. They are *real* property and *personal* property. Real property mainly refers to the land and things or items that are permanently attached to it, such as plant life, ground minerals, and even buildings such as houses or offices. Things that grow on the property, such as trees, flowers and various other plants are considered part of the real property and are generally included with the land as a whole. Any fixture that causes damage to the property when it is moved is considered a real piece of property. When a person owns real property, they have more rights to its surrounding areas such as surface rights or air rights.

Personal property refers to property that is more tangible and moveable, such as furniture, swing sets, or mobile fixtures. Although plant life is generally seen as real property, it can be classified as personal property if it is superficially planted and can be moved when the property is sold. Personal property does not generally include many rights to the land and subpart rights.

Sometimes, personal property can become real property if it later becomes a permanent fixture of the land. For instance, if a house is built on a secure and sturdy foundation and cannot later be moved from the property, it has become part of the real property. However, a home such as an RV or mobile home can be moved from the property at any time, so it remains a piece of personal property.

Land Characteristics

There are many characteristics to describe land and land function. The main two that are considered are the physical characteristics and the economic characteristics.

Physical characteristics of land:

- **Immobility** – Land cannot be moved in its entirety, therefore it is considered immobile. Although pieces can be removed or replaced, the original part of the land still remains and will continue to grow.
- **Indestructibility** – Although land can be damaged by storms or disasters, it cannot be ultimately destroyed because it continues to change, adjust and develop over time. This is one of the main reasons land is considered such a valuable asset and investment.

- **Non-homogeneity** – Simply states that no two pieces of land are alike. Note the different features and location of items on each parcel of land and how they differ from the whole 'package'.

Economic characteristics of land:

- **Scarcity** – In many areas, land itself is considered a rarity, and owning a parcel of land can seem even more outrageous. When land is scarce and there is little to own, it not only drives up the face price, but it will also add value as an investment over time.
- **Improvements** – In many cases, minor improvements, such as decorative touches or adding a bathroom will not affect the economic value on the home, and may even work against the owner. However, structural upgrades, such as replacing the roof or replacing a broken wall, can add value to the home since they are improving the initial foundation of it. Many homeowners confuse these two and can make their house not as economic as they'd like.
- **Permanence** – Also known as 'fixity', permanence refers to the lasting potential of the land or property. Owners want to know that their property will be long term in nature and that what they have built on or created and cannot easily be moved or destroyed.
- **Situs** – Situs is the knowledge that some owners prefer specific locations, which can drive the value of the property up or down. Since the preferences of owners and buyers are always changing, this can be hard to determine at one point in time.

Encumbrances

An encumbrance is generally defined as a claim or lien on a parcel of real property. If a property has some sort of encumbrance attached to its title, it can be difficult to determine the proper owner and who has the rights to the property. Specific types of encumbrances include:

- **Encroachment** – A situation in which a structure or fixture is built on another person's property or land, and 'encroaches' on their area. This often happens due to incorrect surveying or incorrect marked boundary lines.
- **Easement** – A certain right to use the real property of another owner, such as paying rent for a building on their land or being allowed access to a privately owned lake. While the individual rights of the easement can vary, the easement is still considered a property right and is treated as such in courts of law.
    - **Easement Appurtenant** – Typically benefits the land and is transferred automatically if the property is transferred to another party – "runs with the land".
    - **Easement in Gross** – Typically benefits the individual or legal party and can be used for personal or commercial use. While this type of easement is not inherited or assignable, it can be transferred for business purposes.

- **Liens** – The official definition is "is a form of security granted over an item of property to secure the payment of a debt or obligation". Many liens require some form of documentation and specific guidelines that need to be followed.
    - **Mechanic's lien** – a lien that exists for real and personal property and initiated by those who have supplied labor or materials to improve the property (carpenters, landscapers).
    - **Material Man's lien** – similar to a mechanic's lien, but applies more to the actual person or company who supplies the actual materials being used.
- **Foreclosure** – a legal process in which the lender tries to recover the balance of a loan after payments have stopped, by selling the asset used as collateral for the loan. This is a very common term/practice with houses and property.
- **Judgment** – A type of lien that is meant to secure payment or property that was awarded in some kind of judgment or settlement.
    - **Writ of attachment** – a court order to seize an asset.
    - **Writ of execution** – written in order to force a judgment made against an asset, usually to collect an asset that has been ordered to be turned over.
- **Tax liens** – A type of lien obtained on the property, including all land rights, imposed by the government's taxing authority – typically used for payment of federal taxes.
    - **Property tax lien** – a lien to seize assets on a property or set of properties.
    - **Federal tax lien** – a lien to seize federal taxes that have not been paid.
    - **State tax lien** – a lien to seize state taxes that have not yet been paid.

Liens can be considered voluntary or involuntary in different cases. A homeowner may choose to enter a lien if he takes out a second mortgage on his home. However, the lien may not be voluntary if the government obtains a lien to the property in order to secure payment for back taxes and fees.

One common example of an involuntary lien is when a contractor is hired for work on the property, but when the owner doesn't pay for the job, the contractor can put a lien on the property to secure his/her payment. Since the general statute of limitations is four years for the contractor to pursue his claim, he can claim a lien long after the work is done. If this happens, the property owner will need to hire a lawyer to either reach a settlement or fight the claim in a court of law.

Ownership Types

When referring to ownership titles, it is important to remind the seller of the property that is it his responsibility to convey the marketable title to the public. The seller must be aware of instances that can make the property 'unmarketable', such as encumbrances, zoning restrictions, or outstanding interests. If the seller cannot produce a clear deed to the property, the buyer will be unaware of the full ownership.

- **Title search** – a process designed to determine if a seller of property has saleable interest, any restrictions or allowance for a property or any liens/foreclosures.
- **Chain of title** – a 'chain' of transfers of a title to a property. It usually involves investigating the line of previous owners up to the current owner.
- **Grantee index** – an alphabetic list of purchasers of the property.

- **Grantor index** – an alphabetical list of sellers of the property.

Terms to remember:

- **Estate in severalty** – a form of ownership in which the tenant owns the property without being joined in interest with another party.
- **Tenancy in common** – a form of ownership in which two parties possess the property simultaneously, created by a deed, final will or court order.
- **Joint Tenancy** – a form of ownership in which two parties own an undivided interest in the property. With joint tenancy, the right of survivorship is applicable. This means that a co-owner cannot designate a new owner to take over his interest when he dies. Instead, the surviving co-owner will automatically take over the decedent's interest.
    - **Unity of time** – interest acquired by both tenants at the same time.
    - **Unity of title** – interests held by co-owners from the same property.
    - **Unity of interest** – both tenants have the same interest in the same property.
    - **Unity of possession** – both tenants have the same right to the property.
- **Tenancy by entirety** – a form of ownership defined in New York as property owned by husband and wife. In order to receive this designation, the couple must be legally married when they obtain the title to the property. Tenancy by entirety is similar to community property rights, which exist only in Arizona, California, Idaho, Louisiana, Nevada, New Mexico, Texas, Washington, and Wisconsin.
- **Sole Proprietorship** – an individual who is the sole owner of a business organization may hold title in the name of the business and the name of the business owner. For example, Jill Jones owns Jill's Jelly Beans. Title to real property can be held as Jill Jones doing business as Jill's Jelly Beans.
- **Partnerships** – a property contract in which two people enter ownership equally together, each sharing in profits and losses from the property. A joint venture is similar to a partnership, usually involves a 'project' and is normally set for a limited amount of time. Under the Uniform Partnership Act which was adopted in New York, the partnership may hold title in the partnership's name as a tenancy in partnership.
    - **General partnership** – basic form of partnership; an association of people or unincorporated company that creates an agreement formed by two or more people and all parties are responsible for action, debts, and liability that occurs on the property.
    - **Limited partnership** – a partnership in which only one person is required to be a general partner, but both parties share in profits, debts and liability from the property.
- **Corporations** – a legal entity that has been incorporated and holds equal rights and liability for the property through a charter.
- **Fee simple estate** – a form of common law ownership; very popular in common law countries but still has restrictions by the government, such as taxation, police power and liability.

Property Descriptions

There are many different types of property and property deeds. Each one gives different characteristics to the property in question and can change the whole context in which someone views it. The three legal descriptions used in New York are:

- **Metes and bounds** – a method of describing real property that uses geography and land features with direction and distances to define and describe the boundaries of the land.
- **Recorded plat** – also known as the lot and block survey system; this system is used for lots in a variety of areas (i.e. heavily populated metropolitan, suburban, and exurbs). Especially used to plot large areas of a property into smaller lots and land areas.

  - Example plat map
  Source: http://en.wikipedia.org/wiki/Lot_and_Block_survey_system
- **Monument** – method that is sometimes used instead of metes and bounds. Surveyors use monument when they are describing large areas of land that may be too expensive to survey.

  Legal descriptions used in other states:

- **Rectangular survey system** – traditional method of surveying property and measures factors such as the precise length of line run, natural materials (flora/fauna), surface and land soil.
- **Government or US public land system** –Most commonly used method to survey and spatially identify land or property parcels before designating ownership, whether for sale or transfer.
- **Congressional townships** – a survey method that refers to a square unit of land that is usually six miles on each side. Each 36 square mile township is divided into 36 one-square mile sections that can be further subdivided for sale.
- **Principal meridians** – method that uses a principal meridian line used for survey control in a large region, which divides townships between north/south/east/west. The meridian meets its corresponding initial point for the land survey.
- **Assessor's parcel number** – also known as an appraisal's account number; a number assigned to parcels of property by the area's jurisdiction for identification and record-keeping. This APN is unique within the particular jurisdiction, and may conform to certain formatting standards that hold identifying information, such as the property type or location within the plat map.

Rights of Government in Land

The government can often draw a fine line as to where they have rights to land and where they don't. However, the U.S. government has the right to take private property for public use through the power of eminent domain and expropriation or taking power.

Escheatment is the transfer of one's property who doesn't have heirs when he/she dies. This process helps ensure that the property is not left unattended and appoints someone accountable for it, so as not to leave it in 'limbo'. Escheatments are commonly done when the owner of the estate passes away or loses ownership, although it can occur voluntarily between willing parties.

Property taxes are required on all land owned/financed in an area and are paid to the government. Multiple areas, or jurisdictions, can tax the same property at a time if it is being utilized in more than one area or claims more than one address. The tax is imposed by the government in which the property is located. It is made payable to the federal or state government. For property tax purposes, the government performs an appraisal of the quantity and value of each property, including real property and any improvements, and tax is assessed in proportion to that value. Appraisals are required by the government to assure that the property is being taxed appropriately.

Ad valorem taxes are taxes created specifically based on the monetary value of the property as a whole. This is the most common type of property tax and is usually created at the time of the purchase of the property, although it can be done on an annual basis as well.

Gains and Losses

A capital gain is realized when the property is sold and the sale price is more than the price that it was initially purchased for. Many jurisdictions impose a capital gains tax and require several forms of documentation to ensure accurate transactions.

Depreciation generally refers to the decrease in value over time. This can occur due to unfavored home modifications, damages, or changes in property costs and prices.

Estates

"Estate" generally refers to a person's property, entitlements or assets, but is usually applied to a large parcel of land that includes the real and personal property. It is usually defined as the houses and grounds of a very large property, including woodlands, farmlands, gardens or landscapes. Estates are generally owned by individual or joint ownership or title by contract.

- **Freehold estate** – an estate that has the exclusive right to the possession and use of the property for an indefinite amount of time.
  Fee simple absolute - the most common type of freehold estate ownership. This gives the owner a variety of rights, such as:
  -The authority to live in, rent or mortgage the property

-The authority to sell destroy or reassign ownership of the property

-The authority to construct buildings on the property

-The authority to excavate minerals, gas and oil

-The authority to refuse the use of property by others

- **Non freehold estate** – an estate similar to a lease or contract situation that holds limited rights and usage to the property and typically has a set or predetermined time period for the tenant.
- **Fee upon condition** – the fees/taxes of the property based on outside circumstances, such as home modifications, outside liens or holds on the property, or changes in the real estate market.
- **Life estate** – an estate that ends at the death of the owner and reverts to the original owner. The owner of the life estate is called the life tenant, and is designated ownership of the land for the duration of their life.
- **Pur autre vie** – "for another's life" - similar to a life estate, it states that a person's life interest will last for the life of another person's life instead of their own.
- **Remainderman** – an individual who inherits property when an estate is terminated from the former owner. This typically happens due to the death of the owner's life estate, but can also be a voluntary act.
- **Life estate in reversion** – a life estate ownership that 'reverts' back to the original owner or grantor.

If an estate wants/needs to be transferred between parties, it is usually done by one of two ways:

Deeds – deeds can be transferred from one party/person to another, usually done through the county office and completed while both parties are present; this process is usually voluntary but can be done involuntarily if ordered by a court of law.

Will/inheritance – deeds transferred after the original owner dies and designates it to another party; if a party is not assigned, the government can take control of the land and use it as they see fit (putting it up for sale or reassigning survey lines).

Governments Controls

Forms of public controls:

- Police power – government entities typically 'control' the rights to the property by creating laws or guidelines that must be followed when owning a parcel of property. Some common examples include development and zoning laws, which designate or restrict what structures or improvements can be made on the property. City codes, such as building or fire codes, often place restrictions on the occupancy of a property and can determine how a property is used or maintained.
- Eminent domain – the power to take private property for public use by a state, municipality, or private person or corporation; some common examples of property taken by eminent domain are for government buildings and facilities, highways or railroads or for public safety hazards.
  - Condemnation – the process of exercising powers of eminent domain

- o Severance damage – payment to a property owner for an inconvenience that is caused once a portion or all of the land is purchased and used under eminent domain.
  - o Inverse condemnation – a situation where the government seizes the property, but fails to pay the compensation required by the 5th Amendment rights of the Constitution.
  - o Consequential damage – damages you can prove occurred because of the failure of one party to meet a contractual obligation; commonly referred to as a breach of contract.
- Environmental Hazards and Regulations – laws, guidelines, and regulations the government puts into place to help monitor and regulate different aspects of the country, including physical property, plant life, animals and surrounding environments.
  - o The Clean Air Act – signed into law in 1970 and was aimed at controlling air pollutants produced by industrial companies. Since 1970, over 40 amendments have been added to the original law.
  - o The Clean Water Act – passed in 1972 and is aimed at controlling water pollution; addresses a popular problem of water dumping by companies and individuals.
  - o National Environmental Policy Act – created after the 1969 Santa Barbara oil spill; it made the entity of the property, commercial or private, responsible for ensuring the safety of the environment, including pollution or any chance of accidents.
  - o Comprehensive Environmental Response, Compensation, and Liability Act (CERLA) – created in 1980, it was designed to be a 'superfund' that supplies resources to hazardous wastes sites, such as oil spills or spilled contaminants. Through CERLA, entities responsible for the spill are also responsible for the cleanup.
  - o The Endangered Species Act – created in 1973 and is designed to provide protection for wildlife and flora that is at risk of becoming extinct; among many provisions, it states that animals considered endangered are not allowed to be hunted or harmed and that state government can seize any land that is needed to preserve the species.
  - o The Safe Drinking Water Act – created in 1974 and was created to ensure the safety and quality of America's drinking water; it is designed to protect drinking water sources, such as rivers, lakes and reservoirs.
  - o The Toxic Substances Control Act – passed in 1976 and regulates any new or existing chemical substances and their use; it requires companies to submit notifications and information regarding any new chemical created and added to the TSCA list.
  - o Residential Lead-Based Paint Hazard Reduction Act – passed in 1992 and aimed at reducing the number of residences that have lead-based paint, as this type of paint has been associated with many health hazards.

Forms of private controls:

Conditions – generally refers to the status of property, such as current structures and how the property is sustained. Many restrictions are attached to the condition of the property and how it will look and appear in the future.

Covenants – simply defined as a promise to uphold a requested action or use; covenant are often added to deed ownerships to restrict actions taken against the property, such as physical changes or structure formations.

Restrictions – strict prohibitions that generally 'restrict' against certain actions or behaviors; with property restrictions, the owner specifically lines out actions that cannot be done on or with the property. This can range from adding structure or modifications to restrictions on ownership and transfer of ownership.

Restrictive covenants and deed restrictions are one method that private land owners use to control the property, even after they have passed ownership to another person or party. These regulations are designed to impose rules that the owner may want to place on the property to future owners regarding new buildings, structures, or use of the land. The restrictions the owner wants to set forth are usually plainly laid out in the deed itself or in an additional covenant and are normally binding to all future owners. One common example is owners of land that restrict any use of commercial building or structures, such as condominiums or apartment buildings.

A homeowner's association (HA) is a corporation or private party formed by a real estate developer and is designed to market, manage or sell homes in a specific subdivision area. These associations are popular in metropolitan areas that group their homes in suburban divisions. Many HAs are managed by the residents that live in the division, although there are higher 'board members' that govern any final rulings or decisions. This is a form of private control because individuals that live in these divisions are often restricted on what they can do with their property, such as modifications, building add-ons or even minor home improvements.

Air Rights

Air rights refer to the air above the earth. Landowners have the right to use, sell or lease that airspace in accordance with zoning ordinances and other laws.

Water Rights

Although water rights vary by state, there are two that are common nationwide. These are riparian rights and littoral rights.

- **Riparian rights** – When dealing with a navigable body of water, the property owner's boundary will reach to the water's accretion line. With a non-navigable body of water, the property owner's boundary will stop at the water's centerpoint.
- **Littoral rights** – Take into consideration the rights of a property owner whose property shares a border with a non-flowing body of water like a lake or ocean.
  Some terms to keep in mind with water rights:
    - Accretion – Natural deposit of soil that results in the steady increase in land
    - Avulsion – When water abruptly changes its course sudden, the rapid decrease in land that results

- Erosion – When water, wind and other natural elements cause a steady decrease in land
- Reliction – When the retreat of water causes a steady increase in land
- Alluvion – When water shifts soil from where it is to another person's land
- Accession – Attaining land due to the soil deposited by natural elements

Individual states issue water permits for the purpose of allotting scarce water resources, this is especially necessary in states in the west.

Other nationally recognized water rights:

- **Natural flow doctrine** – This doctrine says that if a riparian owner's use of the water causes the water to diminish in the amount, quality, or pace, it can be stopped. All riparian owners have the right to have access to the water in its natural state.
- **Doctrine of reasonable use** – As its name states, each riparian owner is entitled to reasonable use of the water. In other words, unless one owner's use severely inhibits another owner's use, it cannot be stopped. "Reasonable use" can be determined by assessing changes to water quantity, quality, velocity, pollution issues, among other things.
- **Doctrine of prior appropriation** - Refers to the water rights that are not linked to landownership. They can be sold and mortgaged in the same way other property can.
- **Doctrine of beneficial use** – States that the first users of the water are priority, but they must use the water in a beneficial manner, within a reasonable timeframe.
- **Doctrine of correlative rights** – Imposes a limit on landowners regarding their share of the water. Generally, this limit is based on the share of land owned by each.

Property Conditions

Property Condition Disclosure Forms

Usually before signing a purchase agreement, but at least before closing, salespersons/brokers are required to provide potential buyers with a document that explains the condition of the property they're looking to buy. If the proper disclosures (varies per state) have not been made, the purchase contract may become unenforceable. A $500 credit from the seller to the buyer will also result. It is also important that rather than salespersons/brokers giving their own description of the property condition, they should encourage the potential buyers to have an inspection done.

The Stigmatized Property disclosure, which is outlined by Article 443-a of the New York Real Property Law is also an important disclosure when comes to the condition of the property. This disclosure covers all residential properties and states a seller or his agent is not required to inform the buyer or his agent that a former occupant had AIDS or other diseases that are not transmitted via occupancy, nor are they required to inform of any deaths that took place inside the property.

Other Disclosure Types

Electrical Service: If none is available at the place being purchased, the buyer or his agent must receive notification.

Utility Surcharge: The buyer or his agent must receive notification if the property being purchased has a gas or electric utility surcharge imposed upon it.

Agricultural Districts: If the property being purchased is partially or fully located in a state-mandated agricultural district, the buyer must receive notification.

The need for inspection

There are many instances where having an inspection done would be warranted, although not carried out. For the real estate purchaser, it is advisable that a thorough, professional inspection is done before agreeing to purchase the property. Not doing so could result in costly repairs down the line for the buyer, or even legal action against the real estate company.

Property Value

Why an Appraisal?

The first step to performing an appraisal is finding out why the appraisal should be done. Here are the more common reasons:

- condemnation: In cases where the government uses eminent domain to acquire property, the owner must be compensated fair market value.
- assessed value: In order to determine the property taxes that must be paid on the property.
- insurance reasons: So the insurance company can establish the most it will pay for a loss.
- estate settlement: In order to verify the value of a deceased individual's estate.
- sales value for owner: To determine how much the property should be sold for.
- loan value: To establish the maximum loan amount that can be secured by the property.
- exchanges: In cases where the owner of a property is going to trade for another property instead of selling it.

How to Estimate Value

What are the steps to the appraisal process?

- Articulate the problem – why is the appraisal being done?
- Decide what information you need.
    - -Are there any factors to take into consideration that will help determine the value?

-What approach should be taken to determine value?

- Identify the highest and best use of the property.
- Determine a ballpark figure of the value of the site.
- Use the market data, cost, and income approaches to identify the property's value.

-Market data: The appraiser selects comps, usually three that have sold within the past six months, and compare their prices to the property being appraised.

-Cost: The appraiser estimates how much it will cost to make improvements to the property. This is known as replacement cost. The appraiser may also estimate how much it will cost to create a duplication of the improvements (reproduction cost). This will give the value of the property.

The land value is also a crucial part in determining the overall property value.

With the cost approach, it is important to remember that in some cases adjustments may need to be made to take depreciation into consideration. There are three types of depreciation: physical deterioration (general wear and tear), functional obsolescence (features of the property that are no longer ideal), and economic obsolescence (aspects that the owner cannot control, such as economic or environmental influences).

The formula for determining value using this approach is:

Value = Replacement or Reproduction Cost – Accrued Depreciation + Land Value

-Income: This approach is common in properties that result in income or some other type of revenue.

The first step is to determine the effective gross income which is done so by adding income from all sources and deducting vacancy and collection losses. Next, subtract maintenance and operating expenses. This will give the net operating income. The capitalization rate is what the owner wishes as a return on investment.

The formula is: Value = Net operating income ÷ Capitalization rate

- Reconcile the values arrived at using the different approaches and decide the most probable value.
- Report findings to client using a narrative appraisal report (lengthy, detailed account of findings) or Uniform Residential Appraisal Report (form report typically used for single-family residential appraisals).

What elements establish value?

Demand for the type of property

Utility (desirable use) the property offers

Scarcity of properties available

Transferability of property to a new owner (lack of impediments to a sale)

Terms to remember regarding value:

- Anticipation: The expected worth of the property while owning it and possible gains when selling it.
- Assemblage (plottage): Bringing together adjoining parcels under the same ownership for purposes such as commercial or residential development. This could potentially increase the worth of the parcels.
- Change: Whether physical, political, economical, social or environmental, all properties can be affected by it and result in an increase or decrease of worth.
- Conformity: Generally speaking, properties that are similar to other properties in the neighborhood typically have higher values than those that are not.
- Competition: Can result in higher or lower priced homes, depending on the number of sellers that are brought into the market. If there are a lot of sellers, that may drive the home prices down, while if there are only few sellers, this could be a shortage of properties which could mean higher prices.
- Highest and best use: The maximum use of a property that is legally allowed, which typically produces the most income.
- Law of decreasing returns: When property improvements do not result in an increase in property value.
- Law of increasing returns: When property improvements do result in an increase in property value.
- Progression: The advantage to a property of being located in a desirable area.
- Regression: The disadvantage to a property being located in a less desirable area.
- Substitution: The idea that a buyer does not want to pay more for a property than he would pay for an equivalent property.
- Supply and demand: More properties and less buyers = Lower prices
  Less properties and same/more buyers = Higher prices

Competitive or Comparative Market Analysis (CMA)

In some states, real estate brokers have the authority to prepare property appraisals. In doing so, the broker must be sure to follow the uniform standards as well as inform the potential buyer that the CMA is not an appraisal.

The purpose of the CMA is to allow the homeowner (seller) and potential buyer to have property range of value in a particular area for a certain period of time. With Comparative Market Analysis, properties that have been sold are used. With Competitive Market Analysis, properties that have been sold as well as those that are listed but have not been sold are used.

Given the range of asking/purchase prices of all the properties used, the homeowner (seller) has a more accurate picture of his own realistic home asking price. A seller who asks for more than what is realistic may not attract much interest, which could in turn prevent him from having a buyer. The potential buyer also has an idea of what a fair offer would be. A potential buyer who offers an amount that is lower than what is fair for the property may insult the seller and lose the opportunity to purchase the property or even negotiate with the seller.

Important Contracts/Documents

A contract is executory when the duties under it have not been completely fulfilled. A contract is executed when the duties under it have been completely fulfilled.

The different contracts/documents are:

New York State Disclosure Form for Buyer and Seller: Should accompany every real estate listing agreement for the sale or rental of residential properties. The form must be read, acknowledged, and signed by the buyer or seller.

Listing: Details of agreement between a brokerage and homeowner regarding the sale of a particular property.

Offer to Purchase: Typically in fill-in-the-blank format and displays the terms of the sale of a property (e.g. price). Contingencies are also included.

Exclusive Agency Agreement: States that only a particular broker can list the property.

Open Listing Agreement: States that a seller will allow a property to be shown by one or several brokers.

Exclusive Right to Rent Agreement: States that the listing agent will receive the rental fee regardless of who rents out the property.

Lease: Contract between a renter and owner/manager. The renter is entitled to use the property for the time outlined in the contract (lease).

Deed: Written document that transfers title to real property.

Mortgage note: An IOU that spells out the terms by which the borrower agrees to repays the loan.

Mortgage deed: Explains the collateral (the property) to be used as repayment of debt in case of default.

Bilateral contract: Both parties have responsibilities to fulfill.

Unilateral contract: Only one party has responsibilities to fulfill.

Purchase and Sale Agreement: Thoroughly explains the responsibilities of each party included in the Offer to Purchase. This document is usually signed once the buyer has completed a home inspection.

There are several key elements included on the Purchase and Sale Agreement to make it valid. These are:

- The names of all parties involved
- A land description
- The sales price
- The amount of earnest money provided by the buyer
- The contract date
- Buyer and seller signatures

The New York Statute of Frauds says that the Purchase and Sale Agreement be in writing. Once signed, the buyer has equitable title, which means he has interest in the property even though the transaction is not fully complete. Once the transaction is fully complete, the buyer has legal title to the property which gives him all of the rights associated with it.

The majority of Purchase and Sale Agreements give buyers the "right to assign", which means they can assign the contract to someone else, however, they are not off the hook for the requirements of the contract in the case where the new assignee does not fulfill his duties under the contract.

Breach of Contract

A breach of contract is when one party of a contract fails to uphold his duties outlined in the contract. When this occurs, the party who is aggrieved can be compensated by doing the following:

- Suing for monetary damages
- Suing for the party who breached the contract to fulfill his duties under the contract
- If the seller is the one wronged, he can sue for liquidated money damages (i.e. keeping the earnest money deposit)
- Both parties agreeing to annul the contract

Termination of an offer

A purchase offer can be terminated if one of the following conditions exists:

- Either of the parties dies
- The timeframe of the offer expires
- The offeror revokes before being informed that the offeree accepts
- Either party becomes bankrupt
- The property is destroyed or condemned
- The offeree rejects a counteroffer

Counteroffers are used in response to the initial offer regarding the sale/purchase of a property. The individual to whom the counteroffer is made may immediately agree with the counteroffer or further negotiate until a mutually agreed upon offer is reached.

In order to be valid, contracts should:

- Include an offer and acceptance
- Explain the consideration to be used (does not necessarily have to be money)
- Outline the objective, must be legal
- Involve competent parties
- According to the Statute of Frauds, must be in writing (unless lease is for a year or less)
- Signed by both parties, giving their consent

Valid/void/voidable contracts

- Valid contract: Legal, binding and enforceable.
- Void contract: Not legal, binding, or enforceable.
- Voidable contract: Binding for one party but not the other.

Financing

What is the Cycle of Real Estate?

1. The property is listed

2. The buyer is qualified

3. The buyer is shown the property

4. The agreement between the buyer and seller is signed

5. The buyer finalizes and secures financing

6. The closing occurs

Mortgage Markets

The two types of mortgage markets are primary and secondary. With the primary market, loans are sold directly to borrowers. In the secondary market, the loans that are executed in the primary market are made to investors.

Common purchasers of home loans are:

- The Federal National Mortgage Association (Fannie Mae) – purchases all types of home loans.
- The Federal Home Loan Mortgage Corporation (Freddie Mac) – purchases conventional loans.

- The Government National Mortgage Association (Ginnie Mae) – purchases FHA and VA loans.

Conventional loans: Loans that have no insurance backing from the government. The lender expects the borrower to pay back the loan or endure a foreclosure of the property.

VA-guaranteed loans: Loans that are backed by the Department of Veteran Affairs that the lender will be compensated in the case of the borrower defaulting. In order to be eligible for such a loan, the individual must be a veteran who has been issued a certificate of eligibility by the Department. In addition, the home the borrower wants to buy must be appraised by an appraiser approved by the VA, at which time the VA will issue a certificate of reasonable value. Other stipulations regarding the holders of VA-guaranteed loans are:

- The loan can only be for 1 – 4 family, owner occupied residences.
- There may be a funding fee associated with the loan, depending on the veteran's category and down payment amount. The funding fee is typically 0 – 10%, but can be more.
- Prepayment penalties cannot be assessed with these loans.
- Although the property can be sold at a later time to another veteran or non-veteran, the current borrower must get a "release of liability" notice from the VA so that he/she is not held liable for possible future foreclosure or deficiency.

Federal Housing Administration (FHA) loans: Loans are administered through HUD and protect the lender in case the borrower defaults on the loan.

Stipulations regarding FHA loans are:

- The FHA decides on the maximum amount in loan amounts.
- During closing, the borrower must pay an upfront mortgage insurance premium.
- Prepayment penalties cannot be assessed with these loans.
- The loan can only be for 1 – 4 family, owner occupied residences.
- These loans may be assumed. However, if a new borrower assumes the loan of an existing borrower, both would be responsible in the case of a deficiency due to a foreclosure.
- Lower than normal down payments may be acceptable. However, if the borrower pays less than 20% down payment, he may be required to purchase private mortgage insurance.

Rural Housing Service: The loans offered through the agency are geared toward supporting family farms and finance rural housing.

State of New York Mortgage Agency (SONYMA): Offers a below-market interest rate as well as low down payments and no pre-payment penalties. Closing assistance is also available. The program must allocate a specific percentage of the funds for properties in distressed areas.

Construction loan: Given to a developer or builder on a short-term basis. Funds are received according to construction completion phases. Once built, the builder/developer must obtain long term financing.

Blanket mortgage: A developer or contractor is given funds to purchase several lots of land. With this type of mortgage, a release clause is common, which means the developer/contractor can sell a land parcel while maintaining the mortgage on the rest of the property.

Package mortgage: Personal property and real estate are used as collateral.

Demand mortgage: Allows the lender to require payment whenever it wants to.

Purchase money mortgage: The seller of the property is financing for the buyer.

Junior (second) mortgage: Loan in addition to the primary mortgage. In cases where default occurs, this loan may or may not be paid, depending on whether or not the primary loan is fully paid.

Open-end mortgage: Gives the borrower the option of borrowing additional funds on top of what is initially borrowed, up to a certain amount, without having to complete documentation to rewrite the mortgage.

Wraparound mortgage: Merge a new loan and existing loan. Payment is made on both mortgages to the wraparound mortgagee, who then forwards the payments to the appropriate mortgagee.

Variable (adjustable) rate mortgage: Over the life of the loan, the interest rate can increase or decrease, depending on the Treasury Bill Index. There is a cap set on how much the rate can increase during each rate change period and life of loan.

Balloon loan: Starts of charging a lower than normal fixed-rate loan, but after a certain amount of time, will "balloon". The time at which the loan balloons varies with each lender, but is typically 5, 7, or 10 years. Once the loan balloons, the borrower must pay off the loan.

Shared equity loan: The lender loans the funds at a low interest rate in exchange for a portion of the property's equity.

Equity loan: A second mortgage. It is used to access the equity in the home, to be utilized for making improvements to the property or other reasons.

Negative amortization: The rate of an adjustable rate mortgage increases, but the payment each month stays the same. This results in the payment not being enough to pay the principal and interest, which means the deficit amount is tacked on to the outstanding principal balance.

Straight (term) loan: Loan that is interest only. The total loan amount is due at the maturity date of the loan.

Fully amortized loan: Loan that is principal and interest. At the maturity date, the loan will be paid in full.

Partially amortized loan: Loan that is principal and interest. This is short term, so a balloon payment will be made at the maturity date.

Fixed rate loan: Set interest rate over the life of loan. Term, fully amortized and partially amortized loans can include this feature.

How Does the Buyer Secure Financing?

Once the buyer completes a mortgage application, the lender (savings and loan association, commercial bank, mutual savings bank, cooperative bank, credit union, mortgage company, life insurance company, or private lender) completes several steps in deciding whether or not to approve the application. These steps are: 1. Have an appraisal done of the property in question 2. Evaluate the buyer's potential to pay the loan 3. Review the buyer's credit history

Purchase and Sale Agreement forms typically include a financing clause. This means that language is included in the form to protect the buyer in case he does not receive the funding necessary to purchase the property. If funding is not received, he can withdraw his application and receive any earnest money deposits made.

Terms regarding funding

Discount rate: Interest rate charged by the Federal Reserve Bank to financial institutions that loans are made to.

Prime rate: Interest rate charged by banks to preferred borrowers.

Mortgage rates: Rates used for long term loans.

Origination points: Fee paid by borrowers for loan being approved. Each point is 1% of the loan.

Discount points: Paid by the borrower at the start of the loan in order to get a lower interest rate for the life of the loan.

Truth-in-Lending Act: Enacted by Congress in 1968 as a part of the Consumer Protection Act. It is also known as Regulation Z and applies to lenders who conduct more than 25 consumer credit transactions in a year, has more than 5 transactions in a year with a residence used as a security, and/or offers credit to consumers.

Equal Credit Opportunity Act: Creditors are prohibited from discriminating against applicants during credit transactions on the basis of race, color, religion, national origin, sex, marital status, or age.

Home Mortgage Disclosure Act: Financial institutions are required to make annual disclosures about home purchases, refinances, etc. regarding 1 – 4 unit residences.

Community Reinvestment Act: Promotes the idea that commercial banks and savings associations work to help fulfill the financial needs of consumers in all areas, low to high income.

Fair Credit Reporting Act: The collection, disbursement, and utilization of consumer information is regulated via this Act.

Fair and Accurate Credit Transactions Act: Once every twelve months, consumers are able to obtain a free credit report from each of the three credit reporting agencies (Equifax, Experian, and TransUnion).

Gramm-Leach-Billey Act: Financial institutions are required to safeguard the sensitive information of their consumers a well as explain to them the company's information-sharing practices.

Contracts / Agency

Leases

Leases are enforceable when signed by both the landlord and tenant. Leases include a description of the property and do not have to be recorded.

Leases commonly used:

Gross lease: States that the landlord is responsible for paying expenses (i.e. property taxes, insurance, and maintenance costs). Apartment complexes typically use this type of lease.

Net lease: States that the tenant is responsible for paying expenses (i.e. property taxes, insurance, and maintenance costs).

Percentage lease: States that the tenant will pay a percentage of gross sales as rent as well as a base rental amount. This lease is usually used in leases including shopping centers.

Operating stop (expense stop) lease: The tenant and owner share expenses. Typically, the owner will pay a certain amount and the tenant will pay anything that is above that amount.

Office-building lease: A combination of a gross and net lease. The initial expenses are paid by the landlord, then each tenant pays a pro rata amount of the expenses that exceed that.

Graduated lease: States the changes that take place in rent (increase or decrease) over the lease's term.

Ninety-nine year lease: Used in cases like when the owner does not want to sell or the tenant wants to use its funds on capital improvements. Many times used for commercial development.

Leases may be assigned, meaning the individual who originally signed the lease as lessee transfers the entire remaining lease to a third party. Another option for transferring a lease is to sublet, which means only part of the lease is transferred. Whether the original lessee assigns or sublets a lease, the original lessee is still on the hook for the lease being honored. In order to remove the original lessee as responsible, novation must be imitated. Novation is when the original lease is substituted for a new lease. Not all leases allow for the lease to be transferred to another lessee.

What are the Obligations of the Lessor and Lessee?

Lessor:

- Utility services (Lessee typically has to pay for these services, but the lessor must make them available)
- Property that is inhabitable
- Property that does not violate sanitary and/or building codes
- Allow the lessee to have quiet enjoyment of the property
- Not interfere with the lessee's right to a constructive eviction if property is inhabitable or lessor does not allow lessee to have quiet enjoyment of the property
- If collects a security deposit from the lessee (must be deposited into an interest bearing account) and the lessee lives in the apartment for a year or more, the lessee is entitled to the interest paid by the bank (5% or interest paid, whichever is less)

Lessee:

Use the property in the proper manner:

- Keep the property clean
- Use property appliances and fixtures as they are designed to be used
- Do not destroy property or allow others to do so

Additional Considerations for Leases:

Possession and Habitability

In New York, tenants are entitled to inhabit a "livable, safe, and sanitary" apartment. In other words, landlords that do not provide things such as heat and running water are violating this rule. The possession and habitability law is required for cooperative apartments, but not condominiums.

Improvement

As per New York's Multiple Dwelling Law and Multiple Residence Law, the landlord is responsible for keeping the building in good shape.

Rent Control

Rent control is observed in 51 municipalities of New York. An example of how rent control is implemented is the Maximum Base Rent system, which is set for each individual apartment. The landlords are allowed to raise the rent 7.5% each year until it reaches the Maximum Base Rent amount.

In the case of a rent controlled apartment becoming vacant, it becomes rent stabilized or decontrolled.

Rent Stabilization

This protects tenants from steep rent increases while still being allowed to renew their leases. "Rent stabilization" is known as Emergency Tenant Protection Act in places outside of New York City.

Decontrolled Rent-Regulated Unit

All units that are rent controlled become decontrolled when a tenant moves out, unless the tenant leaves under severe circumstances, such as being harassed.

Options

An option allows an individual to purchase a property at a certain amount if done so within a specified timeframe. Options are created by the property owner and must be in writing. Options are assignable without approval from the property owner.

Agency Law

An agent is the one who represents the fiduciary interest of his/her client. There are two types of agencies: single and dual. In a single agency, the agent works on behalf of either the buyer or seller. In a dual agency, the agent works on behalf of the buyer and seller. In the case of a dual agency in the state of New York, it is allowed as long as informed consent and disclosure are present.

The fiduciary duties are:

Obedience

Loyalty

Disclosure (of material facts concerning the transaction)

Confidentiality

Accountability (of funds)

Reasonable care

A real estate company can either be set up so that all agents in the company have the same relationship with the customer OR only the agent listed on the disclosure form can represent the customer.

There are several relationship options between the agent and potential buyer or seller. These are:

- Seller's agent – Represents the seller in all aspects of the transaction and owes all fiduciary duties to the seller.
- Buyer's agent – Represents the buyer in all aspects of the transaction and owes all fiduciary duties to the buyer.
- Facilitator – Brings the buyer and seller together but does not act on behalf of either party as agent. Does not owe fiduciary duties to either party.

- Designated seller's and buyer's agent – Represents his/her client (either the buyer or seller) and owes all fiduciary duties to client. If the client agrees, the agent can be "designated" as the client's only agent.
- Dual agent – Represents the buyer and seller. All fiduciary duties cannot be given to either party. In New York, this is only allowed if disclosure and written consent are present.

Listing Types

Open: States that the broker will get paid a commission if (s) he secures a buyer, which results in the sale of the property. This can be done between a seller and as many brokers (s) he would like. If the listing broker does not sell the home, but rather the homeowner or another broker, the listing broker does not get paid the commission.

Exclusive agency: The seller can only enter into agreement to sell with one broker. If the broker actively sells the house or the house is sold through MLS, the broker will be paid the commission. If the homeowner sells the house on his own, he will not pay commission to the broker.

Exclusive right to sell: States the listing broker will receive the commission on the sale of the property regardless of who actually sells it.

Net: States that the homeowner will receive a specific amount from the sale of the property. Anything received over that amount will go to the listing broker. This type of arrangement is illegal in New York.

Multiple listing service (MLS): System used to display information all members have with regard to real estate property they have for sale.

Termination of Agency

Agency contracts can be terminated by:

- completion of the objective
- time limit expiration
- rescission
- revocation
- death of the principal or broker
- property destruction
- bankruptcy of either party

How are agents paid?

Agents guarantee payment for services by working under some type of agreement (i.e. contract, listing agreement, or buyer-agency representation agreement).

According to *Tristam's Landing versus Wait* decision, the broker who is entitled to the commission is the one who has "procured a ready, willing, and able buyer."

What is a commission split?

When properties are sold, the commission paid for the sale is dividing among many parties. This can include a co-broker, broker-owner, and agent. Different real estate offices choose different ways to split the commission. For example, some offices take off the top a fee that covers operating expenses, while others may charge the agent a set monthly fee that takes care of overhead.

The New York Commission Escrow Act

This act applies to one- to four- unit residential properties, individual condominiums, and cooperatives. It helps protect brokers and sales agents and their right to receive all the commissions due. The seller must deposit with the County Clerk any amounts that are not paid to the broker. The seller must also sign a written listing agreement.

If necessary to start a lawsuit to receive the remaining owed funds, the broker must file an Affidavit of Entitlement with the County Clerk.

Licensing requirements in New York

What Are the Types of Licenses?

Real Estate Broker: For a fee, this individual performs the above activities for another person.

Real Estate Salesperson: Individual cannot perform negotiations but can perform the above activities. A salesperson must always work under the cover of an employer broker. If the salesperson or broker is a non-resident, she can hold a New York real estate license, but is required to take the New York licensure exam and if not one of the states with which New York has a reciprocity agreement, work or maintain an office in New York.

Reciprocity is when a state does not require a New York licensee to pass their exam or have an office in their state in order to practice real estate in their state, and New York extends the same to licensees in these states.

States with which New York has reciprocity:

- Arkansas
- Colorado
- Connecticut
- Georgia
- Massachusetts
- Mississippi
- Oklahoma

- Pennsylvania
- West Virginia

What Makes One Eligible for Licensing?

An individual is eligible for a salesperson license if he:

- Is at least 18 years old
- Fulfills 75 hours of qualifying course(s)
- Successfully completes the exam
- Obtains broker sponsorship

An individual is eligible for a broker's license if he:

- Is at least 20 years old
- Is a licensed salesperson and has been actively employed by a broker for two years, has three years' equivalent real estate experience, or a combination of the two
- Fulfills 120 hours of qualifying educational instruction
- Successfully completes the exam

Under normal circumstances, a real estate license is valid for two years. Agents will renew their license online and can do so up to three months before it is set to expire. In addition, 22.5 hours of approved continuing education must be completed. If the salesperson / broker does renew their license before it expires, the license is set to inactive status. With an "inactive" license, individuals cannot practice real estate. The licensee has two years from the date of expiration to renew the license. If not, she will have to re-take the NYS exam and submit another application and fee.

There are many activities in New York, as related to real-estate that require a license to perform when a fee is charged. These include:

- sales
- exchanges
- purchases
- rentals/leases
- negotiates
- offers
- listing
- options
- advertise real property
- prospecting
- loan negotiating
- apartment search

What activities do not require a real estate license?

- Attorneys allowed to practice in New York Courts
- Public officers while performing official duties
- Individuals under the judgment or order of the court
- Tenants' associations and nonprofit organizations
- Building superintendents and maintenance personnel

Statutory Requirements Governing Activities of Licenses

Advertising requirements:

- Misleading or false advertising is prohibited by brokers
- Advertising without disclosing the fact that the broker is a real estate broker is forbidden
- Advertising property under the salesperson's name is not allowed
- Advertising that's done in a way that directly or indirectly discriminates against any group is prohibited

Salespersons cannot be self-employed, but must be hired by a real estate broker as an employee or independent contractor. Brokers can compensate salespersons via payment, fees, or commissions. Brokers are responsible for the actions of their salespersons.

Brokers are also responsible for maintaining a place of business and making the Board aware of any changes regarding location. A copy of the broker's license must be displayed in an area of the office that is visible to the public. In addition, the broker must let the Board know all of the agents affiliated with the firm. If an agent leaves, the Board must be informed...if a new agent joins the firm, the Board must be informed.

Clients should not be advised by the agent to avoid securing the representation of an attorney at any point of the transaction.

Sherman Anti-Trust Act

The Sherman Anti-Trust Act prohibits many business practices that could unfairly restrict marketplace free competition. Some of these include:
- No price fixing
- Real estate companies cannot offer services in only particular geographical areas
- Real estate companies cannot consciously direct business away from other real estate companies
- Salespersons/brokers cannot create organizations that unfairly exclude qualified brokers from having access to marketing and sales information.

Settlement and the Conveyance of Property

Settlement procedures: Who brings/does what?

Seller:

- Deed
- Current property tax certificates
- Insurance policies
- Termite inspections
- Survey maps
- Keys, garage door openers, etc.

Additional documents that the seller may have to provide in the case of selling an income-producing property, include:

- Leases
- Operating statements
- Estoppel letters from the tenants
- Maintenance contracts

Buyer:

- Monies (good funds)
- Survey
- Insurance policy
- Flood insurance policy
- Termite certificate

The closing agent/officer:

- Ensure signatures are correctly executed
- Make sure copies are made and distributed to appropriate parties involved
- Issue checks, if applicable
- Forward the deed to be recorded

Attorneys for the buyer and seller may be present at the closing.

All applicable disclosures must be presented at closing (e.g. Lead-based paint).

Before closing takes place, the majority of lenders require a termite inspection of the property, appraisal, and proof that the buyer has insurance that covers the property in the case of fire, flood, casualty, or wind damage. This all done to ensure that the property is sufficient collateral.

Purpose of closing/settlement

Right before the closing takes place, the buyer and his broker (if applicable) do a final walk-through of the property to make sure it is in the condition agreed upon by the seller and buyer.

Real Estate Settlement and Procedures Act

Consumers complained about closing costs with regard to purchasing real estate as well as the procedures associated with purchasing real estate. As a result, the Real Estate Settlement and Procedures Act (RESPA) was passed.

RESPA refers to residential transactions that involve first mortgage loans made on 1 – 4 family residences, cooperatives, and condominiums.

With RESPA, it's important to remember several key acts that are illegal:

- Fees paid for services not rendered and kickbacks are strictly prohibited under the Act.
- Also prohibited is the requirement of buyers to purchase title insurance from a specific title company.
- The amount of advance property tax and insurance payments lenders can require of borrowers must be no more than 1/6 or 2 months' worth of annual property taxes.

Deeds

The deed is the legal document used to show a transfer of ownership from the seller (grantor) to the buyer (grantee). In New York, the deed must be in writing and meet the state's other requirements of a valid deed (i.e. contain the name of the grantor and grantee, include acts of conveyance-granting clauses, provide evidence of consideration, have the legal description of the property, habendum clause, limitations and subject to clause, signature of the grantor, acknowledgment/recording, and delivery and acceptance). This gives a constructive notice of the transfer of ownership.

There are three main types of deeds commonly used in New York, including full covenant and warranty deed, bargain and sale deed, and quitclaim deed.

Full Covenant and Warranty Deed: Considered the strongest type of deed with regard to the guarantee of title. This type of deed typically includes the following six covenants:

- Covenant of seisin – "Grantor covenants that he is seised of said premises in fee."
- Covenant of right to convey – The grantor is assuring the grantee that he has the ability to convey title as well as the title to convey.
- Covenant against encumbrances – The grantor is assuring the grantee that there are no encumbrances against the property other than that which is in the deed itself.
- Covenant of quiet enjoyment – The grantor is assuring the grantee that he will have quiet enjoyment of the property.

- o Covenant for further assurances – The grantor is assuring the grantee that he will execute any assurances in the future as necessary in order to rectify any problems or deficiencies in the title.
- o Covenant of warranty – The grantor is assuring the grantee that he will defend the title against lawful claims that may arise.

Bargain and Sale Deed: The grantor assures that he has "good title and possession of the property."

Quitclaim deed: Grantor conveys interest that he has in property but does not give word regarding warranty of said property.

Other deeds that are used in various states include:

Sheriff's deed: Transfers title of property after it being auctioned off due to foreclosure or some other court-related action.

Tax deed: Transfers title of property sold at an auction to take care of unpaid taxes.

Gift deed: Does not require consideration in order to be paid by the grantee.

There are several key elements included in the deed to make it valid. These are:

- Identification of all parties involved
- "Granting clause"
- Consideration
- Details of the rights transferred
- Legal property description
- Correct execution
- Grantor must state the deed is his "free act and deed" and notarize if the deed is to be recorded at the registry of deeds

Torrens System

The Torrens System, also known as Land Court, is used to register land. Most land in New York is recorded, but some is registered. The title of registered land is searched by the Land Court. In the case of registered land, the owner is provided with a certificate of title instead of a deed.

New York Transfer Taxes (Revenue Stamps)

Unlike some states, New York charges a tax stamp when real property is transferred from one to another. The actual tax stamp amount depends on the price of the property purchased. The tax stamp rate in New York is $4.00 per $1000. It is paid at closing by the seller.

In addition to the standard New York Transfer Tax, New York City imposes an additional 1% transfer tax when the sales price of the residential property is $500,000 or less. If the price is more than $500,000, the additional tax amount is 1.425%. For properties other than residential, the additional tax is 1.425% for properties $500,000 or less. Non-residential properties over $500,000, the rate is 2.625%.

Flip Tax

A tax that many cooperatives charge when units transfer ownership.

Real Property Transfer Report

All real estate property transfers in New York must be documented in this report. The form accompanies the deed(s) and a filing fee payment in the amount of $125 for residential and farm properties. It is $250 for all other properties. The seller pays the fee.

Laws Regarding Fair Housing and Consumer Protection

Federal

Federal Civil Rights Act of 1866: Regarding individual home sellers and real estate agencies, they are not allowed to racially discriminate against anyone when it comes to selling, leasing, or any other activities with real or personal property.

Federal Fair Housing Act of 1968 (Title VIII): The discrimination of individuals based on sex, race, color, religion, national origin, handicap, and familial status is strictly prohibited with regard to the sale or rental of housing or vacant land.

Acts that are prohibited:

- Choosing not to sell or rent to someone who is in a protected class. Protected classes include color, race, religion/creed, ancestry / national origin, gender, handicap, or familial status.
- Modifying services or conditions for different people as a way of discriminating against someone in a protected class.
- Advertising in such a way that discriminates against someone in a protected class, which would therefore prevent the sale or rental of a residence.
- Dishonestly telling an individual that a property is unavailable, as a way of discriminating against them.
- Blockbusting: Making money by encouraging homeowners to rent or sell their properties by telling them individuals of a protected class are moving into their neighborhood.
- Redlining: Changing the terms of a home loan of a person in a protected class as a way of discriminating against them.
- Preventing individuals from full participation in organizations that engage in the rental or sale of residences (e.g. multiple listing service).
- Steering: Encouraging individuals to gravitate toward or away from certain neighborhoods based on protected class.
- Stating in an appraisal report that the value of a property is impacted by any of the above prohibited activities.
- Including notes with discriminatory preferences.

- Negatively interfering with anyone who is exercising his rights.

Additional Information About Protected Classes Covered:

Familial status deals with preventing discrimination against children or families with children.

Discriminating against handicapped (mentally and physically) persons by not making reasonable accommodations regarding policies or necessary changes to the premises is prohibited.

Since 1991, homes that are four-family or larger are required to be handicapped accessible for first floor units. In homes where elevators are present, units on upper floors must also be handicap accessible.

The 1968 Federal Fair Housing Act covers residential property.

What does Title VIII Not Cover?

- The sale or rental by an individual who owns three or less properties and does not use a broker, engage in discriminatory advertising, and have not sold another property in the last two years.
- The rental of rooms in an owner-occupied, multi-family home with two or four units, providing no salesperson is used and he has not engaged in discriminatory advertising.
- The sale or rental of a property by a religious organization to a person of the same religion (for non-commercial purposes), providing no prohibited restrictions are enforced.
- The rental of properties managed by a private club for members for purposes other than commercial.
- Elderly housing that meets particular HUD rules.

Individuals who believe they have been discriminated against can file a complaint with HUD or civil action with the court.

If it is proven that the individuals have indeed been discriminated against, the offender may face penalties such as civil penalties, monetary fines, and court costs, among other things.

New York State General Law

NYS Human Rights Law-Article 15 of the New York Executive Law

The law prevents discrimination in many areas (including real estate [residential and commercial], employment, education, amusement attractions, and others). In addition to the protected classes covered by federal law, the NYS Human Rights Law includes protected classes for individuals who are 18 years or older, marital status, sexual orientation, and military status. There are no exemptions to this state law with regard to race, but other exemptions do exist.

New York Real Property Law and DOS Regulations

A tenant who becomes pregnant while living in the property cannot be evicted under this law. Also, families with children cannot be discriminated against with regard to the property being rented to them.

New York City Commission on Human Rights

Residents living in the five boroughs (Manhattan, The Bronx, Brooklyn, Queens, and Staten Island) are covered under this law. The law covers discrimination in the sale or lease of property. It includes the additional protected classes of alienage or citizenship status, lawful occupations, partnership status, and lawful source of income.

An exemption to this law includes two-family owner-occupied housing when the house is not made available through any form of advertising.

New York Anti-Predatory Lending Law

This law refers to loans that are no more than $300,000 and for one- to four- unit primary, personal residences. There are several restrictions on high-cost (subprime) loans for first and second mortgages.

NYS Mortgage Foreclosure Law (2009)

- The 90-day pre-foreclosure notice includes all New York loans rather than just for subprime loans.
- Early mandatory settlement conferences are for all NY residential borrowers rather than just subprime loan borrowers.
- Both parties of the foreclosure must reach a mutual agreement.
- NY tenants are entitled to a written notice outlining a foreclosure action. They are also allowed to stay in the home for 90 days or until the lease term expires (whichever is longer).
- The plaintiff in a foreclosure case must make sure the foreclosed property is in good condition.
- Upfront fees cannot be paid to brokers who provide consulting services of distressed properties.

Lead Paint Law

There is a federal and state law that real estate agents must abide by regarding lead paint disclosure requirements.
For homes built before 1978, the prospective buyer must be provided with a Department of Public Health Property Transfer Notification Certification that informs the buyer of whether or not the seller is aware of lead paint anywhere on the property. The seller must provide reports about it. The buyer then has ten days to have a test completed to check for lead paint. This process is done before the prospective buyer signs a Purchase and Sale Agreement.

If the prospective buyer decides he would like to continue with the purchase, he must be given a Lead Paint Notification and Tenant Certificate Form. Also, if the new tenant has a child who lives in the property that is under the age of 6, the current owner must delead.

Additionally, potential hazards such as those regarding smoke detectors must also be addressed. Within 60 days of closing on the property, the fire department must inspect and issue a smoke detector certificate saying the smoke detectors in the property are sufficient and properly working. Homes that are three-family or larger must also have hard-wired smoke detectors in common areas of the home. Homes that are six-family or larger must have hard-wired smoke detectors everywhere in the property.

Insurance

There are two basic types of policies for individuals to choose from:

Monoline policy – A policy that includes one type of coverage (e.g. liability)

Package policy – A policy that includes several types of coverage (e.g. liability and property)

- Liability insurance: Coverage that protects against claims of negligence or inappropriate behavior that results in property damage or bodily injury.
- Property insurance: Coverage that protects against financial loss in the case of:
  - fire, windstorm, hail, tornado, vandalism, smoke damage, and other physical damage that occurs against personal property or the home
  - theft of the owner's personal property
  - injury that occurs to someone on the property because of the homeowner's negligence

Management of Property

Condominiums

Units can be owned by an individual fee simple estate, which means in the case of payment default, only that individual owner is penalized, not all other owners.

The condominium master deed explains details of the property, each unit, and land and common area percentage ownership for each buyer. In addition to the master deed, a unit deed exists. A unit deed is provided each time the sale of a unit takes place. The unit deed includes bylaws, by which each owner agrees to abide by. The bylaws describe the condominium association and its legal authority.

There are typically fees associated with condominium ownership that are paid monthly. The amount due depends on the percentage of ownership for each owner.

Common areas of the condominium are for the use of each owner, unless designated as a limited common element (e.g. balcony).

If a condominium owner fails to pay monthly condominium fees, a priority lien may be assessed against the property, under the Super Lien Bill. Priority liens take precedence over first mortgage holder liens.

Cooperatives

Cooperatives are unlike condominiums in they have one owner, a corporation. There is a blanket mortgage on the property. The corporation is responsible for paying ad valorem taxes.

The buyers of each unit are considered stockholders, as once they make the purchase, they are given a stock certificate in the corporation. With ownership, the buyer has a "proprietary unit lease" which means they can occupy the property for the life of the corporation.

The downside to ownership in a cooperative as opposed to a condominium is that if one shareholder defaults on his monthly payment, the other shareholder tenants are affected and they must come together to make up the shortage.

Condop

A particular building in which ownership in a condominium and cooperative is present in that one building. Although there aren't many currently in existence, this hybrid structure is known for lower down payments for prospective buyers. There also typically less restrictions than those found with purchasing cooperatives. Owners also have more freedom when it comes to selling, subletting or even making modifications to the property.

Subdivisions

"Subdivision" is used to describe when large tracts of land are divided into smaller parcels that will be for sale. The land is improved (added infrastructure, etc.) and typically regulated by local, state, and federal law. The plat will be recorded, showing lots, blocks, etc.

If the subdivision includes greater than 25 lots, exceeding 20 acres and are offered for sale, crossing state lines, HUD (Federal Interstate Land Sales Full Disclosure Act) requires that several reports be filed.

Real Estate Investment

There are many reasons individuals and companies choose to invest in real estate. Typically, investing is done to obtain a form of income or profit.

Terms to keep in mind:

Rate of return- The percentage of income an investor receives form an investment.

Liquidity- An asset's ability to be converted to cash.

Leverage- Using borrowed funds. A high amount of borrowed funds that one has access to, means that he has a great amount of leverage.

Cash flow- The amount of cash one has in an investment property once operating costs and other expenses are deducted.

Cash-on-cash return- A percentage that represents the ratio before-tax cash flow: total amount of cash invested.

Tax shelter- A way of shielding income from taxation.

Capitalization rate- The amount (in percentage) an investor will receive in net income.

Analysis of Income, Rate, and Value (IRV) - Income is the money received. Rate is an annual percentage that typically relates to interest rate, capitalization rate, or commission rate. Value is the amount the unit costs or is worth.

Examples of types of investment properties:

Multifamily-

- ✓ Condos
- ✓ Cooperatives
- ✓ High-Rise Apartments

Retail-

- ✓ Outlet Mall (100,000 – 300,000 square feet)
- ✓ Free Standing Retail
- ✓ Strip Mall Center (8,000 – 30,000 square feet)

Office-

- ✓ Single Tenant Office
- ✓ High-Rise Tower (more than 20 stories)
- ✓ Office Over Retail

Health Care-

- ✓ Nursing Home
- ✓ Rehabilitation Facility
- ✓ Ambulatory Care

Industrial-

- ✓ Self-Storage
- ✓ Heavy Manufacturing
- ✓ Warehouse

Commercial Leases

Usable square footage- The amount of square footage that is physically used by the tenant.

Rentable square footage- The amount of square footage the tenant pays for, but may not be fully usable.

Effective rent- The actual amount the landlord receives in rent after deducting concessions and other expenses.

Loss factor- The lost areas of a property, or areas that are not considered usable for an individual tenant (e.g. hallways and elevators).

Add-on factor- Usable square feet divided by rentable square feet. Tenants pay for rentable square footage rather than just usable square footage.

Real Estate Math

The Real Estate Math section of this guide should not be taken lightly. Most state exams include around 10% math questions, but you don't have to be a mathematician to effectively complete this part. Use this review to refresh your understanding of or learn arithmetic, algebra, geometry, and word problems. You will also have the opportunity to practice with the included sample problems for each math topic.

Some of the math question types you may come across on your exam include:

- Area
- Percents
- Loan-to-Value Ratios
- Points
- Equity
- Qualifying Buyers
- Prorations
- Commissions
- Proceeds from sales
- Mortgage Recording Tax
- Property Tax Rate
- Real Property Transfer Tax
- Competitive Market Analyses
- Income Properties
- Depreciation

Use the following to help you complete the math questions.

Tips for Completing Math Questions

Before taking the exam, and specifically before completing the math portion of the exam, there are a few things you may want to keep in mind:

Leave No Question Unanswered

Although you may not know the answer to every question right off the top of your head, it is advisable that you answer every question to the best of your ability. You immediately have a 1 in 4 chance of getting the answer correct. There are also some instances where an answer choice is clearly not correct, which betters your chance for selecting the right answer.

Use a Calculator

You must confirm with the testing center before taking the exam, but some states allow the use of a calculator. However, you shouldn't solely rely on the calculator as this can slow you down, but using it to work out some mathematical equations can prove to be very helpful.

Utilize Scrap Paper

Let nothing take the place of scrap paper. While using a calculator can help you get the answer quickly, writing your thought process on scrap paper provides information for you to refer to in case you get stuck.

Review! Review! Review!

Avoiding an incorrect answer can be something as simple as checking your work.

Math Review

Basic math skills in the areas of arithmetic, algebra, geometry, and word problems will be necessary. Here's a review.

Arithmetic

Multiplication

"Factor" is the term used to describe the two numbers that are being multiplied. The answer is known as the product.

Example:

2 x 5 = 10   2 and 5 are the factors. 10 is the product.

A multiplication problem can be presented in a variety of ways.

- You may see a dot between the two factors, which denotes multiplication:
  $2 \cdot 5 = 10$

- The use of parentheses around a part of one or more factors denotes multiplication:

  (2)5 = 10

  2(5) = 10

  (2)(5) = 10

- A number next to a variable denotes multiplication:

  2a = 10

  Multiply "2" and "a" to arrive at the product of 10.

Division

The divisor is the number "divided by"; while the dividend is the number the divisor is going into. The result is the quotient.

Division is similar to multiplication by the fact that there are several ways to present the problem.

12÷3 = 4

12/3 = 4

$\frac{12}{3}$ = 4

Decimals

The key to understanding decimals is knowing each place value.

Here is a table to help you remember:

4	6	3	2	6	.	5	7	9	1
Ten Thousands	Thousands	Hundreds	Tens	Ones	Decimal	Tenths	Hundredths	Thousandths	Ten Thousandths

Using the above table, this number would be expressed as: 46,326.5791

It is also important to understand how to round decimals. If the number immediately following the number you must round is 5 or greater, you increase the preceding number by 1. If the number immediately following the number you must round is less than 5, drop that number and leave the preceding number as is.

Example:

0.236 = 0.24

0.234 = 0.23

Adding Fractions

Adding fractions with like denominators is a simple operation. You add the numerators together and leave the denominator as it appears.

Example:

$$\frac{3}{5} + \frac{1}{5} = \frac{4}{5}$$

Adding fractions with unlike denominators requires you to find the least common denominator. The least common denominator is the smallest number that each of your denominators can divide into evenly.

Example:

$\frac{4}{6} + \frac{3}{4}$ The least common denominator is 12 because 6 x 2 = 12 and 4 x 3 = 12.

Once you have determined the least common denominator, each fraction should be converted to its new form. This is done by multiplying the numerator and denominator by the appropriate number in order to arrive at the least common denominator. Next, you add the new numerators, which gives you the final answer.

Example:

$$\frac{4}{6} + \frac{3}{4} = \frac{2(4)}{2(6)} + \frac{3(3)}{3(4)} = \frac{8}{12} + \frac{9}{12} = \frac{17}{12}$$

Subtracting Fractions

Subtracting fractions with like denominators is a simple operation. You subtract the numerators and leave the denominator as it appears.

Example:

$$\frac{3}{5} - \frac{1}{5} = \frac{2}{5}$$

Subtracting fractions with unlike denominators requires you to find the least common denominator. The least common denominator is the smallest number that each of your denominators can divide into evenly.

Example:

$\frac{8}{9} - \frac{3}{6}$ The least common denominator is 18 because 9 x 2 = 18 and 6 x 3 = 18.

Once you have determined the least common denominator, each fraction should be converted to its new form. This is done by multiplying the numerator and denominator by the appropriate number in order to arrive at the least common denominator. Next, you subtract the new numerators, which gives you the final answer.

Example:

$\frac{8}{9} - \frac{3}{6} = \frac{2(8)}{2(9)} - \frac{3(3)}{3(6)} = \frac{16}{18} - \frac{9}{18} = \frac{7}{18}$

Multiplying Fractions

When multiplying fractions, the denominators of the fractions can be alike or different. Either way, the operation is performed the same.

Multiply the numerators and denominators.

Example:

$\frac{4}{7} \times \frac{3}{5} = \frac{12}{35}$

Dividing Fractions

When dividing fractions, you actually multiply the fractions by their reciprocals.

You find the reciprocal of a number by turning it upside down. For example, the reciprocal of $\frac{3}{8}$ is $\frac{8}{3}$.

Solve the problem.

$\frac{18}{24} \div \frac{2}{4} = \frac{18}{24} \times \frac{4}{2} = \frac{72}{48} = \frac{3}{2}$

Percent

"Percent" is used to describe a portion of a whole, with the whole being 100.

How do I change a decimal to a percentage?

This operation is simple. Move the decimal two places to the right of the number, add a percentage sign, and voila!

Example:

.32 = 32%

.04 = 4%

.1 = 10%

How do I change a fraction to a percentage?

The first step in converting a fraction to a percentage is to change the fraction to a decimal. Do so by dividing the denominator into the numerator. From here you move the decimal two places to the right of the number, and then add the percentage sign.

Example:

$3/6$ = .5 = 50%

$1/4$ = .25 = 25%

How do I change a percentage to a decimal?

Simply slide the decimal two places to the left of the number and take away the percentage symbol.

Example:

69% = .69

4% = .04

How do I change a percentage to a fraction?

Divide the number by 100. Reduce to lowest terms.

Example:

$$25\% = \frac{25}{100} = \frac{1}{4}$$

$$62\% = \frac{62}{100} = \frac{31}{50}$$

How do I change a percentage that is greater than 100 to a decimal or mixed fraction?

To change to a decimal:

Add a decimal point two places to the left of the number –

298% = 2.98

600% = 6.0

980% = 9.8

To change to a mixed fraction –

$$275\% = \frac{275}{100} = \frac{200}{100} + \frac{75}{100} = 2 + \frac{3}{4} = 2\frac{3}{4}$$

$$275\% = 2\frac{3}{4}$$

$$550\% = \frac{550}{100} = \frac{500}{100} + \frac{50}{100} = 5 + \frac{1}{2} = 5\frac{1}{2}$$

$$550\% = 5\frac{1}{2}$$

Conversions Commonly Seen in Real Estate:

Fraction	Decimal	Percentage
½	.5	50%
¼	.25	25%
1/3	.333…	33.3…%

2/3	.666...	66.6...%
1/10	.1	10%
1/8	.125	12.5%
1/6	.1666...	16.6...%
1/5	.2	20%

Algebra

Equations

To solve an equation, you must determine that is equal to the unidentified variable.

Things to remember about equations:

- There are two parts to an equation. They are separated by an equal sign.
- An operation performed in an equation must be done in each part.
- When beginning to solve the equation, priority #1 is to get the variables on one side and numbers on the other.
- You will usually have to divide both parts of the equation using the coefficient. This will enable the variable to equal an exact number.

How do I check an equation to make sure it is correct?

Once you've solved the equation, take the number equal to the variable and input into the original equation.

Example:

$x = 15$

Original equation: $\dfrac{x}{3} = \dfrac{x+35}{10}$

$\dfrac{15}{3} = \dfrac{15+35}{10}$

$\dfrac{15}{3} = \dfrac{50}{10}$

$$5 = 5$$

Algebraic Fractions

Example:

How do I solve subtraction on two fractions with different denominators?

$$\frac{x}{6} - \frac{x}{12}$$

$$\frac{x\,(2)}{6\,(2)} - \frac{x}{12}$$

$$\frac{2x}{12} - \frac{x}{12} = \frac{x}{12}$$

Geometry

Terms to remember:

- **Area** – Refers to the space inside a two-dimensional figure.
- **Circumference** – Refers to the linear distance around a circle.
- **Perimeter** – Refers to the total distance around a two-dimensional figure.
- **Radius** – Refers to the distance from the center point of a circle to its perimeter.

Area

Area refers to the space inside a two-dimensional figure.

In the triangle below, the area is the part that is shaded green.

= Area

Area Formulas for Various Shapes

Circle: $A = \pi r^2$

Sphere: $A = 4\pi r2$

Rectangle: $A = lw$

Square: $A = s^2$

Triangle: $A = \frac{1}{2} bh$

Parallelogram: $A = bh$

What do the above letters/symbols mean?

A: Area

π: 3.14

r: Radius

l: Length

w: Width

s: Side length

b: Base

h: Height

Examples of area:

Area of circle

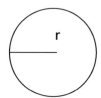

Area of rectangle

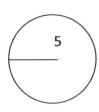

8 mm

3 mm

$A = \pi r^2$

$A = \pi \times (5 \times 5)$

$A = \pi \times 25$

$A = 3.14 \times 25$

$A = 78.54$

$A = lw$

$A = 8mm \times 3\ mm = 24\ mm^2$

Perimeter

Perimeter refers to the total distance around a two-dimensional figure.

It is simply calculated by adding together all of the sides of the figure.

Example:

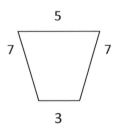

Perimeter = 7 + 7 + 5 + 3 = 22

Circumference is the perimeter of a circle.

Formula for circumference: C = 2πr

Word Problems

Understanding word problems is crucial to doing well on the math problems of the Real Estate Exam, as these make up a significant portion of the math problems found on the exam.

Before knowing how to solve the problems, you must understand what the problem is asking.

Terms you will commonly see:

- **Increase**
  What operation do you perform?
  Answer: Addition

  Example:

  A number is increased by 7, which means $x + 7$.

- **Less than**
  What operation do you perform?
  Answer: Subtraction

  Example:
  A number less than 12, which means $12 - x$.

- **Product or times**
  What operation do you perform?
  Answer: Multiplication

  Example:

  A number times 8, which means $x(8)$.

- **Times the sum**
  What operation do you perform?

Answer: Multiply a number by a quantity

Example:

Six times the sum of nine and a number, which is $6(9 + x)$.

- **Of**
  What operation do you perform?
  Answer: Multiplication

  Example:

  5% of 100 is 5, which means 5% x 100 = 5.

- **Is**
  What operation do you perform?
  Answer: Equals

  Example:

  10 is 20 minus 10, which means $10 = 20 - 10$.

- **The use of two variables**
  What operation do you perform?
  Answer: Whatever the equation states

  Example:

  A number y exceeds 3 times a number x by 8, which means $y = 3x + 8$.

Creating and Using Variables in Word Problems

In order to solve some word problems, you may be required to create and use variables. The first step in doing so is to determine what you know and don't know regarding the equation.

Examples:

Perry made $5 more dollars than Billy in his paper route.
What do you know? Perry made $5 more
What don't you know? The amount that Billy made

So,

The amount Billy made is x and the amount Perry made is x + 5.

Pam made 3 times as many A's on her report card as Jan.

What do you know? Pam made 3 times as many A's as Jan

What don't you know? The number of A's that Jan made

So,

The number A's Jan made is x and the number of A's Pam made is 3x.

Greg has 4 more than 2 times the number of marbles that Shelly has.

What do you know? Greg has 4 more than 2 times the number of marbles Shelly has

What don't you know? The number of marbles Shelly has

So,

The number of marbles Shelly has is x and the number of marbles Greg has 2x + 4.

Percentage Word Problems

There are three main types of percentage word problems. All three types follow the same formula for calculating the result.

Formula:

$$\frac{\text{part}}{\text{whole}} = \frac{\#\ \%}{100}$$

Calculate the problem substituting the appropriate information in the above formula.

Keep this in mind:

- On the percentage side, 100 will always be the denominator.
- If you are not provided with a percentage amount to use as the numerator, use a variable.
- On the number side, the number always equals the whole (100%). In the word problem, this number follows the term "of".
- On the number side, the numerator is the number that's equal to the percent.

Examples:

How do you find the percentage when you know the number?

What is the number that is equal to 40% of 95?

\# %

$$\frac{x}{95} = \frac{40}{100}$$

Cross multiply:

$100(x) = 40(95)$

$100x = 3800$

$$\frac{100x}{100} = \frac{3800}{100}$$

$x = 38$

Answer: 38 is 40% of 95

How do you find the number when you know the percentage?

40% of what number is 38?

\# %

$$\frac{38}{x} = \frac{40}{100}$$

Cross multiply:

$100(38) = 40(x)$

$3800 = 40x$

$$\frac{3800}{40} = \frac{40x}{40}$$

$95 = x$

Answer: 40% of 95 is 38

How do you find what percentage one number is of another?

What percentage of 95 is 38?

#	%
38	x
95	100

$$\frac{38}{95} = \frac{x}{100}$$

Cross multiply:

100(38) = 95(x)

3800 = 95x

$$\frac{3800}{95} = \frac{95x}{95}$$

40 = x

Answer: 40% of 95 is 38

Calculating Rate

Calculating cost per unit, interest rate, and tax rate are common problems found on the real estate exam. The purpose of rate is to compare two amounts, using various units of measure.

Rate formula: $\frac{x \text{ units}}{y \text{ units}}$

Calculating cost per unit

Example:

How much do 2 square feet cost if 250 square feet cost $2,500?

Answer:

$$\frac{2,500}{250} = \$10 \text{ / square foot}$$

Therefore, 2 square feet cost $20

Interest rate

The formula for simple interest is:

Interest = principal x rate x time

Basic Percentage

Determining basic percentage.

Example:

How do you calculate 53% of $3,645?

Answer:

Convert 53% to a decimal by moving the decimal two units to the left of the number.

53% = .53

Multiply the result by $3,645.

(.53) (3645) = $1,931.85

$1,931.85 is 53% of $3,645.

Percentage: Interest

How do you calculate the rate of interest being charged?

Example:

Paul Billings borrowed $22,000. He is paying $1,200 / year in interest. What is the interest rate he is being charged?

I = principal x rate x time

The principal amount is $22,000

The interest amount is $1,200

Rate = x

Time = 1 year

Using the formula, Interest = principal x rate x time, solve for x.

$1,200 = 22,000(x)(1)$

$1,200 = 22,000x$

$$\frac{1,200}{22,000} = \frac{x}{22,000}$$

$.055 = x$

Convert the decimal to a percent. Do this by moving the decimal two places to the right.

$.055 = 5.5\%$

Area of Various Figures

Rectangles

Keep in mind: The formula for area in a rectangle is: Area = (length) (width)

Example:

Theresa purchased two small lots of land. One is 70 feet by 20 feet and the other, 80 feet by 30 feet. What is the total square feet of land that she has?

Answer:

$A = (70)(20) + (80)(30) =$

$A = 1400 + 2400 = 3800$ square feet

Theresa has a total of 3800 square feet in land.

How do you find the length of a rectangle if you only know the area and width?

Keep in mind: The formula for area in a rectangle is: Area = (length) (width)

Example:

Theresa has 2400 square feet of land that is 30 feet in width. What is the length of the land?

Answer:

$2400 = (x)(30)$

$\dfrac{2400}{30} = \dfrac{(x)(30)}{(30)}$

$x = \dfrac{2400}{30}$

$x = 80$ feet

Triangles

Keep in mind: The formula for area in a triangle is: Area = $\dfrac{1}{2}$ bh

Example:

For their small business, Paul and Sally Green are buying a triangular piece of land. The base of the property is 150 feet. The side that is perpendicular to the base is also 150 feet. What is the total number of square feet for the property?

Area = x

Base = 150

Height = 150

$x = (\dfrac{1}{2}$ or .5$)(150)(150)$

$x = (\dfrac{1}{2}$ or .5$)(22{,}500)$

$x = 11{,}250$ square feet

Circles

Keep in mind: The formula for area in a circle is: $A = \pi r^2$

Example:

Gill is using a circular prop on a circular piece of land for a special project. The radius of the circular land area is 23 feet. What is the area of the prop?

For "π", use 3.14.

What do you know?

Radius = 23

π = 3.14

Area = x

Solve.

$A = \pi r^2$

A = (3.14)(23)(23) = 1,661.06 square feet

The area of the prop is 1,661.06 square feet.

Loan-to-Value Ratios (LTV)

Problems regarding Loan-to-Value Ratios typically involve percentages.

A mortgage loan for 25% is at an 85% LTV. The interest on the original balance for year #1 is $21,474. When securing the loan, what was the value of the property? Round to the nearest penny.

Solve.

Step #1: Determine the loan amount.

What do you know?

25% of the loan amount is $21,474.

Loan amount = x

In equation form this means:

($21,474) = (20%) (x) OR ($21,474) = (.2) (x)

$$\frac{21{,}474}{.2} = \frac{.2x}{.2}$$

x = $107,370

The loan amount is $107, 370

Step #2: Determine the value of the property.

What do you know?

Loan amount = $107,370

Loan-to-value ratio = 85%

Value = x

$107,370 is 85% of the value

In equation form this means:

(85% or .85) (x) = $107,370

$$\frac{.85x}{.85} = \frac{107{,}370}{.85}$$

x = 126,317.64

The value amount is $126,317.64

Points

"Point" is the term used to describe loan discounts. Each point represents a percentage of the face amount of the loan. For example, 3 points means 3% of the face amount of the loan.

Example:

Burt is attempting to obtain an $80,000 FHA mortgage loan. In order to do so, he must pay a 2-point discount (2%). What is the discount amount?

Answer:

Before solving the problem, convert the percentage to a decimal.

2% = .02

What do you know?

Amount of the loan = $80,000

Points = .02

Amount of the discount = x

x = (.02) (80,000)

x = $1,600

Equity

How do you calculate the value of a home?

Example:

John owns a home of which he has three mortgages. The first mortgage balance is $190,000. The second mortgage balance is $20,000 and third mortgage balance, $10,000. The equity in John's home is $50,000. What is the value of John's home?

In this problem, the value of the home is the total of all three mortgages plus the equity.

Answer:

$190,000 + $20,000 + $10,000 + $50,000 = $270,000

The value of the home is $270,000.

Qualifying Buyers

Megan is attempting to qualify for an FHA loan to buy a home. Her ratio requirement is 34/41. She makes $75,000 / year and has a $900 monthly car payment. What is her maximum PITI payment?

Answer:

First, divide Megan's annual income by the number of months in a year (12).

$75,000 ÷ 12 = $6,250

Megan's monthly income is $6,250

Next, determine the front-end qualifier by multiplying Megan's monthly income by the front-end portion (in decimal form) of the ratio.

$6,250 (.34) = $2,125

$2,125 is the front-end qualifier

Lastly, determine the back-end qualifier by multiplying Megan's monthly income by the back-end portion (in decimal form) of the ratio. Then subtract Megan's debt amount from this number.

$6,250 (.41) = $2,562.50 - $900 = $1,662.50

$1662.50 is the back-end qualifier

The maximum PITI is $1,662.50. PITI is the lower of the two qualifiers.

Prorations

During settlement, there is typically a reconciliation that needs to take place regarding money that is owed as of the settlement date. The best way to remember who owes what is by remembering the simple fact that he who uses the service is the one who has to pay for it. When calculating these figures, unless otherwise noted, you must always use a 30-day month and 360-day calendar year.

Example:

Mr. Perkins paid his 2012 property taxes in the amount of $2,400 one year in advance. He sells his house to Mr. Dickinson in April 2012 and settles in May of that same year. With regard to the amount paid in taxes, how much do the two gentlemen owe each other?

What do you know?

	Mr. Perkins	Mr. Dickinson
How many months paid for?	12 ($2,400)	0 ($0)
How many months used/will use?	4 ($800)	8 ($1,600)
How many months should he **be** reimbursed for?	8 ($1,600)	0 ($0)
How many months should he reimburse for?	0 ($1,600)	8 ($1,600)

Mr. Dickinson should be debited $1,600. Mr. Perkins should be credited $1,600.

Commissions

Commission calculation problems are common. They usually seek to determine a percentage, but they may also ask for a dollar amount.

Example:

The broker made her first home sale for $127,000. The total amount of commission is $7,700. What is the broker's commission rate?

Answer:

What do you know?

Home price: $127,000

Commission: $7,700

Commission rate: x

In equation form, this means:

127,000x = 7,700

Solve.

$$\frac{127,000x}{127,000} = \frac{7,700}{127,000}$$

x = 0.060

Change to a decimal and round to the nearest whole percent.

0.060 = 6%

Example:

An agent made a 6% commission on the sale of a home. The sale price was $345,867. The agent made another 6% commission on the sale of a $243,542 home. What is the total dollar amount the agent received in commission on the two homes?

Determine the commission amount on the first home sale.

$345,867 (.06) = $20,752.02

Determine the commission amount on the second home sale.

$243,542 (.06) = $14,612.52

Add together the two commission amounts.

$20,752.02 + $14,612.52 = $35,364.54

Total commission = $35,364.54

Sale Proceeds

Example:

The agent is working with the homeowner to determine the list price for the homeowner's home in order to meet the homeowner's desire to at least net $30,000. The current mortgage balance is $235,000 and commission to take into consideration is 7%. If they list and sell the property at $300,000, will the homeowner net at least $30,000?

What do you know?

Expenses: Total - $256,000

      Mortgage balance: $235,000

      Commission: $21,000

Sale price: $300,000

$235,000 + $21,000 = $256,000

$300,000 - $256,000 = $44,000

The homeowner will net $44,000. Therefore, he will net at least $30,000.

Mortgage Recording Tax

The taxes for recording a mortgage is at the state and local level (two separate taxes are collected and combined). The total amount varies by city or county.

As an example, in New York City, if the principal amount of the mortgage is less than $500,000, the tax rate is $2.05 for each $100. However, if it is a one- or two- family house, it is $1.75 for each $100 for the first $10,000 of the principal.

If the principal amount of the mortgage is $500,000 or more, the tax rate is $2.175 for each $100. However, if it is a one-or two- family house, it is $1.875 for each $100 for the first $10,000 of the principal.

Example:

Bill and Marcia have a mortgage for their $423,000 two-family home. What is the amount of the mortgage recording tax?

$423 x $2.05 = $867.15

Tax reduced by $0.30 for each $100 of the first $10,000 of the principal.

$10,000 ÷ $100 = $100 x .30 = $30

$867.15 - $30 = $837.15

Property Tax

Property tax questions are solved using percents and rates.

Example:

Laurie Collins lives in Purple County. The tax rate for Purple County is $5.89 per hundred of assessed valuation. Ms. Collins shares that she pays $2,550 in taxes. What is her property assessment? Round answer to nearest 10 cents.

What do you know?

Taxes = $2,550

Tax rate = $5.89 per hundred (%)

Assessment = x

$5.89 is 5.89%. Convert the percentage to a decimal: .0589

.0589 of the assessed value of the house is $2,550, which means:

(.0589) (x) = 2,550

Solve.

$$\frac{.0589x}{.0589} = \frac{2,550}{.0589}$$

x = $43,293.718

Rounded to the nearest 10 cents, the answer is $43,293.70.

How do you determine the tax rate if you know the amount of taxes paid and assessment amount?

Example:

Mrs. Ferguson said her taxes are $1,300 and property assessment $40,000. What is the tax rate percentage?

What do you know?

Taxes = $1,300

Assessment = $40,000

Rate (%) = x

In equation form, this means:

($40,000) (x) = 1,300

Solve.

$$\frac{40,000x}{40,000} = \frac{1,300}{40,000}$$

x = .0325

Convert to a percentage.

The rate is 3.25%

Real Property Transfer Tax

The New York property Transfer Tax Rate is $4.00 / $1000 of the home's sale price.

Example:

A homeowner sells her house for $432,000. How much does she owe the state for transfer tax?

There are 432 ($1,000s) in $432,000. Therefore, you multiply the tax rate per $1,000, which is $4.00 times 432.

$4.00 x 432 = $1,728

The transfer tax amount for the sale of a $432,000 home is $1,728.

New York Transfer Tax Example:

A homeowner sells his property for $297,765. The transfer tax is $1,191.06. If the tax amount is calculated per $1,000 of the sale price, what is the rate (per $1,000) of the tax amount?

Answer:

What do you know?

Sale price: $297,765

Tax amount: x per $1,000

Tax stamp amount: $1,191.06

Solve.

$$\frac{\$297,765}{\$1,000} = \$297.77$$

$1,191.06 = (x)(\$297.77)$

$$\frac{\$1,191.06}{\$297.77} = \frac{(x)(\$297.77)}{(\$297.77)}$$

$4.00 = x$

The tax stamp rate is $4.00 per $1000.

Competitive Market Analyses (CMA)

CMAs help sellers get a better understanding of the market value of their property, which could in turn help them decide on the sale price. Although very useful, it is important to note that CMAs are not appraisals.

CMA problems are solved by using measurable aspects of comparable properties to come to a specific value.

Example:

Mr. Stone has the blueprint for two homes he would like to build. Home A is 62' x 94' in size and will cost $234,985 to build. Home B is 90' x 112' in size. If each house costs the same per square foot to build, how much will it cost to build Home B?

Answer:

Remember, the formula to find Area for a rectangle is: A = lw.

Area of Home A: 62(94) = 5,828 square feet

Area of Home B: 90(112) = 10,080 square feet

Cost to build Home A / square foot: $\dfrac{\$234,985}{5,828}$ = $40.32

Cost to build Home B = 10,080($40.32) = $406,425.60

Income Properties

Example:

Bob, a local real estate investor is interested in buying an income property that creates gross income in the amount of $270,500. He discovers that the operating costs of this property will equal 65% of the gross income. Ideally, he would like to acquire a 15% return. With his desire to have a 15% return, what is the most he can pay for the property?

Answer:

What do you know?

Gross income= $270,500

Operating costs= 65% of $270,500

Net income = Gross income – operating costs

Desired return= 15%

Most the investor can pay = x

Step #1:

Determine the dollar amount of the operating costs. Start off by converting the percentage to a decimal.

65% = .65

Operating costs = (.65)(270,500) = $175,825

Step #2:

Gross income – Operating costs = Net income

$270,500 - $175,825 = $94,675

Step #3:

The investor wants his net income to be 15% of what he pays for the property. Convert the percent to a decimal, and then determine the most he can pay.

15% = .15

$94,675 = (.15)(x)

$$\frac{\$94,675}{.15} = \frac{(.15)(x)}{.15}$$

$$\frac{\$94,675}{.15} = x$$

$631,167 (Rounded to the nearest dollar)

Depreciation

You may encounter "depreciation" problems on the exam, but those representing the straight-line method are the only ones you will probably see.

The formula for the straight-line method of depreciation:

$$\frac{replacement\ cost}{years\ of\ useful\ life} = annual\ depreciation$$

If the depreciation rate is not given, you can calculate it dividing the total depreciation, which is 100%, by the useful life of the building.

For example, if a building has 25 years of useful life, then you will use this calculation:

$$\frac{100\%}{25} = 4\%$$

This means that the building has an annual depreciation rate of 4%.

Example:

It has been determined that the replacement cost of a 15 year old building is $90,000. Since it has 35 years of useful life left, how much can be charged to annual depreciation?

What do you know?

Replacement cost = $90,000

Useful life = 35 years

Using the formula $\frac{\text{replacement cost}}{\text{years of useful life}}$ = annual depreciation, calculate annual depreciation.

$$\frac{\$90,000}{35} = \$2571 \text{ (Rounded to the nearest dollar)}$$

Example:

The annual depreciation of a building is $3245. What is the total depreciation of a 19 year old building?

annual depreciation x age of building = total depreciation

$3245 x 19 = $61,655

Total depreciation = $61,655

Example:

The replacement cost of a building is $62,000. The total depreciation of said building is $19,354. What is the current value of the building?

replacement cost – depreciation = current value

$62,000 - $19,354 = $42,646

Current value of the building = $42,646

Summary

It is our hope that this Real Estate Math review has helped reinforce your knowledge of the topics you will most likely see on the math section of the Real Estate Exam. For those of you who feel like you could use a bit more of a refresher, feel free to take the included practice exams over and over until you feel confident that you can triumphantly complete the Real Estate Exam. Good luck!

Real Estate Glossary

>A

abandonment giving up the right to possess a property, building or real estate area through non-use and intention.

abstract of title the background of a property listing legal transactions and information.

abutting sitting next to another property.

acceleration clause an addendum that forces the borrower to repay the entire loan upon the lender's insistence for specific reasons listed in the clause.

acceptance agreement to an offer.

accretion increase of the amount of land by natural deposits of soil on onto the property.

accrued depreciation the total loss of value on the property.

accrued items the additional costs still outstanding at the close of the real estate deal, such as interest, insurance, HOA fees or taxes.

acknowledgement agreement to fulfill admitted responsibility.

acre a section of land that is 4,840 square yards or 43,560 square feet in area.

actual eviction a step-by-step procedure to remove renters from property.

actual notice specific information given to a party, such as a tenant, landlord, buyer or seller.

addendum a clause that provides more specific information to clarify a contract.

adjacent property or buildings next to each other but might not touch each other.

adjoining property or buildings next to each other that do touch each other.

adjustable rate mortgage a loan rate that changes throughout the period of the loan. Sometimes called a variable rate or flexible rate.

adjusted basis the final cost of a property after improvements are added and deductions or reduced value are subtracted.

adjustment date the date agreed upon by the buyer and seller for financial changes.

administrator a court-appointed individual who executes a person's estate if there is not a will.

ad valorem tax property tax on the current value of the land.

adverse possession The ways by which a person may acquire property, such as through purchase, inheritance or other methods, including without payment as in a squatter.

affidavit a sworn promise before a person in authority.

agency a professional company who can act on behalf of another, such as a real estate agency or a title agency.

agent a professional individual who can act on behalf of another, such as a real estate agent or a title agent.

agreement of sale a contract between two parties to buy/sell property, usually over time.

air rights the right to air space above a property, separate from the property land itself.

alienation placement of ownership of property from one person/company to another person/company.

alienation clause an addendum to the mortgage contract that keeps the borrower from reselling the property without paying the lender.

allodial system a national system overseen by law that monitors property ownership.

amenities "extras" on a property that make it worth more or more attractive to buyers. Location or kitchen upgrades are two examples of amenities.

amortization paying off the principle and interest on a debt with equal payments until the debt is repaid.

amortization schedule the time frame set up over which the principle and interest of the debt is repaid.

amortize to pay off the principle and interest on a loan.

annual percentage rate (APR) the percentage above the principle added onto the loan over 12 months. It includes additional costs, such as closing costs and fees, and not just interest rates.

anti-deficiency law a statute that stops the lender from pursuing the buyer for a loss on a property after a foreclosure sale.

anti-trust laws national laws that encourage free market trade and practices and prohibit the restriction of such.

apportionments the division of costs, such as fees and HOA responsibilities, between the seller and purchaser.

appraisal assessing the worth of land or property by a professional, qualified person who is usually licensed.

appraised value the worth of the land or property as determined by the licensed professional.

appraiser a professional, qualified person so licensed by the state to determine the value of land or property.

appreciation growth in the worth of real estate.

appurtenance an attachment to land or edifices that now conveys with the property.

arbitration dispute resolution through the use of a third party.

ARELLO an online company that encourages the cooperation of decision makers in the real estate business.

assessed value the tax-related value put on a property.

assessment the placement of tax-related value on a property.

assessor a professional who determines the tax-related value of a property.

asset something of value that belongs to a person, such as cash, property, bonds, etc.

assignment the transfer of a mortgage from one agency to another.

assumption the process of the buyer taking over the seller's mortgage.

attachment placing a legal hold on a property to pay for a judgment.

attest to agree to the truth of a document by signing it.

attorney-in-fact a person who acts as a legal representative for another; does not need to be a professional lawyer.

avulsion transfer of land because water, such as a stream or brook, changes course.

balloon mortgage a mortgage with small payments due for a specified period, such as three to five years with a lump sum or balloon due at the end of the mortgage.

balloon payment the lump payment at the end of a balloon mortgage.

bankruptcy the legal discharge of most debts through the courts.

bargain and sale deed a document transferring property from seller to buyer without guaranteeing the validity of the transfer.

baseline a line in surveying that runs east to west and acts a point of reference for corresponding lines that run north to south.

benchmark a fixed point of reference by which elevation is marked.

beneficiary the recipient of the profits that occur as a result of someone else's actions

bequest similar to an inheritance, a transfer of personal property through a will.

betterment an upgrade to property.

bilateral contract a contract, such as a rent agreement, when both parties agree to comply with or not comply with certain terms.

bill of sale a legal paper that transfers ownership of property from one person (company) to another.

binder money paid to hold a property for set terms.

biweekly mortgage payments made on real estate every two weeks as opposed to once a month. In some cases, this reduces the time needed to pay off the loan.

blanket mortgage a mortgage owned by the same person on at least two properties.

blockbusting an illegal process that involves scaring residents of an area into selling their property at reduced prices so that an agent can take advantage them.

bona fide legal adjective that describes faithful, trustworthy actions or people.

bond a type of insurance money that protects a professional against loss.

boot a sum of cash included in a buyer/seller agreement to even out exchange.

branch office a satellite or another office that is at separate place from headquarters, for example, the headquarters are in New York City with branch offices in Queens, the Bronx and Brooklyn.

breach of contract breaking a binding agreement illegally.

broker professional or entity that is qualified through classes and licensed to buy or sell property.

brokerage a firm that employs one or more real estate professionals; real estate company.

broker's price opinion (BPO) an estimate on the worth of real estate by a professional in the industry.

building code state and local legislation that regulates new edifices or structural changes or existing ones.

building line an invisible boundary line around the property. The building must stay within this boundary.

building restrictions state, local and neighborhood guidelines or constraints that guide how it is built or determine property use.

bundle of rights privileges associated with property ownership, such as residency or use.

buy down payment by the buyer of added fees or points to the seller or lender for a lower interest rate.

buyer's broker a real estate professional who searches for a property and conducts negotiations in order to purchase the property.

bylaws procedural guidelines used to conduct business or meetings at an organization like a homeowner's association.

>C

cancellation clause a section in a contract that permits parties to nullify the obligations of the contract.

canvassing surveying or soliciting an area to see if people are interested in selling their home.

cap the maximum increase in interest for a mortgage with changing rates.

capital funds used to generate more money.

capital expenditure money spent to improve the value of real estate.

capital gains tax taxation on the proceeds from a property sale.

capitalization the total yearly potential earnings on a property, such as a rental.

capitalization rate a percentage that can be used to compare investment opportunities. This is determined by dividing the yearly capitalization by the cost of the property.

cash flow the final amount of income generated from a rental property after income and expenses.

caveat emptor Latin expression meaning "let the buyer beware." Serves as a warning to the buyer.

CC&R covenants, conditions and restrictions – The bylaws for a group of homeowners.

certificate of discharge an IRS document that enables the government to waive taxes on a property.

certificate of eligibility formal document from the Veteran's Administration that proves the person qualifies for a VA loan.

certificate of reasonable value (CRV) the maximum value permitted for a VA mortgage.

certificate of sale permits the buyer to receive the title for the purchase of the property.

certificate of title an official decision on the ownership, status or availability of a piece of real estate through public documents.

chain of title the legal document that tells the history of a piece of real estate.

chattel any property someone owns except real estate.

chattel mortgage the use of personal property as security for debt repayment.

city an incorporate group of residences larger than a town or village.

clear title a document of ownership that is completely valid.

closing the final legal transfer of property ownership through the signing of official papers.

closing costs the monies associated with the sale of property, such as inspection fees.

closing date the actual date the property will transfer from the buyer to the seller.

closing statement a final summary of all costs involved in the sale of real estate.

cloud on the title a questionable title as to the availability for sale.

clustering a group of residential buildings used to maximize land use.

codicil an addendum to a will that explains additions or deletions to the document.

coinsurance clause a clause in an insurance policy that divides financial responsibility for a loss between at least two parties.

collateral something of value that promises the repayment of a loan.

collection efforts to acquire delinquent rent or mortgage payments.

color of title a title that is invalid although it seemed to be valid initially.

commercial property real estate set aside for business use.

commingling combining the funds of two parties into one account

commission the payment that a broker or real estate agent receives for the sale of a property, usually a percentage of the sale price.

commitment letter a document from the mortgage company that informs the borrower regarding loan approval and the terms of said approval.

common areas regions of a neighborhood or apartment complex that all residents share, such as a pool, playground or parking lot.

common law originating in England, law based in part on traditions and in part on the courts.

community property real estate and chattel shared by 2 parties, usually husband and wife. Comparable sales: Homes in the area that interested parties can assess to determine the worth of a piece of real estate.

comparative market analysis (CMA**)** assessing the worth of real estate through the value of similar pieces of real estate in the area.

competent parties someone who can legally sign a contract.

competitive market analysis (CMA) a list of benefits of the property and a comparison to other homes in the area. **condemnation** taking over ownership of a property, usually by the government, and paying the owner for the real estate.

condominium similar to apartments, individual residences in a building or area with common areas shared jointly by all residents.

condominium conversion the transfer in ownership in a condominium from one owner to many for each residence.

conformity the belief that similar pieces of real estate will retain their worth.

consideration a legal enticement that attracts the buyer to sign the contract.

construction mortgage a two-part loan – first, to pay for construction costs and next to pay for the home. Usually the borrower pays interest only payments until the home is finished when the mortgage transitions into a regular loan.

constructive eviction when a tenant moves out of a residence because of the poor quality of the residence without being liable for rent.

constructive notice public record and therefore common information to all.

contingency certain requirements that must be met to fulfill the contract, such as sale of the buyer's home so that he can afford the new residence

contract a legal arrangement between two legal parties that establishes certain conditions that will happen.

contract for deed a deferment of the price of the property for a specific time frame.

conventional loan financing to obtain a piece of property or real estate.

conversion option an agreement that the buyer can change an adjustable interest rate to a fixed rate. There is a cost associated with this option.

convertible ARM an agreement that the buyer can change an adjustable interest rate to a fixed rate. There is a cost associated with this option.

conveyance the legal transfer of property from one party to another.

cooperative ownership in shares of a common residential building, similar to an apartment, which allows the owners to live there.

corporation a company acts as its own business with liability and management.

cost approach a way to assess real estate value by starting with the worth of the property, subtracting costs and adding improvements.

counteroffer saying no to a real estate offer and then suggesting a different offer.

covenant specifications included in the deed requiring obligations or restrictions on real estate use.

covenant of seisin a legal verification that the owner has the right to the property.

credit available financial backing for real estate that needs to be repaid in the future.

credit history a list of borrowers or lenders who have lent the individual money and a history of how they have fulfilled their financial obligations.

cul-de-sac a semi-private road with a circular type of dead-end at the end, usually adds value in real estate.

curtesy a man's ownership of some or all of his spouse's property even if she will deny him such ownership.

cartilage the area in close proximity to a residence, including other buildings, but not including open lands away from the home.

>D

damages financial or other compensation to the hurt party for tangible or intangible losses.

datum a horizontal reference point used to make vertical measurements.

DBA "doing business as" – sometimes used as an "also known as" name for a company.

debt money or property that is owed to another and must be repaid.

debt service repayment over a specific time frame, usually of a mortgage, including interest and principal.

decedent a person who passed way, often used to discuss their estate, will, inheritance or other financial matters.

dedication a gift of property for the benefit of all and the receipt of land by authorities.

deed the official, written proof that transfers and verifies property ownership.

deed-in-lieu used instead of a foreclosure, the property owner returns the property deed back to the lender to avoid a public record of foreclosure in some cases.

deed of trust a type of mortgage used in some jurisdictions.

deed restriction part of the deed that prevents the owner from certain land uses.

default failure to make a loan payment within a certain time frame, usually within 30 days of the due date.

defeasance clause the legal option that the lender has to repossess delinquent payments or the property from the borrower in case of a default.

deficiency judgment a legal document ordering the collection of the difference between what a borrower owes to the bank and the sale price of a home.

delinquency late payment on a loan.

density zoning regulations that prohibit more than a certain number of homes in an area.

depreciation a reduction in the value of an asset because of financial, physical or use.

descent the passing down of property to an heir if the deceased person has not left specific provisions.

devise a gift of real estate to an heir through a will.

devisee the person who receives a gift of property from a will.

devisor the person who gives a gift of property to another through a will.

directional growth the direction in which a city is expanding.

discount point money paid to the mortgage holder to reduce the interest payment. The more money that is paid, the lower the interest will fall.

discount rate the interest rate that a bank will pay to the Federal Reserve to borrow cash for short-term loans.

dispossess legal process of eviction.

dominant estate (tenement) property that benefits from the shared use of land on a neighboring property.

dower a woman's ownership of some or all of her spouse's property even if his will denies her such ownership.

down payment cash, as part of the cost of real estate, paid separately from the financing.

dual agency a real estate agent or broker who acts on behalf of two or more parties in a sale.

due-on-sale clause the clause that requires the loan to be repaid to the lender when the real estate is sold.

duress a person feels threatened into doing something, such as selling property.

>E

earnest money money to prove the buyer's serious intent of purchasing the home.

easement an agreement that one person has the privilege of use of another's land.

easement by necessity the need to walk on someone else's property by necessity.

easement by prescription accepted use of property by another person that is unnecessary. This becomes legal when it occurs over a certain number of years, such as a short cut through a neighbor's yard.

easement in gross accepted use of property that remains with the individual and does not convey with the property. For example, when the home is sold to a different owner, the easements are not passed to the new owner.

economic life the length of time when real estate will continue to earn money.

effective age the age of the building based on the condition of the building.

emblements different types of farming crops considered part of property.

eminent domain the purchase of private property by the government for public purposes.

encroachment part of real estate that crosses property boundaries onto another's property.

encumbrance assessments against a property, such as delinquent HOA fees, any mortgages or easements that impact the value.

equitable title the right someone who has to a property when they commit to buy it although the deal is not yet finalized.

equity the worth of the property above the mortgage or other debts on the property.

equity of redemption the reclaiming of real estate by the mortgage holder because of foreclosure.

erosion slow wearing away of land by natural elements, such as flooding.

escalation clause passing on increased expenses to tenants, such as fuel or HOA fees.

escheat real estate goes to the state if a person dies without a will and without any heirs.

escrow money or something of value held in trust by a third party until the completion of a specific transaction.

escrow account monies collected from the buyer that the lender holds in reserve to pay property taxes and homeowner's insurance.

escrow analysis a yearly review that assesses the monies collected in escrow to ensure that the amount is correct. It may be increased or decreased at that time to reconcile the account.

escrow disbursements the use of the escrow account to pay taxes, insurances and expenses.

estate all of a person's property.

estate for years time frame during which a person accesses land or property.

estate tax the tax on the worth of the assets when a person dies. A certain portion of the estate is exempt.

estoppel certificate written confirmation that the borrower signs stating that the mortgage amount is correct.

et al. Latin for "and others;" used to refer to property ownership by several people, "Jane Doe, et. al."

et ux. Latin for "and wife".

et vir. Latin for "and husband".

eviction the process by which a person is legally removed from a property.

evidence of title official paperwork that proves that someone own the property.

examination of title history of the title although not as complete or detailed as a title search.

exchange similar business or investment properties that can be traded tax-free per IRS Code 1031.

exclusive agency listing a binding legal agreement that gives a single broker permission to sell real estate for a certain time frame.

exclusive right to sell a binding legal agreement that gives the real estate agent the right to collect the commission if anyone else sells the property during the specified time frame.

exculpatory clause permits the borrower to give back the real estate to the lien holder without personal responsibility to repay the mortgage.

execution when a creditor wants to enforce the payment of the debt, they will require the debtor to turn over the property.

executor/executrix the person established by the deceased to perform estate duties. Executrix is a female who performs these duties.

executory contract a legal agreement that is awaiting action by at least one party for completion.

executed contract a completed contract.

express contract a contract that details all aspects of the contract, such as offer, acceptance and consideration.

extension agreement a mutual decision to lengthen the time frame for a contract.

external obsolescence a reduction in the worth of a specific home improvement because of something separate from the real estate that decreases the worth of the home.

>F

fair housing law a national statute that prohibits discrimination in any housing dealings because of race, color, sex, religion, family status, handicap or national origin.

fair market value what the property will sell for according to both a buyer and seller.

Federal Housing Administration (FHA) a government agency that guarantees loans to make housing easier to obtain.

Federal National Mortgage Association (Fannie Mae) a federal organization that helps keep the home loan market solvent by purchasing notes from bankers.

Federal Reserve System the government banking system that oversees banks, offers services and sets national economic policy.

fee simple full and complete ownership of real estate.

FHA-insured loan a mortgage that is backed by the government through the FHA. VA loans are also backed by the government.

fiduciary relationship a person who acts on another's behalf in business or general matters.

finder's fee money that the realtor pays to a third party who finds a buyer; usually illegal.

first mortgage the first loan taken out on a home, usually in chronological order, but not always.

fixed-rate loan a loan where the interest rate remains the same throughout the loan term.

fixture personal property affixed to the building that conveys with the building when it is sold.

flip tax tax paid by seller when closing on a cooperative

foreclosure the process by which a buyer loses the property because of failure to pay the debt, which result s in the public sale of the real estate in order to pay as much of the debt as possible.

forfeiture seizure of property because of criminal actions or failure to fulfill a contract.

franchise when a business owner pays to use a company name in return for company backing, such as member brokerages.

fraud deceptive actions intended to mislead another person and harm them

freehold estate continued ownership or stake in a property as compared to a temporary stake or a lease.

front foot the measurement at the front of the home nearest the street; used to compare home value especially on the same street

functional obsolescence the decrease in worth on the real estate except those caused by wear and tear

future interest a right to real estate that will come to pass in the future.

>G

general agent someone who can do any job duties related to the business on behalf of the principal. A real estate agent acts as a special agent.

general lien a mortgage that covers more than one property owned by the same person.

general warranty deed a guarantee that the title is free and clear of other claims against it for the protection of the buyer.

government-backed mortgage a loan that is backed by the federal government as contrasted with a conventional loan.

Government National Mortgage Association (Ginnie Mae) a federal agency that supplies funding for government loans.

government survey system a process of dividing land into rectangle sections in order to set area boundaries.

graduated lease a rental agreement that permits periodic adjustments in rental price increases.

grant the exchanging of real estate to another individual through a deed.

grant deed the legal document used to transfer real estate to another.

grantee the person who receives the real estate; buyer.

grantor the person who sells the real estate.

gross income all financial gains received for real estate before any losses or expenses on the property.

gross income multiplier a way to assess the profitability of property arrived at by dividing the total price paid by the monthly rental rate.

gross lease a rental agreement when the landlord pays all costs associated with the property, including HOA fees, repairs, taxes and more.

gross rent multiplier a way to assess the profitability of property arrived at by dividing the total price paid by the monthly rental rate

ground lease a lease of land only, not of buildings.

guaranteed sale plan a contract between the seller and the real estate agent/broker. The broker promises to buy the property for predetermined terms if the property does not sell by a certain date.

guardian a person who the court deems legally responsible for someone who is incapable of managing their affairs.

>H

Habendum clause "To have and to hold" that specifies any restrictions on property; fee simple absolute.

hamlet a small, populated area; municipality.

heir someone who receives property, often through a will after a death.

hereditament anything either tangible or intangible given through a will.

highest and best use the most productive use of real estate that will provide the greatest financial return over a specified period of time.

holdover tenancy a renter who stays on the property when the lease ends.

Holographic will a handwritten will signed by the person who makes the will; does not need a notary or witness.

home equity conversion mortgage (HECM) Reverse mortgage or when a lender makes payments, usually monthly, to a homeowner.

home equity line of credit a loan available to homeowners based on the equity in the home, similar to a credit card.

home inspection a professional assessment of the real estate that closely examines the property.

homeowner's insurance an insurance policy that covers the property and contents against all types of natural and other damages, includes liability.

homeowner's warranty insurance coverage that protects the buyer against any defects in the residence.

homestead permitted by some states, protects a residence against lawsuits or judgments up to certain limits.

HUD Housing Urban and Development Department, federal agency that regulates some aspects of the housing industry.

hypothecate a promise of something as pledge for a loan without physically relinquishing that item. Most home owners live in their primary residence through this method unless they own the residence free and clear.

>I

implied contract an informal contract, not in writing, yet enforceable by the courts.

improvement work done on land or property that increases worth, additions or upgrades that are more consequential than repairs.

income capitalization approach a specific formula used to assess the income-producing worth of a property.

income property real estate that earns money for the owner.

incorporeal right intangible rights associated with real estates, such as easements and future income.

indemnify to insure against loss.

independent contractor the employment status of most real estate agents; those who work independently and do not have an employer/employee relationship.

index an assessment of the current financial atmosphere by the government; used to adjust prices.

industrial property real estate used for non-residential but business purposes, such as a warehouse or manufacturing property.

inflation an increase in overall costs and expenses that results in a decrease in what money will buy.

initial interest rate the first or starting rate for an adjustable mortgage.

installment a scheduled payment toward the reduction of debt, such as a mortgage.

installment contract a binding, legal, written agreement that sets a schedule for the loan payments.

installment loan a loan that is repaid in periodic payments at a set schedule; sometimes secured by personal property.

installment sale payments made to a seller over a longer period of time in order to defer taxes.

insurance money paid to an indemnity holder to reduce the expenses associated with the specific emergency being insured, such as flooding or earthquakes.

insurance binder temporary proof of insurance until the permanent paperwork is completed.

insured mortgage financial backing for a loan that protects the lender against default, sometimes called PMI.

interest a legal right to real estate or other property; B. The amount a lender charges a borrower for the loan above the principal, usually specified as a percentage.

interest accrual rate how often the interest accrues, such as daily, weekly or monthly, until it is paid to the lender.

interest rate the amount a lender charges a borrower for the loan above the principle, usually specified as a percentage.

interest rate buydown plan a plan that uses money from a still uncompleted home sale to reduce the interest rate and the monthly costs to the buyer.

interest rate ceiling the maximum percentage rate cap on an adjustable rate mortgage.

interest rate floor the lowest percentage rate minimum on an adjustable rate mortgage.

interim financing a transitional loan to bridge the time frame until the buyer can obtain permanent financing, for example a construction loan.

intestate without a legal will or without any will at all.

invalid not legally enforceable, such as a will or a contract.

investment property real estate purchased for the purpose of generating income.

>J

joint tenancy more than one individual who owns property in common, usually related individuals.

joint venture more than one entity who works toward the same professional goal, usually a temporary arrangement for a specific purpose.

judgment the court order that sets the amount one person or entity owes another in the event of a default, such as a loan or in an eviction.

judgment lien a lender's right to claim the property of the borrower because of a judgment.

judicial foreclosure court order to force the sale of real estate to pay off debt. The satisfaction of debts will stop foreclosure.

jumbo loan a property loan above the normal limits.

junior mortgage a loan that will only be satisfied after the first mortgage.

>L

laches the delay of the time period during which a legal claim can be enforced.

land solid real estate, separate from water or air.

landlocked property that is not accessible to public roads except through a neighboring property.

lease a legal contact that lasts for a specific time period during which the owner allows the renter to possess the property.

leased fee a restriction on property because of a rental/lease agreement.

lease option the renter can decide to buy the property under certain conditions.

leasehold property subject to a long-term rental agreement.

legal description authoritative confirmation of a property through written, technical means.

lessee tenant of real estate property.

lessor landlord of real estate property.

leverage the mortgage used to purchase a home or business.

levy a legal order of payment of any money due.

license legal permission, such as the temporary use of property.

lien financial assessment against real estate that must be paid when the land is sold.

life estate a lifelong interest in a specific real estate that ends when the owner dies.

life tenant someone who can stay on the real estate property until their death.

liquidity the availability of cash when using assets, such as property or real estate.

lis pendens Latin for "suit pending." Notice of possible restrictions on title when a lawsuit is filed.

listing agreement a contract between a real estate agent and client that pays commission to the agent no matter how the buyer finds the property.

listing broker the real estate agent who lists the property.

littoral rights the shore land next to an ocean or very large water body that the property owner has rights to.

loan borrowing money from another entity.

loan officer a representative for the lender or a representative for the borrower to the lender who may also look for loans.

lock-in the borrower pays a fee to guarantee a certain interest rate for a specific time period, especially if the borrower thinks the interest rates will rise.

lock-in period the time frame of the lock-in, such as 90 days.

lot and block description a legal process of finding real estate based on its lot and block identification within the housing area.

>M

management agreement a legal agreement between an owner and a property manager for a percentage of the rental generated.

margin a flat percentage to adjust interest rates up or down according to the index used in adjustable rate mortgages.

market data approach a comparison of recent property sales to assess real estate worth.

market value in real estate, price range between the maximum purchase price and minimum purchase price.

marketable title a free-and-clear title.

mechanic's lien a hold on the construction and on the real estate that guarantees payment for the work done on the property.

metes and bounds specific description of the land that identifies all boundaries of the real estate.

mill one-tenth of a penny; used for taxation.

minor a person who is not of legal age to make a binding decision.

misrepresentation a misleading verbalization even if unintended.

modification a legal alteration to a contract.

money judgment a court order that orders a financial payment.

month-to-month tenancy a rental agreement that can be extended or cancelled each month.

monument a landmark or immovable object used to decide the land locations.

mortgage a loan on property that uses the property itself as security for the repayment of the property.

mortgage banker a bank that finances loans for others, which are then sometimes purchased by federal agencies.

mortgage broker an agency that researches and finds loans for others but does not finance them.

mortgage lien the financing on a piece of real estate that obligates the buyer to the holder.

mortgagee the person/agency who lends money in a real estate transaction

mortgagor the person/agency who borrows money in a real estate transaction.

multi-dwelling units a building, such as an apartment complex, that has separate living units but only one property loan.

multiple-listing system (MLS- also multiple-listing service) a group of real estate agents that lists all the available properties for sale, which gives a buyer a wide range of choices.

mutual rescission an agreement to void a contract by all involved parties.

>N

negative amortization a deferment of interest payments on a loan, which is added on to the principal and results in an eventual increase in the payments over time and a loss of value on the home.

net income when all bills have been paid, the earnings that remain.

net lease the renter, as opposed to the landlord, pays costs, such as HOA fees, repairs and upkeep.

net listing any funds above the original price of the property that are paid to the real estate agent, illegal in some   places.

net worth the positive, monetary difference between the value of assets and liabilities.

NYC Commission on Human Rights discrimination that takes place in the sale, rental, or lease of property(housing, land, and commercial space) is managed through this agency.

New York Commission Escrow Act offers a process that allows real estate agents to collect commissions they are owed.

NYS Department of Environmental Conservation (NYSDEC) protects land, water, animals and their habitats in the state of New York.

NYS Department of Health (NYSDOH) regulates drinking water safety as well as other health issues in New York.

NYS Human Rights Law helps eradicate discrimination in real estate (commercial and residential), employment, educational institutions, and public facilities.

NYS Mortgage Foreclosure Law defends the rights of borrowers who are facing default or foreclosure.

NYS Uniform Fire Prevention and Building Code outlines the minimum standards for the construction and renovations of buildings.

no cash-out refinance sometimes called a "rate and term refinance," the borrower receives no cash, but the money is used to recalculate the loan and related costs.

non-conforming use a code violation related to property use that is permitted because it was "grandfathered in." In   other words, the property owner began the questionable property use before the zoning ordinance took effect.

nonliquid asset something of worth that is difficult to convert to cash.

notarize to witness the veracity of a signature.

notary public a person with the legal and official authority to witness the veracity of a signature.

note the written loan that admits debt and promises repayment.

note rate the interest rate on a loan or mortgage.

notice of default official notification that the borrower has defaulted and that the lender can take additional legal remedies.

novation the substitution of one party for another party in a contract.

>O

obligee a person requesting a certain duty in their favor.

obligor a person required to perform a certain duty, often under bond.

obsolescence a decrease in worth because of outdated design or construction, such as a home without a dishwasher or cable hook-up.

offer a suggestion or expression of desire to buy or sell real estate.

offer and acceptance the suggestion or expression of desire to buy or sell real estate and the acceptance of the offer by the other party.

open-end mortgage a loan with smaller amount than the maximum funds that a borrower can access from the lender.

open listing more than one real estate agent can list the property; the first to close the sale is the one who receives payment .

opinion of title legal authentication that the title is clear.

option an agreement that allows a buyer to purchase a property at a specific price if done so within a specific time period.

optionee the person who has available choices.

optionor the person who gives or sells the available choices.

ordinance a statute or legislations related to property use.

original principal balance the loan amount before the first payment is made.

origination fee fees assessed to the borrower that cover loan expenses related to the title, appraisal and credit checks.

owner financing the seller provides the buyer with the loan; the buyer does not go through a bank.

ownership possession of property.

>P

package mortgage a combination loan that covers both the residence and the land.

parcel a section of real estate under the person who owns it.

participation mortgage a loan that permits the holder to receive a portion of the profits from the property.

partition equal division of property between all owners.

partnership business relationship between 2 or more parties subject to debt and tax laws.

party wall a wall that divides 2 properties with ownership rights for both users.

payee the seller who receives money or something of value.

payor the buyer who gives the payee money or something of value.

percentage lease a rental payment determined by sales volume of the renter with a minimum rental amount.

periodic estate a rental agreement that goes for a specific time frame, such as month-to-month.

personal property (hereditaments) anything either tangible or intangible given through a will.

physical deterioration decrease in property worth because of normal wear, failure to repair or things breaking .

PITI principal, interest, taxes and insurance payment; usually the total of all payments due on the property.

planned unit development (PUD) zoning permission to design a subdivision with flexibility and creativity .

plat description of a section of land that provides detailed information about the area.

plat book public information with the description of a section of land that provides detailed information about the area.

plat number the number associated with each lot in a plat.

plottage combining small sections of real estate into a larger parcel.

PMI private mortgage insurance; used to cover the default of the loan.

point one percent of the loan amount; monies paid to entice a lender to loan money to the borrower, sometimes used in exchange for a reduction in the interest rate on the loan.

point of beginning the exact same starting and ending point on a land survey as the survey borders and encloses the property.

police power the government's ability to address the overall well-being of the community.

power of attorney the legal right for one person to perform duties for another either some or all of the time.

preapproval qualifying a buyer prior to actual purchase of the home.

prepayment paying costs or monies due early, sometimes as escrow funds.

prepayment penalty the expenses associated with early pay-off of a loan.

prequalification preapproval, sometimes in writing, before the buyer can purchase the home.

prescription receiving the right to a property through common use, such as a squatter, or adverse possession.

primary mortgage market the original buyer of a loan, such as a bank or savings and loan, which may then be sold on the secondary mortgage market for a profit.

prime rate the lowest available interest rate a lending institution charges on short-term loans to businesses.

principal the face value of a loan or mortgage, separate from the interest, taxes and insurance.

principal meridian an imaginary north/south line used as a reference point in surveying to describe land.

probate to confirm the authenticity of a will.

procuring cause a method of deciding if the real estate agent earned a commission, legal expression that means the goal was realized through the actions.

promissory note a written statement of a promise to pay.

property management oversight of different aspects of property, such as collecting payments, upkeep, leasing units, cleaning units.

property tax real estate tax based on worth that is collected by the government.

prorate to equally divide a financial assessment between a buyer and a seller, for example as HOA fees or property taxes.

pur autre vie "For the life of another;" use of property that one individual gives another, as long as the third person is alive.

purchase agreement also called contract of sale or agreement of sale; a written contract between a buyer and seller.

purchase money mortgage a mortgage loan that the purchaser gives the seller as partial payment for property.

>Q

qualifying ratios the ratio of the buyer's debt when compared to the buyer's income, which must be below a certain percentage for a lending institution to offer the loan.

quitclaim deed a release of rights in a property without confirming the validity or the rights of the person who keeps the deed.

>R

range A six mile wide area of land. Using the rectangular survey system, it is numbered East or West.

ready, willing, and able a buyer who is ready to buy and follows through with the requirements needed to close the sale.

real estate land, the air above it, the ground under it and any buildings.

real estate agent a person who acts on the behalf of another to make a transaction with a third party.

real estate board a group of professional agents who belong to the National Association of Realtors.

real estate broker a person who acts on the behalf of another to make a transaction with a third party.

Real Estate Settlement Procedures Act (RESPA) a law that informs buyers of their rights by requiring the lender to give updated information to the borrower throughout the home buying process.

real property real estate; physical land and structures on the land.

REALTOR a professional real estate agent.

recording the official documentation related to a change in property title, such as a sale or transfer.

rectangular survey system a survey method of dividing land into squares and grids.

redemption period a time frame when an owner can buy back real estate that was foreclosed.

redlining illegal action of refusing to lend money to an individual in a lower socio-economic area without considering the circumstances of the individual.

refinance transaction obtaining a new loan on real estate and paying off the first loan using the same real estate as collateral.

Regulation Z federal requirement that a lender must disclose all terms of a loan, including the APR.

release clause a section in a contract that allows the buyer to pay off part of the loan, which then frees a piece of the real estate from the loan.

remainder estate the real estate that passes to another individual when the first individual's rights in the real estate end.

remainderman the individual who real estate goes to when a life tenant dies.

remaining balance the amount still left to pay on a loan.

remaining term the length of time still left to pay on a loan.

rent payment for temporary use of property; lease.

replacement cost the amount of money needed to replicate an edifice so that it can fulfill previous functions.

reproduction cost the amount of money needed for an exact replica of an edifice.

rescission the negating of a contract so that it is no longer in effect.

restriction (restrict covenant) prevents the real estate from being used in certain manners, either in the deed or through local laws.

reversion the landlord's right to take possession of rental property when the rental agreement ends.

reversionary interest the interest the remainderman has in the ownership of the real estate as it passes to them when a life tenant dies.

reverse annuity mortgage a property loan used for a person with high equity when the lender makes yearly payments to the home owner.

revision alteration or change (e.g. contract).

right of egress (or ingress) the right to leave real estate; the right to go to real estate.

right of first refusal the option an individual or entity has to fulfill a legal agreement before another person or entity meets those obligations.

right of redemption the owner's privilege to take possession of real estate when the financial obligations of the loan have been met even during the process of foreclosure.

right of survivorship the remaining survivor's right to take over the interest of the deceased survivor.

riparian rights water rights in close proximity to a person's real estate.

>S

safety clause an extender clause or protection clause that gives the broker commission if a buyer who sees the home returns later to close the sale.

sale-leaseback the sale of the real estate to a new owner and the new owner rents the real estate back to the original owner.

sales contract a legal agreement between a buyer and seller to finalize a sale.

salesperson a professional and licensed real estate agent or broker.

salvage value used to determine depreciation; the worth of a property or asset when its service is over.

satisfaction a document that verifies and confirms the mortgage payoff.

second mortgage a mortgage obtained after the first mortgage used for a down payment, refinancing or cash.

section a unit of measurement in the government rectangular system, one-square mile.

secured loan a loan that uses collateral in the case of default.

security the real estate used as collateral in case of default when money is borrowed.

seisin the owner who holds the title to the property free and clear.

selling broker the real estate agent who finds a buyer for the property.

separate property property that belongs to only one spouse as opposed to both spouses.

servient tenement property that gives shared use of land to a neighboring property for their good.

setback a boundary away from the edge of the property that must remain free of buildings.

settlement statement (HUD-1) a full accounting of all the monetary transactions that occur in a property sale.

severalty independent interest of real estate by a person.

special assessment a financial levy against real estate to pay for something of benefit to that real estate.

special warranty deed a deed that pertains only to the title under the person issuing it, not to any title issues from previous title holders.

specific lien a mortgage or lien against only a specified part of the real estate.

specific performance mandate by the court that the party in a contract fulfill their duties.

standard payment calculation a process of calculating monthly equal payments needed to pay the balance owed on a mortgage at the present interest rate.

statute of frauds legal necessity for real estate contracts to be written.

statute of limitations a time period after which someone cannot file a law suit.

statutory lien a legal obligation on the property, such as taxes.

steering illegal action when only certain racial or cultural groups are shown a property.

straight-line depreciation the total depreciation divided by the number of years of depreciation.

subdivision a division of land into lots upon which homes are built.

sublet to rent from another renter.

subordinate a lesser priority, as in a subordinate mortgage that would be paid off only if the first mortgage was satisfied in a foreclosure.

substitution replacing the market worth of one piece of real estate for another piece of real estate, usually viewed as indifferent by buyers.

subrogation the legal substitution of one individual for another individual, with all rights passing onto the new party.

suit for possession eviction lawsuit after a break of contract by a renter.

suit for specific performance a lawsuit filed by the buyer for breach of contract in property sale. The court can either require the seller to pay damages and expenses or complete the sale.

survey the boundaries of a parcel of real estate; a map of the property surveyed.

syndicate a group of people or entities who join resources to invest in real estate.

>T

tax deed a legal document that places a claim on real estate because of owed taxes.

tax lien a hold placed on real estate because of owed taxes prior to filing the tax deed.

tax rate the rate at which an individual property is taxed; calculated by dividing all funds needed by all properties within the locale.

tax sale the sale of real estate because taxes have not been paid.

tenancy at sufferance a renter who can no longer legally remain on the property because the lease has ended.

tenancy at will an agreement the owner provides to the renter that ends upon if and when the landlord decides to end it. The renter can also terminate the lease.

tenancy by the entirety equal rights to property shared between spouses, the real estate passes to the surviving spouse upon death of a spouse.

tenancy in common equal rights to property shared between individuals without surviving rights but determined through a will upon one party's death.

tenant renter who pays the landlord a fee for property use.

tenement a fixture that remains as part of the land.

testate a person who dies with a legal will in place.

"Time is of the essence" following a contract according to time specifications to prevent delays in fulfilling the contract.

time sharing a piece of real estate owned by more than one person; each person has the right to a specific time at the property.

title legal proof and verification of property ownership.

title insurance insurance that covers the owner from problems with the title.

title search scrutiny of legal records to review the rights to and encumbrances against real estate.

Torrens system a short-cut type of title registration available in some jurisdictions without going through the lengthy process of a title search.

township a section of land in the government rectangular survey system; six-square miles.

trade fixtures fixtures, such as furniture and appliances, used in a specific business; may convey with the property upon the expiration of the lease.

transfer tax an assessment levied when a title passes from one person or entity to another.

trust a holding that transfers the real estate to the trustee for the beneficiary.

trustee the person who keeps the real estate for the beneficiary.

Truth-in-Lending Law federal requirement that a lender must disclose all terms of a loan, including the APR.

>U

underwriting similar to insuring; validating the policy.

undivided interest shared rights and ownership of property among all owners.

unilateral contract one party has a duty to fulfill a certain responsibility in the contract but the other party does not.

unsecured loan a loan that uses no collateral but may be based on the borrower's credit worthiness.

useful life the period of time during which improvements will yield income.

usury charging a higher than maximum interest rate; illegal.

>V

VA-guaranteed loan a mortgage backed by the government agency, the Veteran's Administration, which promises repayment to the lender for the main residence.

valid contract a legally binding contract that will hold up in a court of law.

valuation estimation of the price of real estate.

variance a deviation from zoning laws that permits the owner to violate zoning code.

vendee buyer of personal property.

vendor seller of personal property.

village a small grouping of residential properties and other buildings.

void contract a written agreement that cannot be enforced even when signed.

voidable contract a written agreement that becomes unenforceable after it is signed.

>W

waiver the abdication of certain rights.

warranty deed a legal right of protection against any type of claim.

waste specified abuse of mortgage or rental property that causes damages.

will legal document that transfers ownership of property to another upon the death of the person who writes the will.

wraparound mortgage a property loan that combines a first mortgage with a second mortgage at a higher loan amount and higher payment.

writ of execution an order that permits the court to sell the person's real estate, such as after a foreclosure.

>Z

zone a section regulated by local rules and conditions, such as a business zone that is prohibited from residential housing.

zoning ordinance a regulation that specifies the type of property use permitted in the area.

Real Estate Sales Exam I

1. A couple executes a sales contract on their home after several counter-offers with the buyer. In this case, the seller is:

a) the mortgagee

b) the grantor

c) the grantee

d) the mortgagor

2. The Cambridge family bought a house with a lot size of .25 of an acre. This is equivalent to:

a) 10,890 feet

b) 43,560 feet

c) 11,000 feet

d) 5,250 feet

3. A primary residence is sold for $527,000 by a couple in the 28% tax bracket. The home was originally purchased 8 years ago for $313,000 where the family lived there the entire 8 years. How much will be paid in capital gains?

a) $59,920

b) $32,100

c) $ 214,000

d) none of the above

4. An owner-occupied 4 unit dwelling worth $525,000 generates $4500 in income from 3 units and $150/mo from the onsite laundry. If the current owner typically yields roughly 9% annually on his investment, what is the monthly effective gross amount?

a) $4350

b) $6000

c) $4905

d) $4650

5. A brother is moving out of the country and decides to sell his home to his sister for $275,000, making this the latest sale in that area. The sister decides to pay cash, as she says she will later get a home equity loan for $200,000. Recent sales comps of very similar homes had values of $325,000. Based on the information provided, what is best estimate of the market value of the subject property?

a) $325,000

b) $200,000

c) $275,000

d) not enough information provided

6. When can a landlord choose to **not** rent to someone with children?

a) Never, children are protected under Fair Housing

b) If the unit has evidence of lead paint

c) A lease of an owner occupied 3- family home

d) Someone on a temporary lease

7. A seller provides written permission allowing his listing broker (who has a fiduciary obligation to the seller) to work with the buyer. This relationship is known as:

a) Dual agency

b) Sub agency

c) Special agency

d) Implied agency

8. A homeowner purchased a home for $300,000 on a 30 year FHA loan with an interest rate of 4.25%. If he wants to do cash out conventional refinance and eliminate the MIP, what is the max amount that the new loan balance can be based on a future home value of $350,000?

a) $276,500

b) $310,000

c) $300,000

d) $240,000

9. A valid contract is _____.

a: Verbal agreement
b: A 10 month lease

a) both a and b

b) b only

c) neither a nor b

d) a only

10. A brother is moving out of the country and decides to sell his home to his sister for $275,000, making this home the latest sale in that area.   This sister puts 20% down and finances $220,000. Recent sales comps of similar homes had values of$485,000. Based on the information provided, what is the market value?

a) $485,000

b) $220,000

c) $225,000

d) not enough information provided

11. Which best describes an example of emblements?

a) cherry tree, apple tree and tomato plants

b) cherry tree, apple tree and peach tree

c) tomato, lettuce and onion crops

d) none of these

12. Nine states recognize this system of property ownership where the husband and wife have equal interest in property acquired through marriage. This is_____.

a) common-law

b) community property

c) commingling

d) common title

13. A dad who owns his house free and clear decides to take out a HELOC and let his son make the payments. He also signs a quitclaim deed to transfer the home into his son's name. What clause might the lender enforce?

a) co-insurance clause

b) acceleration clause

c) due-on-sale clause

d) cancellation clause

14. In New York, which of the following situations would NOT allow for the termination of a contract?

a) agreement of the parties

b) full performance

c) impossibility of performance

d) none of the above

15. The Federal Home Loan Mortgage Corporation primarily purchases which loan types:

a) FHA

b) owner-financed notes

c) VA

d) conventional

16. Sally works for ABC Bank. Her job duties are to gather documents, review application for accuracy, package the loan and take each file from pre-approval to closing. What is most likely her job title?

a) underwriter

b) processor

c) loan officer

d) appraiser

17.   Which of the following does not loan money directly to borrowers?

a) insurance company

b) mortgage broker

c) cooperative bank

d) private lender

18. Jay decides that he's ready to move out of his parent's home and purchase his own home. He has a roommate who will be moving in so he would like at least a 3 bedroom house. What should his 1st step be?

a) get prequalified by submitting a mortgage application

b) purchase new furniture

c) pick out a house

d) purchase a new car to go with the new house

19. Mike and Kathy have $30,000 or 10% down to purchase their 1st home. Their loan officer prequalifies them for several different loan types. They decide to go with the following

scenario: purchase price: $300,000 with a loan amount of $300,000 and $6450 funding fee. What type of loan did they choose?

a) conventional

b) FHA

c) VA

d) negative amortization

20. A lender offers you a very low interest of 2.75% in exchange for part of your equity. What type of mortgage is this?

a) balloon

b) shared equity

c) wraparound mortgage

d) equity loan

21. Sellers Keith and Rita execute a standard purchase and sale agreement on November 1st. The contract also states that by Nov 15th their agent should receive a mortgage commitment letter. November 14th, the buyer's agent sends over a letter that the buyer has been unable to secure financing. They should expect:

a) their earnest money deposit back

b) to withdraw from the transaction

c) both a and b

d) a only

22. House and Home Realty Brokerage leased a 2 family residence for $1500/mo for each unit. Tenant 1 wrote a check to cover the 1st month's rent and deposit and tenant 2 paid by money order. Which is the best representation of what the brokerage must do?

a) make and keep a copy of all funds collected from each tenant

b) nothing as long as the broker received the money that is sufficient

c) Only copy the money order because a check is a legal record

d) Tell the tenant to pay the owner directly

23. Kimberly finds the home of her dreams, cozy bungalow built in 1932. Her agent suspects that the home may have lead-based paint. Kimberly has how many days to test for lead-based paint?

a) 5

b) 3

c) 7

d) 10

24. The governor appoints 5 members to the Board of Registration of Real Estate Brokers and Salespersons. How many members are not licensed agents?

a) 5

b) 0. all are licensed

c) 2

d) 3

25. An appraisal is done on a unique property that sits on 42.5 acres. The approach the appraiser will more than likely use is _____.

a) assumption

b) cost

c) income

d) market data

26. Jill secures a 15 year fixed conventional home loan. This loan was more than likely purchased by which investor?

a) FNMA

b) insurance company

c) an orb

d) GNMA

27. A homeowner has an existing mortgage balance of $120,000 with a mortgage payment of $1375. He puts an ad in the newspaper to sell his home, owner financing where he will offer the buyer a new note based on a sales price of $258,000 at 5 %. The buyer decides to use this financing to purchase the home. Based on the information given, what type of mortgage is this?

a) wraparound mortgage

b) junior mortgage

c) package mortgage

d) none of these

28. When determining whether a buyer is a good credit risk, the lender needs to evaluate:

a) borrower's credit, the borrower's ability to pay, and homeowner's age

b) ability to pay, property, borrower's 401K

c) borrower's credit, future expected value of the property, job stability

d) property, ability to pay, credit

29. When a buyer chooses to pay discount points, her goal is to receive_____.

a) cash back at closing

b) a lower interest rate

c) principal reduction

d) none of these

30. Kevin's sister decides she wants to purchase a home and needs to get prequalified. Kevin's sister's best friend James is a loan officer at the bank and tells him once the loan closes he will give him a referral fee. Which statement is true?

a) As long as James gives Kim the HUD information booklet within 3 days, he can pay a referral fee

b) James is protected under RESPA

c) James must disclose the referral amount on the GFE

d) Fees and kickbacks to individuals who do not provide a loan is prohibited

31. Members of the Board of Registration of Real Estate serve a term of _____ years.

a) 5

b) 2

c) 7

D) 10

32. The purpose of which of the following is to enforce a minimum standard for the construction and renovation of buildings?

a) NYS Mortgage Foreclosure Law

b) NYS Office of Parks, Recreation and Historic Preservation

c) NYS Uniform Fire Prevention and Building Code

d) NYS Human Rights Law

33. Another name for a HUD-1 is _____,

a) Good Faith Estimate

b) Uniform Settlement statement

c) Truth-in-Lending document

d) Housing Uniform document

34. A homeowner attempts a refinance on his home only to find out that the home has 2 liens from the previous owner that were never paid off. Who should he contact?

a) The title insurance company

b) the escrow office

c) the loan officer

d) a real estate attorney

35. All listing types below allow the seller the right to sell their property on their own without paying a commission, EXCEPT_____.

a) an exclusive agency

b) Open

c) exclusive right to sell

d) none of the above

36. Kurt receives a letter that an expressway is being built where his property sits. The state offers to purchase his home. What right are they (the state) exerting?

a) escheatment

b) foreclosure

c) adverse passion

d) eminent domain

37. A family leases a home with a pool. The contract states that the owner will pay property taxes and insurance, but the tenant must pay the pool and yard expenses. This is known as a _____ lease.

a) percentage

b) gross

c) net

d) month to month

38. Mr. Green has purchased new energy efficient windows, put weather stripping around the doors and replaced his old wall heater with a new central air and heat system. Mr. Green has _____ his home.

a) weatherized

b) energized

c) overhauled

d) redlined

39. How many municipalities in New York have rent control?

a) 51

b) 3

c) 22

d) 10

40. The total commission for the sale of a $449,000 property is 6%. The listing states that they will offer 3.5% to a co-broker who brings a buyer which ends in a successfully closed transaction. How much will the listing broker net after his sales agent, who is on a 45/55 (listing broker gets 55%) split, is paid?

a) $26,940

b) $15,715

c) $6174

d) $11,225

41. Several first time home buyers purchasing homes in a community redevelopment area noticed that they were not offered a fixed rate loan by the developer's lender. They were only offered adjustable rate mortgages. This is most likely an example of _____.

a) economic adjustments

b) redlining

c) conforming

d) steering

42. Susie has been a licensed sales agent for over a year and would like to pursue her broker's license. What must she do?

a) be at least 25 years old

b) be a salesperson for at least 2 years

c) complete 200 hours of a qualifying course

d) all of the above

43. All are true except:

a) real estate licenses are valid for 2 years

b) an inactive sales agent cannot collect referral fees

c) the fee for renewing a salesperson's license is $137

d) a salesperson must take continuing education in order to remain in active status

44. FHA insured loans protect the:

a) lender

b) realtor

c) seller

d) buyer

45. In New York, what is the percentage of the mansion tax collected from the purchasers of a two-family home that costs $1 million or more?

a) 1

b) 3

c) 5

d) 2

46. A tenant signs a 1 year lease where the owner allows him to occupy the property during this time. This is an example of _____.

a) fee simple

b) freehold estate

c) time share

d) non-freehold estate

47. What type of mortgage is also known as a "term mortgage"?

a) ARM

b) Straight

c) Purchase Money

d) GPM

48. When someone who is upside down with their mortgage gets permission to sell their house for less than they owe, this process is known as:

a) short sale

b) foreclosure

c) deed restructure

d) deed-in-lieu of foreclosure

49. "OLD CAR" stands for:

a) obligation, litigation, disclosure, care, access, real estate

b) obedience, loyalty, dedication, confidentiality, accountability, realtor

c) obligation, license, disclosure, confidentiality, accountability, reasonable care

d) obedience, loyalty, disclosure, confidentiality, accountability, reasonable care

50. In what type of mortgage is the borrower's down payment deposited in a savings account with the lender?

a) Pledged Account

b) Straight

c) Purchase Money

d) GPM

51. A broker's license can be revoked if he:

a) fails to return deposit funds to client when requested

b) commingles business and personal funds

c) fails to pay the agent his commission split

d) all of the above

52. A person dies leaving no will and no heirs. The decedent's property would transfer by:

a) adverse possession

b) state

c) escheat

d) laws of descent

53. Describe the ownership of a property if 4 cousins, Keenan, Kelly, Shon, and Marcia   are joint tenants and Marcia sells her interest to cousin Michael. The new deed will read:

a) tenants in common with Keenan, Kelly and Shon

b) tenants in will

c) joints tenant Keenan, Kelly and Shon

d) Marcia is not allowed to sell her interest

54. A transaction where the seller agrees to finance the loan of the buyer is called:

a) hard money loan

b) blanket mortgage

c) conventional loan

d) purchase money mortgage

55. A 2,980 square feet home sells for $328,000. If it sits on an acre lot, what is the price/ square feet the home sold for?

a) $94

b) $110

c) $116

d) $154

56. A lot recently sold for $198,000. It is 378' x 296'. What was the cost/acre?

a) $67,074

b) $70,774

c) $77,774

d) $77,042

57. If Michelle sells her home, but then remains in the property by becoming a tenant of the new landlord, this is known as

a) testate

b) wraparound mortgage

c) leaseback

d) freehold

58. A homeowner puts a $104,250 down payment on a $417,000 home. What percentage is the down payment?

a) 25%

b) 18%

c) 20%

d) 30%

59. "Age" is a protected class under which of the following?

a) NYC Commission on Human Rights

b) Fair Housing Amendments Act of 1988

c) Housing and Community Development Act of 1974

d) Civil Rights Act of 1866

60. An investor gets a 30 year loan due in 15 years. This is a:

a) VA loan

b) package mortgage

c) balloon

d) open-end mortgage

61. Easements appurtenants are created by which of the following?

a) necessity and intent

b) implication

c) prescription

d) all of the above

62. The most probable price that an informed purchaser might pay is the:

a) sales price

b) broker price opinion

c) market value

d) assessed value

63. A lender prequalifies a couple for a loan amount up to $375,000 with a 3.5% down payment. What booklet must he give them within 3 days of application?

a) an information booklet prepared by HUD

b) a booklet on the explanation of closing costs

c) Regulation – Z booklet

c) HUD-1 booklet

64. When a borrower makes a down payment less than 20% and gets an FHA loan, what monthly charge should they expect to be added to their mortgage payment?

a) property taxes

b) funding fee

c) mortgage insurance premium

d) equity loan payment

65._____ backs rural development loans.

a) a life insurance company

b) FHA

c) Freddie Mac

d) Ginnie Mae

66. The sales comparison approach is also known as the:

a) appraisal process

b) market data

c) replacement cost

d) cost

67. "DUST" is a term associated with:

a) licensing

b) title

c) appraisals

d) conformity

68. If there are more homes on the market than buyers, there is:

a) regression

b) more supply than demand

c) substitution

d) law of decreasing return

69. If a 3 family home is valued at $769,000 and the cap rate is 9% ,what is the annual net operating income?

a) $69,210

b) $85,444

c) $100,000

d) $71,000

70. Tim inherits his family's farm which has suffered years of neglect. He decides to take an equity loan on the property, so his realtor orders an appraisal. While doing the appraisal, the appraiser sees obvious physical deterioration and also notices that a bathroom was never added to the home, it still has an outhouse. The lack of an inside bathroom is a _____.

a) functional obsolescence

b) physical deterioration

c) economic obsolescence

d) accrued depreciation

71. Another name for the Federal Fair Housing Act is _____.

a) Fair housing

b) Title VIII of the Civil Rights Act of 1968

c) Federal Civil Rights Act of 1866

d) Consumer Protection Law

72. Which of these is NOT an appurtenant right?

a) water rights

b) subsurface rights

c) air rights

d) civil rights

73. All of these are grounds for license suspension or revocation EXCEPT

a) commingling personal and business funds

b) acting as an undisclosed dual agent

c) owing no fiduciary duties to clients while acting as a facilitator

d) practicing real estate with an inactive license

74. All have right of survivorship EXCEPT

a) tenancy in common

b) tenancy by entirety

c) joint tenancy

d) none of the above

75. The best form of ownership is:

a) pur autre vie

b) leasehold

c) fee simple

d) freehold

76. Mary and John owned their home as joint tenants until Mary died. Which statement is true?

a) John now has to sell his home.

b) If there is a loan on the property, the lender will call the loan due.

c) John will become the sole owner

d) John will have to move

77. In New York, which of these is NOT one of the most common legal descriptions used?

a) principal meridian

b) metes and bounds

c) description by reference, lot and block

d) monuments

78. A licensed agent who is associated with a brokerage is a:

a) broker

b) salesperson

c) processor

d) escrow agent

79. Overlooked by many homeowners, which is NOT a cost of owning a home?

a) repairs

b) interest paid on the mortgage loan

c) personal property taxes

d) maintenance

80. Which is MOST likely to influence a person's decision to purchase a home in a certain location?

a) street signage

b) school ratings

c) high number of planned unit developments

d) loan types

81. The only time a broker can add personal funds to the escrow account is

a) never

b) to maintain a minimum balance in the escrow account

c) to purchase investment property using the escrow account

d) if a purchaser asks the broker to hold funds

82. Income received from annuities is known as:

a) Passive activity income

b) Active income

c) Unrealized income

d) Portfolio income

83. Mr. and Mrs. Sellers signed the purchase and sales agreement in which they are selling their home to the Buyer family. The Buyers have moved forward in getting all inspections, appraisals etc ordered on the property, however the Sellers are now feeling sad and desire to terminate the contract. Which statement is true?

a) they are the owners and maintain the right to terminate the contract at any time

b) they may be forced to sell their home as the contract is legal and binding

c) if they offer to return the buyers deposit and pay other incurred expenses the Buyers must accept this and allow them to terminate the contract

d) none of the above are true

84. Which of the following ads will require more disclosures?

a) We have no money down loans

b) VA, FHA and conventional loans offered here

c) APR is 4.5% on a 30 year fixed loan

d) The interest rate is 4.375% per year

85. A missing _____ could cause a home to not pass an FHA inspection.

a) refrigerator

b) freestanding stove

c) cooktop

d) washer/dryer

86. Larry is purchasing a home that has $20,000 in needed repairs but he doesn't have $20,000. What loan is a good option for him?

a) FHA 203(b)

b) FHA 203(k)

c) FHA 203(c)

d) FHA

87. The minimum age in New York to receive a salesperson's license is:

a) 21

b) 25

c) 16

d) 18

88. In New York when an agent provides information that another agent has requested, this term is known as:

a) cooperate

b) equity share

c) co-broker

d) commission split

89. In New York, to apply for a broker license, an individual must be at least___ years old.

a) 18

b) 21

c) 20

d) 25

90. In New York, how many years of experience must an individual have in order to apply for a salesperson license?

a) one

b) five

c) three

d) none

91. Jim does a lot of home improvement projects, so he built a shed on his neighbor Jerry's land.   Jim has used this shed continuously for over 20 years. Jim can pursue a claim of _____ in order to gain title the property.

a) adverse possession

b) eminent domain

c) servient tenement

d) concurrent ownership

92. An ad reads "2 story traditional 1500 square foot home in Albany, New York for sale. Asking $423,000. Please call Rhonda at 857-455-8234. From a legal perspective, the ad is missing:

a) Rhonda's last name

b) Rhonda disclosing that she is a broker

c) number of bedrooms and bathrooms

d) Rhonda disclosing her brokerage's name and that she is a licensed broker

93. What is a broker's commission fee percent if she sells a building for $673,225 and her fee earned is $16,830.62?

a) 2.5%

b) 6.5%

c) 3.5 %

d) 4.0%

94. Another name for loan fees is:

a) application fee

b) credit report fee

c) discount points

d) broker's fees

95. The Federal Civil Rights Act was passed in

a) 1968

b) 1866

c) 1868

d) 1986

96. The _____ sets the minimum requirements for appraisals.

a) RESPA

b) MLS

c) TILA

d) USPAP

97. A section is:

a) 2 square miles

b) a city block

c) 27,878,400 square feet

d) 43,560 acres

98. In New York, what is a salesperson's fee and term of licensure?

a) $50 every 2 years

b) $100 every year

c) $50 every year

d) $100 every 2 years

99. Which is not covered under the fair housing laws?

a) a SFR that is corporate owned

b) elderly housing that meets certain Department of Housing and Urban Development guidelines

c) a 2 -4 unit dwelling that is not owner occupied

d) a home owned by an individual who owns more than 3 properties

100. Within a 3 year period, an owner has been found guilty of sending discriminatory letters to his tenants. The owner may have to pay civil penalties up to _____ if this is his 1st offense:

a) $25,000

b) $10,000

c) $50,000

d) $20,000

Real Estate Sales Exam I Answers

1. b. The couple (owner) is conveying title to the real property.

2. a.   1 acre = 43,560   43,560 * .25 = 10,890 feet

3. d.   None of the above. The property is a primary residence which has been lived in over 5 years with a profit less than $500,000.

4. d.   The effective gross amt is $4500 + $150 (the sum of all income generated.)

5. a.   The transaction is "non-arms length" because they are related.

6. c.   The children are generally protected under Chapter 151B (Fair Housing) except when an occupant requests a temporary lease

7. b. Subagency requires that the listing broker obtain written permission from the seller and that the fiduciary duties are to the seller.

8. a. To eliminate the mortgage insurance premium, the loan to value must be below 80%.

9. a. A contract is defined as an agreement between 2 or more persons or entities and they can be written or verbal.

10. a. This is an arm's length transaction because the brother and sister are related; therefore the sold price cannot be included with non-arm's length sales comps.

11. c. Emblements are crops that are annually cultivated.

12. b. Each spouse has equal interest in property acquired during marriage.

13. c. Because the borrower has transferred the property, the lender is allowed to demand full payment.

14. d. In New York, a contract can be terminated if any of the following are present: 1. agreement of the parties 2. full performance 3. impossibility of performance 4. operation of law.

15. d. Fannie Mae and Freddie Mac purchase conventional loans.

16. b. Processors prepare the loan package for the underwriter

17. b. Mortgage brokers bring borrowers together with lenders.

18. a. The 1st step to obtaining home loan financing is to submit the application.

19. c. VA loans offer 100% financing and include a funding fee.

20. b. Shared equity is when the lender offers a low interest rate in exchange for a portion of the equity.

21. c. This contract was written with a financing contingency in which the purchase was given a date to secure financing.

22. a. The property manager is required to make and keep a copy of collected funds for 3 years.

23. d. Under the Lead Paint Law, the buyer gets 10 days to test for evidence of lead paint.

24. c. 2 of the members must be unlicensed and are members to represent the public.

25. b. The cost approach is used when the appraiser has difficulty finding comps.

26. a. FNMA purchases conventional loans.

27. a. The new mortgage will include the remaining balance on the existing first mortgage.

28. d. The lender must do an appraisal, ensure the borrower has means to repay the mortgage and meet the lender's credit score.

29. b. Points charged by a lender are to lower the rate for the buyer.

30. d. RESPA prohibits several types of payments to persons who did not perform a service.

31. a. The term is for 5 years.

32. c. This is true for all buildings in New York, not just residential properties.

33. b. A HUD-1 is also known as a Uniform Settlement Statement.

34. a. The title insurance companies protect the holder from defects in the title.

35. c. An exclusive right to sell listing allows the broker to receive a commission no matter who sells the property.

36. d. Eminent domain gives the government the right to take private property for public use.

37. c. In net lease, the tenant pays the maintenance and operating expenses.

38. a. Because he made energy efficient improvements he has weatherized his home.

39. a. New York City uses Maximum Base Rent. Landlords can raise rent up to 7.5% each year until the rent reaches the maximum base rent amount.

40. c. Subtract the listing broker's commission from the total commission percentage. Then multiply that number to the home sales price. Then multiply that number by the listing broker's split with his agent.   6- 3.5= 2.5% x 449000 = 11225 x 55% = 6174.

41. b. The lender only offered 1 loan type to homebuyers purchasing in the area which is more than likely a low to moderate income area.

42. b. To be a broker in New York, she has be at least 20 years old, complete 120 hours of a qualifying course, and be a salesperson for 2 years or 3-year equivalent .

43. c. The fee for renewing a salesperson's license is $127.

44. a. FHA insured loans protect the lender in the event the borrower defaults.

45. a. A 1% mansion tax is collected from purchasers of one-, two-, or three- family homes, cooperatives, or condominiums that cost$1 million or more.

46. d. Non-freehold estates give the holder of the estate the right to occupy the property until the end of the lease.

47. b. With this type of mortgage, a borrower is responsible for only paying interest for a specific amount of time. After that, he must pay the principal.

48. a. Short sale is when the bank gives the homeowner the permission to sell the home when they owe more than it's worth.

49. d. "OLD CAR" is an acronym used to remember the agent's fiduciary duties to their client.

50. a. The borrower makes increasing payments, to which withdrawal forms from the savings account are added.

51. d. A broker cannot mix business and personal funds, refuse to pay client their escrow funds when requested and hold out on paying his sales agent.

52. c. When no heirs can be found, the state can lay claim to the property.

53. a. Joint tenants can transfer title but the new owner becomes a tenant in common with the other joint tenants. For joint tenancy to be valid everyone has to go on title at the same time.

54. d. A purchase money mortgage is when the seller holds the financing for the borrower.

55. b. Price/ square feet is found by dividing the price by the square feet. 328000/2980 = 110.

56. d. Multiply the lot dimensions 378 x 296 = 111,888 square feet. Determine how many acres the lot is. An acre is 43,560 square feet; therefore divide 111,888/ 43,560= 2.57 acres. Divide the cost of $198,000 by 2.57 = $77,042.

57. c. New landlord leases property back to the tenant.

58. a. Divide the down payment by the sales price. 104,250/417000 = .25 or 25%.

59. a. "Age" is a protected class under NYC Commission on Human Rights and NYS Human Rights Law.

60. c. In a balloon mortgage the final lump sum is due at the balloon termination date.

61. d. Easements appurtenant are created by necessity and intent, prescription, grant or reservation (deed), implication, and condemnation.

62. c. Market value is the most probable price that an informed buyer will pay.

63. a. Per RESPA , a lender or mortgage broker must give a borrower a copy of a HUD prepared information booklet within 3 days of application.

64. c. FHA provides mortgage insurance to protect the lender in case default and the borrower pays a monthly fee along with their mortgage payment.

65. d. The Government National Mortgage Association (Ginnie Mae) is a major purchaser of government-backed mortgage loans.

66. b. The Market Data approach is also known as the Comparison approach.

67. c. DUST is an acronym for the elements that establish value and is associated with appraisals.

Demand for the type of property

Utility (desirable use) the property offers

Scarcity of properties available

Transferability of property to a new owner

68. b. There's a larger inventory of homes than there are buyers

69. a. Value x Cap rate = Net Operating Income

769000 x .09 = 69210

70. a. Functional obsolescence highlights features that are no longer considered desirable.

71. b. The Federal Fair Housing Act broadened the prohibitions against discrimination in housing to include sex, race, color religion, national origin, and handicap familial status in connection with the sale or rental of housing or vacant land.

72. d. The most common appurtenant rights are profit, license, air rights, subsurface rights, and water rights.

73. c. A facilitator (non-agent) owes no fiduciary duties to clients

74. a. Tenancy in common does not have right of survivorship. Tenancy by entirety is a form of joint tenancy and has along with joint tenancy right of survivorship.

75. c. Fee simple is a type of freehold estate and is the best form of ownership because the owner has the right to occupy or rent the property, sell or transfer ownership, build on and mine for minerals and restrict or allow the use of the property to others.

76. c. Joint tenancy includes the right of survivorship, the surviving co-owners share equally in the deceased owner's interest.

77. a. In New York, there are three common legal descriptions used. They are: metes and bounds, description by reference, lot, and block, and monuments.

78. b. A licensed agent who is associated with a brokerage is a salesperson.

79. c. Personal property taxes are taxes on personal property not real property.

80. b. School ratings can influence whether a person purchases in a certain area.

81. b. A broker can mix business and personal funds if the broker needs to add funds to maintain a minimum balance in the escrow account.

82. d. Interest, annuities, dividends, and royalties are known as portfolio income.

83. b. Because the contract is legal and binding, if the Sellers don't move forward, they will be in breach of contract and the Buyers can sue for specific performance.

84. a. The ad should disclose the loan amount, down payment and APR and terms of repayment.

85. c. FHA minimum property guidelines state that the home must be delivered in safe, secure and sound condition. A free standing stove could be considered personal property, but a cooktop (because it is attached) is a part of the home.

86. b. FHA 203(k) is FHA's Rehabilitation Loan Insurance Program.

87. d. New York minimum age for a real estate salesperson license is 18.

88. a. In real estate when an agent provides information that another agent has requested this is to cooperate.

89. c. For a salesperson license, one must be at least 18 years old. To apply for a broker's license, one must be at least 20 years old.

90. d. To apply for a salesperson license, one is not required to have any experience. However, to apply for a broker's license, one must have experience of two years as a salesperson or three-year equivalent.

91. a. Adverse possession is a method of acquiring title to another person's property through court action after continuous use for over 20 years.

92. d. The broker must disclose her name and that she is a licensed broker.

93. a. Divide the total commission earned by the sales price. 16830.62/673225 =.025 x 100 = 2.5%.

94. c. Discount points are loan fees that the buyer can pay to get a lower interest rate.

95. b. The Federal Civil Rights Act was passed in 1866 to prohibit discrimination on the basis of race.

96. d. The Uniform Standards of Professional Appraisal Practice (USPAP) sets the minimum requirement for appraisals.

97. c. A section is 640 acres. (640 acres/acre) x 43560 sq ft = 27,878,400 square feet.

98. a. The fee and term of licensure for a sales person is $50 every 2 years. It is $150 every 2 years for a broker / associate broker.

99. b. The Federal Fair Housing Act does not cover housing for the elderly that meets certain HUD guidelines.

100. b. Under the Federal Fair Housing Act a person can pay civil penalties up to $10,000 for the 1st offense.

Real Estate Sales Exam II

1. MY TOWN Realty gets a listing to sell a home. The broker appoints one of his sales agents (with permission of the sellers), Melissa represent the sellers. During one of the open houses, a couple comes in and decides to make an offer, so they call the broker at MY TOWN, who then assigns one of his other sales agents, Keith to represent the buyers. In this case the broker is acting as a:

a) non-agent

b) designated seller's and buyer's agent/dual agent

c) single agent

d) principal agent

2. A buyer secures a 1st mortgage for $243,750, puts down 15% and the seller carry's back 10%. What was the sales price of the home if she paid full asking?

a) $250,000

b) $300,000

c) $375,000

d) $325,000

3.   All are true statements regarding appraisal reports EXCEPT?

a) they can be verbally delivered

b) they must be delivered on the Uniform Residential Appraisal Report

c) must use guidelines set forth by USPAP

d) they can be delivered in writing

4. Seller competition in the market usually results in:

a) higher home prices

b) lower home prices

c) anticipation

d) progression

5. The disposition, control, right of possession and enjoyment are all:

a) zoning ordinances

b) Intangibles

c) corporeal

d) the bundle of rights of ownership

6. All are real property EXCEPT

a) air rights

b) refrigerator

c) oak tree

d) pond

7. In New York, how many hours of a qualifying course is necessary in order to obtain a broker's license?

a) 75 hours

b) 300 hours

c) 120 hours

c) 40 hours

8. A church, which has 501(c) 3 status is exempt from paying:

a) a mortgage

b) property taxes

c) hazard insurance

d) licensing fees

9. Anthony sells his condo to Michael. Besides getting a certificate 6(d) what other certificate must he obtain?

a) insurance

b) 21(e)

c) property tax

d) freehold

10. Matthew decides to purchase a home, so he gives his landlord of 2 years a 30 day notice. If his security deposit was $1345 and the bank interest rate (where the landlord held his deposit) was 1%, how much money should he expect back?

a) 1545.38

b) $1345

c) $1358.45

d) $1435

11. Even though Jennifer's lease ended over a month ago, she has not moved out. What type of tenancy does she now have?

a) tenancy at will

b) tenancy for years

c) tenancy for period to period

d) tenancy at sufferance

12. Realtors are members of the

a) NAREB

b) NRA

c) NAR

d) REBAC

13. A lender needs to set a listing price on one of their foreclosed homes. They will more than likely order a(n):

a) mortgage payment history

b) appraisal

c) assessed value report

d) BPO

14. Which one is an example of commercial real estate?

a) a 21 unit apartment complex

b) a store for rent

c) a store front with apartments on the second floor

d) loft apartments

15. Julian refuses to pay his condo association fees; he runs the risk of the association placing a priority lien on his property. This Bill is known as the

a) Priority Lien

b)NYSAR

c) New York Human Rights Law

d) Super Lien

16. Fructus naturales refers to:

a) real property

b) emblements

c) natural fruit

d) annually cultivated crops

17. An exploration company purchases the rights to any minerals and oil from an owner. The owner now owns all rights EXCEPT the following

a) subsurface

b) water

c) air

d) surface

18. A manufactured home is proven by:

a) mortgage deed

b) mortgage note

c) bill of sale

d) purchase contract

19. Cheri was so happy when she received checks from her lender where she could use them to pay her contractor. She took out a(n) _____mortgage.

a) equity

b) land sales

c) purchase money mortgage

d) primary

20. Bill negotiated the lease for his new apartment on the phone and told the landlord that he could sign the lease and meet in person within 3 days. However, Bill experienced an emergency and had to fly out of town right away, so he told his twin brother Will to meet the landlord and sign the lease for him. The lease is:

a) valid

b) void

c) voidable

d) illegal

21. In 2 days, Jackie was anticipating going to her home loan closing, but instead she received a call from her agent that the home had an old 2nd lien on it that the seller said he paid off. What term best describes the title?

a) the title is free and clear

b) the title is encumbered

c) the title is vested

d) the title is clouded

22. Due to the economy and a loss of jobs in the area. Home prices have fallen by 46% and are now valued at about $372,000. Based on the information, what

was the average home price?

a) $866,000

b) $689,000

c) $668,000

d) $888,888

23. Janet's landlord locked her out of the building she lives in New York, New York. She decides that she wants to file a lawsuit against him but finds that he has filed bankruptcy. She must file her case with which court?

a) Janet cannot file a lawsuit; she must go before the bankruptcy court

b) Judicial

c) Housing

d) District

24. A couple, who had their home listed with Any Town Brokerage, hosted a Christmas party. One of the guests from the party loved the home and came back over to ask them several questions about the house and get a formal tour. He ended up purchasing the home and the sellers did not have to pay Any Town Brokerage any commission. What type of listing did they have with Any Town?

a) dual

b) net

c) open

d) exclusive agency

25. An apartment purchaser receives shares and a limited partnership. What type of apartment was purchased?

a) condo

b) cooperative

c) multi unit

d) 3 family home

26. In New York, what amount of surety bond must a person submit with a broker license application?

a) $20,000

b) $40,000

c) $10,000

d) $70,000

27. Balance contributes to value when:

a) there is homogeneity in a neighborhood

b) there are diverse land uses

c) there is conformity

d) there is regression

28. If an agent is found to have violated Massachusetts fair housing laws, his license can be automatically suspended for_____ days.

a) 60

b) 120

c) 30

d) 90

29. Mrs. Tenant vacated her apartment because her landlord turned off the water. This was a(n):

a) adverse eviction

b) lease back

c) constructive eviction

d) contractual eviction

30. In a 99-year lease, the buyer typically receives all bundle of rights EXCEPT:

a) enjoyment

b) possession

c) control of use

d) none of the above

31. Which of the following makes direct loans?

a) Rural Housing Service

b) State of New York

c) Department of Veterans Affairs

d) Federal Housing Authority

32. Which of the following is NOT a disclosure that the Truth in Lending Act requires?

a) amount financed

b) finance charge

c) APR

d) none of the above

33. What type of tenancy does a tenant who lives in public housing have if they have additional tenant protections?

a) tenant at will

b) tenant with written lease

c) tenant by regulation

d) tenant at sufferance

34. Another name for a tenant at will is _____.

a) yearly lease

b) common tenancy

c) sublease

d) month to month

35. For a fixed rate conventional loan, what is the maximum percentage in total obligations the borrower can have?

a) 31

b) 28

c) 41

d) 36

36. For an adjustable rate conventional loan, what is the maximum percentage monthly housing expense the borrower can have?

a) 31

b) 28

c) 36

d) 41

37. A seller will pay 3% in closing cost. If the sales price is $378,499 and the buyer is putting down a 20% down payment, which is the amount paid by the seller?

a) $ 2270

b) $9084

c) $3000

d) $11,355

38. For an FHA loan, what is the maximum percentage monthly housing expense the borrower can have?

a) 26

b) 38

c) 31

d) 24

39. Mike and Dana are renting a unit in their 1946 2 family home to a couple with a 5 year old child. What must they (Mike and Dana) do in accordance to the Lead Law?

a) delead

b) give the new tenants a Lead Paint N

c) have the tenants sign an escalation lease

d) provide the tenants a stock certificate

40. Stan and his business partner decide to sell their 4 unit property. They find another 4 unit property in a town closer to where they live which will make it easier to manage. What product can they use that may ease their current tax burden from the sale?

a) 1031 exchange

b) owner financing

c) hard money loan

d) equity loan

41. If you are a tenant in a property that has been foreclosed, your tenancy will:

a) terminate and you must immediately move out

b) automatically convert to a written lease with the lender

c) automatically turn into a tenancy at will

d) turn into an option to purchase

42. Sharon was told that her front and back end numbers were 48/55 and that she did not qualify for a home loan at this time. These are called _____.

a) LTV

b) qualifying ratios

c) cost per unit

d) income to debt ratios

43. Farmer Jedd has _____ rights in that he is able to allow his horses to drink from the river next to his property.

a) mineral

b) air and surface

c) littoral

d) riparian

44. Regarding New York High-Cost (Subprime) Loans, which of these is TRUE?

a) The lender can increase the interest rate when the borrower defaults.

b) The lender may not charge hidden fees.

c) The loan can be made to unqualified buyers.

d) The loan is allowed to cause negative amortization.

45. An agent lost her wallet with her real estate license. In order to get a duplicate, she must_____.

a) complete the change of name form on the Board's website

b) misplaced license form

c) retake the test

d) only send in the appli00000000cable fee, no form is needed.

46. Mitzi is a licensed agent but no longer wishes to perform real estate. The **only** thing she needs to do is:

a) send a resignation letter to her broker

b) send a resignation letter to the Board

c) do not pay the renewal fee

d) tell the Board members in person when they have a meeting

47. In New York, a 1st time homebuyer is someone who hasn't owned a property for
_____ years.

a) 4

b) 5

c) never owned a home

d)3

48. The Taxpayer Relief Act was passed in:

a) 1997

b) 1986

c) 1977

d) 2001

49. Flood insurance is

a) always optional

b) required in certain areas

c) automatically included in the hazard insurance policy

d) only available to homeowners purchasing properties financed by rural housing

50. Patty has gotten a loan pre- approval from **Conservative** Trust Bank. More than likely, her housing expense ratio does not exceed _____ percent.

a) 38

b) 20

c) 28

d) 33

51. How much must a mortgage broker applicant submit with the application for an investigation fee?

a) $2,700

b) $200

c) $1,500

d) $500

52. Under the cost approach, the formula for determining value is:

a) Replacement or reproduction cost – Accrued Depreciation + Land Value = Value

b) Accrued Depreciation – Replacement or reproduction cost + Land Value = Value

c) Replacement or reproduction cost + Accrued Depreciation - Land Value = Value

d) Replacement or reproduction cost + Land Value – Accrued Depreciation = Value

53. All are examples of a protected class EXCEPT:

a) children

b) veterans

c) elderly

d) All of the above

54. How much must a mortgage broker applicant submit with the application for a fingerprint processing fee?

a) $475

b) $325

c) $265

d) $105

55. The _____ pledges the property as collateral.

a) mortgage lien

b) mortgage deed

c) mortgage note

d) collateralization note

56. Land, "bundle of legal rights", and permanent, human-made additions are

a) personal property

b) emblements

c) real property

d) real estate

57. Lisa and Mike are remodeling their home. The contractor unloads a truckload of drywall and tile in front of their house. The delivered items are

a) personal property

b) encumbrances

c) real property

d) real estate

58. Which is NOT one of the "bundle of rights"?

a) right to transfer the home to a relative

b) right to live in the home

c) right to refuse entry into the home

d) right to run a neighborhood casino

59. Which economic characteristic of Real Estate best represents the following example? Two identical homes built by the same developer are located on Milford Street, which is a street that separates 2 cities, Old City and New City. House A is in New City and sits on the west side of the street and house B sits on the east side of the street and is in Old City. Because it is a newer area, homeowner's believe that the school district in New City is better than Old City.

a) relative scarcity

b) area preference

c) supply and demand

d) improvements

60. A granddaughter inherited a home worth about $225,000 that her grandparents lived in for 50 years. This home had a great deal of sentimental value to her so because of this she decided to remodel the home to her taste, which costs her well over $380,000 in remodeling costs. While the home's value did increase to $300,000, the appraiser did tell her that she over-improved the home for that neighborhood. What type of value does this home now have?

a) objective

b) indestructible

c) subjective

d) immobility

61. How much must a mortgage broker applicant submit with the application for each branch office fee?

a) $500

b) $1,000

c) $750

d) $325

62. Of the following, which is NOT a component of a rate lock?

a) loan program

b) interest rate

c) points

d) none of the above

63. Who can issue a junior mortgage?

a) Freddie Mac

b) the VA

c) the seller

d) RHS

64. Kelley, Marvin and Andrea are joint tenants. When Andrea dies, Kelley and Marvin remain as joint tenants. When Marvin dies, Kelley now holds title as a sole owner. Kelley now holds title in _____.

a) common

b) severalty

c) entirety

d) life estate

65. Greg has an ocean front property where he is able to freely enjoy the ocean at any time. He has _____ rights.

a) bundle of rights

b) alluvion

c) riparian

d) littoral

66. A _____ is divided into 36 sections.

a) city

b) township

c) Commonwealth

d) acre

67. In a deed, *ET ux* means

a) and wife

b) everyone

c) and others

d) and husband

68. Abraham bought a property and later learned that his great grandfather's father may have owned that property. What can he order that will show the property ownership history?

a) deed of trust

b) legal description

c) certificate of title

d) chain of title

69. A chattel mortgage would more than likely be used in a transaction with all of the following EXCEPT

a) car

b) furniture

c) single family residence

d) mobile home

70. A developer plans to build a new subdivision that is pedestrian friendly. The homes will be on small lots, but the community will have several "green" areas with parks and common areas for the residents. This type of design is known as _____.

a) communal property

b) clustering

c) commingling

d) canvassing

71. Mrs. James' husband passed away about 6 months ago and because she is on fixed income she is finding it difficult to meet all of her expenses due to her husband's remaining medical bills. Because she owns her home free and clear and she would like to remain in it, what loan product might be a good option for her?

a) junior mortgage

b) HELOC

c) primary mortgage

d) HECM

72. Which is NOT a method used to satisfy the requirement for legal description in a deed.

a) the Torrens System

b) the metes and bounds system

c) the lot and block system

d) the government survey system

73. Juliet has lived in her apartment for 4 months and loves it. Because summer is approaching and she does not have air conditioning, she's decided to replace her dining room lighting fixture with a ceiling fan. The ceiling fan will now be a(n)

a) riparian right

b) easement

c) real property

d) personal property

74. A hardship associated with acquiring rental property is

a) the law of increasing returns

b) lack of reserves

c) negative amortization

d) redlining

75. A broker's license is NOT required

a) when an individual sells his candy store business to another individual

b) when he offers to list real property for sale

c) when he offers to sell his parents' home

d) in exchange for 1 month's rent, negotiate the rental of real estate for another individual

76. The ADA is the

a) American Disabled Vets Act

b) American Disposition of Realty Act

c) American Disposal Act

d) American with Disabilities Act

77. Misty works as a sales agent under Real Time Realty in which she is an independent contractor. She should expect all of the following EXCEPT:

a) to assume responsibility for paying her own income tax

b) to compensated on production

c) to receive employee benefits from the broker

d) that she and the broker will have a written contract

78. Manny and Lisa purchased their home 6 years ago for $325,000 where they put down 10%. Their interest rate was 6.5% and after making 72 monthly payments, their loan balance was $268,901.06. Assuming the current market value and the sales price are the same, how much equity does the homeowner have?

a) $32,500

b) $56,098.04

c) $29,200

d) none of the above

79. Every homeowner is entitled to the following income tax deductions EXCEPT

a) loan interest on second homes

b) property taxes

c) discount points

d) penalty-fee withdrawals up to $10,000 from an IRA

80. Byron, a first time homebuyer, bought his home for $72,500 with an FHA loan. The contract was executed April 28th, 2010. Because he had a 60 day escrow, he finally got his keys on June 30th, 2010. How much tax credit money should he expect to get back if he has no other tax liabilities?

a) $7,250

b) $500

c) $8000

d) $7500

81. Which physical characteristic of real estate best describes the following: 2 parcels of land are not identical

a) homogeneity

b) immobility

c) nonhomogeneity

d) a physical characteristic of land

82. All are uses of real property EXCEPT

a) residential

b) grazing cattle

c) cemetery

d) all of the above

83. The first real estate license law was passed in _____ in 1919.

a) Massachusetts

b) New York

c) California

d) Texas

84. A cookie shop owner needs to move to a larger location. When he removed the oven, he repaired the holes from the bolts on the walls and the floors. The oven was a(n)

a) fixture

b) trade fixture

c) real property

d) appurtenance

85. The section on the 1003 that deals with the race or ethnicity and sex of an application is data collected under the

a) Home Mortgage Disclosure Act

b) Community Redevelopment Act

c) Fair Housing Act

c) Federal Civil Rights Act

86. Broker Connie says the following phrases to her clients, "Better sell the house before too many of them move in the neighborhood", "There goes the neighborhood". These are examples of

a) redlining

b) steering

c) blockbusting

d) commingling

87. Randy meets with loan officer Jackie so she can prequalify him for a loan. After talking with Randy she learns that he is unmarried and decides to halt the application process. Randy calls her several times only to receive a voicemail. Since it appears as though Jackie is discriminating against Randy on the basis of marital status, what law is she violating?

a) The Civil Rights Act of 1964

b) The ADA

c) The Federal Fair Housing Act of 1866

d) ECOA

88. Which is NOT a purpose of the License Law?

a) raise revenue

b) to protect the public from incompetent brokers

c) prescribe minimum standards for licensing brokers

d) protect licensed brokers and salespersons from unfair or improper competition

89. Which is the best acronym to help in remembering the 4 government powers?

a) DUST

b) OldCAR

c) PETE

d) PPEDTE

90. Ms. Mary owned the land adjacent to her church and decided to grant it to the church so long as it is used to build a recreation center for the church's youth. This type of estate is known as

a) fee simple

b) determinable fee

c) legal fee

d) conventional life estate

91. Sonja gave her $3500 earnest money deposit to her sales agent. What should her sales agent do next?

a) deposit the check in his (sales agents) personal checking account

b) give the check to the office's transaction coordinator who will then put the check in the company's escrow account

c) cash the check and give Sonja a receipt

d) give the check to the office's transaction coordinator who will then place the check in file folder with Sonja's name on it along with the contract and store them safely in the file cabinet

92. Johnny and Donna visit a new home development and fall in love with the model homes. All of the homes in this subdivision will only have 1 level. After picking a floor plan they like, they ask the sales agent what the cost would be to add a 2nd story media room and bathroom. The sales agent advises the couple that the developers have created a _____ _____ that does not permit 2nd story homes in the subdivision.

a) planning and zoning law

b) inverse condemnation

c) public control

d) deed restriction

93. Ted received a letter stating that the lender had obtained a deficiency judgment against him. Which scenario below best fits what has happened to Ted?

a) One of his creditors from a credit card put his account in collections then filed a judgment against him.

b) The home was sold in an auction for the amount he owed, but because there were no funds to pay the agents the lenders paid it and are now suing Ted for the deficiency.

c) Ted's loan balance and fees were more than the home sold for at foreclosure sale; therefore the lender will claim Ted's other assets in order to satisfy the indebtedness.

d) none of the above

94. When working on behalf of a seller or buyer, an agent must exhibit good business judgment, trust and honesty. This creates a(n) _____ _____.

a) fiduciary relationship

b) faithful performance

c) implied authority

d) special agent

95. Keith is selling his 5 unit complex. He should be prepared to bring all documents below EXCEPT:

a) tax returns

b) lease agreements

c) maintenance contracts

d) estoppels letters from the tenants

96. Baker and Johnson Partnership decides to sell off some their real estate. If each partner holds title as tenants in common, which signatures will be required to convey the real estate?

a) Only 1 signature is required since it is a Partnership.

b) Since each partner holds title, they will each have to sign.

c) They can sign with a stamp in the name of their Partnership.

d) Whenever a Partnership sells real estate, only 2 signatures are required no matter how many partners there are.

97. Theron and Perry are neighbors. Theron builds a fence in which 2 feet of it extends into Perry's property. The fence is an example of a(n)

a) eminent domain

b) encumbrance

c) encroachment

d) easement by necessity

98. A couple residing in a community property state have been married for 5 years. During the marriage, the wife's grandfather decides to give each grandchild their inheritance, which is one of his income producing properties. The property is

a) community property

b) sole proprietorship

c) part of a land trust

d) separate property

99. Real estate ownership by a corporation is a(n)

a) tenancy in sufferance

b) tenancy in severalty

c) joint tenancy

d) none of the above as corporations can own real estate

100. Barbara has been pre-approved for a maximum purchase price of $318,000 based on 90% LTV. What will her down payment?

a) $10,000

b) $6400

c) $ 32,000

d) $23,000

Real Estate Sales Exam II Answers

1. b. Designated buyer's and seller's agent is a designated agent who represents their client and owes fiduciary duties to their client and with the client's permission the agent can be designated by another agent. When the appointing agent designates, another agent in the office to represent the other party to the transaction, the broker will also be a dual agent.

2. d. First. we need to establish that the borrower's down payment and the seller carry back can be added together and treated like it is the borrower's down payment. Second, find the loan to value(LTV) which is 100-25=75% or .75 since we are given the loan amount and now have the LTV we can solve for the sales price: $243,750/.75 = $325,000.

3. b. The appraisal can be verbal or written.

4. b. When sellers are competing there is a lot of demand in the market which drives home prices down.

5. d. The bundle of rights are the property rights which include the right of possession, control, enjoyment and disposition.

6. b. The refrigerator is not attached to the house. The owner can take this with him/her therefore it is personal property.

7. c. Brokers require 120 hours and salespersons require 75 hours.

8. b. Non-profits are exempt from paying property taxes.

9. b. Anthony must provide an insurance certificate showing the new owner and his mortgage holder will be covered under the condominium master insurance policy in order to transfer the property, in Massachusetts.

10. c. In Massachusetts, the landlord is to give the tenant the interest he earned in the bank on the deposit.

11. a. Tenancy at will is a lease without a termination date

12. c. National Association of Realtors

13. d. BPO or broker price opinion is when the mortgage holder gets a broker's opinion of value based on a competitive market analysis.

14. b. Commercial property is used to produce income.

15. d. The Super Lien Bill gives the association the right to impose a priority lien.

16. a. Fructus naturals are considered to be citrus fruit, apples, berries and grapes and remain with the property.

17. a. Subsurface rights are rights below the earth's surface.

18. c. Manufactured homes are considered personal property as most are not permanently affixed.

19. a. Equity mortgage is where the homeowner takes out a portion of the equity on their property and often times lenders will send the borrower checks.

20. c. A voidable contract binds one party but not the other.

21. d. Clouded title is any document, claim, unreleased lien that may impair the title to real property or make the title doubtful.

22. b. First we need to find the LTV which is 100-46 =54% or .54. $372,000/.54 =$688,889.

23. a. If the landlord has filed bankruptcy, the tenant must go before the bankruptcy court.

24. d. An exclusive agency listing means that only 1 listing broker represents the seller. If the property sells through the efforts of the broker, however the seller retains the right to sell the property on their own without paying a commission.

25. b. Cooperatives are apartments owned by a corporation that holds titles to the entire cooperative property.

26. c. This is the minimum amount required.

27. b. Balance is when a neighborhood or town has several different types of land uses.

28. a. An agent's license can be suspended for 60 days if they are found to have violated Massachusetts fair housing laws.

29. c. Constructive eviction is when a landlord has rendered a property uninhabitable and the tenant moves out.

30. b. In a 99 year lease the buyer does not have full ownership.

31. a. The Federal Housing Authority insures loans, while the Department of Veterans Affairs guarantees loans. The State of New York itself does not make loans.

32. d. In addition to the disclosures of APR, finance charge, and amount financed, the Truth in Lending Act requires verbiage that says the total amount of many the borrower will pay toward the mortgage in principal and interest payments.

33. c. Tenants who live in public housing may have additional protections.

34. d. Tenancy at will is a lease without a termination date.

35. d. For a fixed rate conventional loan, the maximum percentage the borrower can have for monthly housing expenses is 28%, for total obligations, it is 36%.

36. b. For an adjustable rate conventional loan, the maximum percentage the borrower can have for monthly housing expenses is 28%, for total obligations, it is 36%.

37. d. Closing Cost can be found by multiplying the sales price by the closing cost percent. 378,499 x .03 = 11,355.

38. c. For an FHA loan, the maximum percentage the borrower can have for monthly housing expenses is 31%, for total obligations, it is 41%.

39. b. According to the Lead Paint Law along with giving the new tenants a Lead Paint Notification and Tenant Certification Form, because the new tenants have a child under 6, Mike and Dana must delead the property.

40. a. By using the 1031 exchange, they deferred the tax on their gain until a future date.

41. c. Turn into a tenancy at will with the new owner

42. b. Qualifying ratios are calculations to determine whether a borrower can qualify for a mortgage.

43. d. Riparian rights are the rights of a landowner whose property is adjacent to a flowing waterway to use the water.

44. b. Although these loans are made to subprime borrowers, there are still many laws lenders must follow.

45. a. The Change of Name or Request for Duplicate License form located on the Board's website under the Applications and Forms link and send in the applicable fee.

46. c. The Board will make her license inactive if she doesn't pay the renewal fee.

47. d. First time homebuyers in most states are individuals who have not owned a home in the last 2-3 years.

48. a. The Taxpayer Relief Act was enacted August 5, 1997.

49. b. Flood insurance may be required if any part of the property is in a flood zone.

50. c. The housing ratio is the front end or housing expense and the back end ratio is the total debt ratio conservative lenders tend to use more conservative ratios.

51. c. When submitting a mortgage broker application, candidates must pay a $1,500 investigation fee, $105 fingerprint processing fee, and $500 fee for each branch office.

52. a. The formula for determining value:

Replacement or reproduction cost – accrued depreciation + land value = Value

53. d. A protected class is any group of people designated by HUD.

54. d. When submitting a mortgage broker application, candidates must pay a $1,500 investigation fee, $105 fingerprint processing fee, and $500 fee for each branch office.

55. b. The mortgage deed pledges the property as collateral.

56. c. Real Property is real estate plus bundle of legal rights.

57. a. Personal property is moveable.

58. d. Illegal purposes uses are not included in the "bundle of rights"

59. b. The economic characteristics of Real Estate are relative scarcity, improvements, permanence of investment and area preference.

60. c. Subjective value is affected by the relative worth an individual places on a specific item.

61. a. When submitting a mortgage broker application, candidates must pay a $1,500 investigation fee, $105 fingerprint processing fee, and $500 fee for each branch office.

62. d. There are four components of a rate lock. These are: loan program, interest rate, points, and length of the lock.

63. c. The seller can offer to carry back a 2nd mortgage.

64. b. Estate in severalty is sole ownership.

65. d. When a landowner's property borders a large non-flowing body of water such as an ocean, the landowner has the right to enjoy the water.

66. b. A township is divided into 36 sections.

67. a. Abbreviation for Latin term *ET uxor* meaning wife.

68. d. A chain of title is a recorded history of conveyances on a particular property.

69. c. A chattel mortgage is used with personal or moveable property.

70. b. Clustering is when a developer groups home sites on a smaller lot and leaves the remaining land for use as common areas.

71. d. A home equity conversion mortgage is another name for a reverse mortgage. This type of mortgage allows an elderly person to remain in their home in which the equity is converted to cash for the homeowner.

72. a. The Torrens System is a system of registering title to land with a public authority.

73. c. The ceiling fan became real property once it got attached to the ceiling.

74. b. Most lenders require 3-6 months of reserves of the PITI payment when purchasing income property which often creates a barrier to entry.

75. a. A license is not required when an individual sells his business.

76. d. American with Disabilities Act.

77. c. A broker cannot offer benefits to his/her independent contractors.

78. b. $325,000 - $268,901.06 = $56,098.04

79. d. Only first time homebuyers can withdraw penalty-free up to $10,000 from their IRA.

80. a. The tax credit was worth 10% of the purchase price.

81. c. No two pieces of land are ever exactly alike.

82. d. All are uses of real property.

83. c. California

84. b. The oven was a trade fixture and because he returned the walls and the floors to their original condition it can be considered personal property.

85. a. The Home Mortgage Disclosure Act (HMDA) requires mortgage lenders to collect and report data to assist in identifying possible discriminatory lending practices.

86. c. Blockbusting is the illegal act of convincing homeowners to sell their properties by suggesting that a protected class is moving into the neighborhood.

87. d. The Equal Credit Opportunity Act prohibits lenders from discriminating against credit applicants on the basis of race, color, religion, national origin, sex, marital status, age or dependence on public assistance.

88. a. The License Law was not enacted to raise revenue.

89. c. The 4 government powers are PETE: Police Power, Eminent Domain, Taxation, and Escheat

90. b. This is a determinable fee estate in which the estate will come to an end immediately if the specified purpose ceases.

91. b. All earnest deposits must be held in the company's escrow account.

92. d. Deed restrictions can control from what can be parked in a driveway to what exterior color the homes can be.

93. c. When the proceeds of the foreclosure sale do not cover what is owed, the lender may claim other assets to cure the indebtness.

94. a. A fiduciary relationship requires that an agent exhibit trust, honesty and good business judgment when working on behalf of the principal.

95. a. He does not have to supply his tax returns.

96. b. Each partner will have to sign since they all hold title.

97. c. The fence is an encroachment because it invades the neighbor's land.

98. d. Once the grandfather conveys the property to her it is separate property.

99. b. Because a corporation is a legal entity, corporate real estate ownership is held as tenancy in severalty.

100. c. The down payment is 100-90= 10% . 10% of 318,000 = 31,800 or 32,000.

Real Estate Sales Exam III

1. A property valued at $275,000 appreciates two percent a year. What is the value of the property after one year?

a) $295,000

b) $280,500

c) $286,000

d) $320,000

2. The 40 classroom hours were waived for Wendy because she took a real property course in
_____ school.

a) business

b) accounting

c) project management

d) law

3. Which of the following is considered residential property?

a) single-family home

b) retail store

c) warehouse

d) land without buildings

4. Of the following, which is commercial property?

a) single-family home

b) retail store

c) warehouse

d) land without buildings

5. Arthur, the owner of 3 two family homes, decides to enlist the help of a property
management company to aid him in managing the properties. What type of contract will he
have with the property manager?

a) a multiple listing agreement

b) a rental agreement

c) a management agreement

d) a multiple use agreement

6. The Federal Reserve Board's Regulation B implements _____.

a) Equal Credit Opportunity Act

b) Truth in Lending

c) RESPA

d) Home Mortgage Disclosure Act

7. The Hemsley family bought a vacation home in Manhattan. Their down payment was 40% and they financed the rest. They became the

a) mortgagee

b) borrower

c) mortgagor

d) lienor

8. Karen, who purchased her apartment in the city for $598,000, tells her friend Samantha that her property tax payment is included in her monthly maintenance fee. Samantha suspects that Karen more than likely purchased a

a) leasehold

b) PUD

c) condo

d) co op

9. The Stemmons family owns 2 thousand acres of land with several trees on the property. Every year they sell the lumber to a timber company. The cut trees are sold as

a) real property

b) personal property

c) not considered property since they are not a structure

d) an appurtenance

10. Marla, a vendee, has an equitable interest in the property located on 926 Elm Street, Any Town, Any State 12345. In this case Marla is the

a) seller

b) grantor

c) purchaser

d) grantee

11. Which of the following is considered industrial property?

a) single-family home

b) retail store

c) warehouse

d) land without buildings

12. An option to purchase a home for $325,000 with 120 days was sold to Heather for $9,000. After 60 days the seller accepted an offer from Heather to purchase the home of $305,000. Which is true?

a) Heather violated the agreement

b) Heather loses her option deposit

c) Both Heather and the seller are in violation of contract law.

d) Heather could make a new offer for $305,000

13. A property is worth $214,000 and it has $156,000 in liens tied to it. This difference is known as

a) the assessed value

b) down payment

c) equity

d) leverage

14. Martha and her daughter made an offer on another home based on their current home selling by a certain date. What type of clause was this?

a) financing

b) contingency

c) recession

d) partial performance

15. An agent meets with a client in their home for the 1ˢᵗ time and the couple decides to sign the listing agreement authorizing the broker as their listing agent. The agent loves the home and believes it would make a great starter home for Jack, her neighbor's son. The agent holds an open house and receives 2 offers along with Jack's offer. These offers are all very similar. Then just before she (agent) leaves to present the offers, she gets a new offer which is much better than the current offers. Even though she really wants Jack to get the home, she shows all offers to her client. Which of the 6 agent responsibilities did the agent demonstrate?

a) loyalty

b) accounting

c) reasonable care

d) confidentiality

16. _____ is when the municipality takes action against a property owner and through the court land process attempts to gain ownership of the property.

a) foreclosure

b) eminent domain

c) taking

d) constructive notice

17. Which is true?

a) FHA is hazard insurance

b) FHA guarantees that the borrower will not default on the loan

c) FHA 203(k) loans are for 1 – 4 investment properties only

d) FHA insures the lender against borrower default

18. Which contract is voidable?

a) a painter is contracted to paint a home, but 2 days before he was to begin the job, the home was destroyed by a hurricane.

b) an owner who grows marijuana in his backyard, agrees to sell it to his next door neighbor

c) an older brother who lives with his younger brother because he is mentally challenged and needs supervised care contracts a landscaping company to begin cutting the yard

d) a buyer makes an offer to purchase and includes a financing contingency

19. According to Massachusetts General Law chapter 244, Sec 14, borrowers have no _____ rights after a valid foreclosure.

a) littoral

b) air

c) redemption

d) mortgage

20. Victor has a section 3 homestead and files his Declaration of Homestead with the Registry of Deeds. How much protection should he expect?

a) $100,000

b) $500,000

c) $110,000

d) $125,000

21. Another name for the government survey method is _____.

a) the rectangular survey system

b) principal surveys

c) base lines survey method

d) principal meridians

22. The Jackson Estate is sold to satisfy a judgment resulting from an $18,000 mechanics lien for work that began on September 15, 2012, subject to a first mortgage lien of $ $310,000 recorded November 17, 2011, and to this year's outstanding property taxes of $14,000. If the

Estate is sold at the foreclosure sale for $350,000, in what order will the proceeds of the sale be distributed:

a) $310,000 mortgage lien; $18,000 mechanics lien; $14,000 property taxes; $8,000 to the foreclosed landowner

b) $18,000 mechanics lien; $310,000 mortgage lien; $8,000 foreclosed landowner; $14,000 property taxes

c) $14,000 property taxes; $8,000 foreclosed landowner; $310,000 mortgage lien; $18,000 mechanics lien

d) $14,000 property taxes; $18,000 mechanics lien; $310,000 mortgage lien; $ 8,000 foreclosed landowner

23. Which is subject to property taxes?

a) Non-profit hospital

b) 100 unit apt complex

c) church

d) golf course operated by the city's parks

24. Kiley, a realtor and interior designer is, more than likely a member of these two associations.

a) NRA and AID

b) NAR and ASID

c) NAR and MAR

d) REA and NRA

25. Public employees use a mill to calculate

a) hazard insurance premiums

b) mortgage interest

c) trash and sewage rates

d) property tax rates

26. Julie owns 5 acres of land that she wanted to sell to Kelvin for $800,000. But before she could sell the land to Kelvin she had to first offer it to Angelica, a holder of the right to purchase the land who decided to exercise her right and follow through with the purchase. What right did Angelica exercise?

a) bundle of rights

b) redemption

c) right of first refusal

d) contingency

27. A developer agrees to purchase 50 acres of land from the owner $600,000. The owner has agreed to carry back 20%. If the developer takes out a construction loan with a 1st - lien position, the landowner will have to agree to a _____ agreement.

a) subordination

b) percentage lease

c) conformity

d) deferred transfer

28. A listing agreement is a(n)

a) future delivery purchase

b) interest in severalty

c) estimated amount for which a party should exchange hands

d) contract between a broker and seller

29. Deprecation is accounted for in which approach

a) market value

b) cost

c) comparative market analysis

d) rent history

30. Although Jesse works as an independent contractor under his broker, the broker is still responsible for all of the following EXCEPT

a) providing a contract which clearly stipulates that Jesse is responsible for paying quarterly federal income tax payments

b) the ethical and legal behavior of Jesee

c) payment of licensing and professional fees

d) provide an agreement which defines compensation amounts

31. Windstorm insurance is mandated by

a) federal government

b) state

c) city

d) county

32. The minimum credit score set by FHA is

a) 530

b) 530

c) 620

d) FHA has no minimum credit score

33. A hearing panel found that Mary was in violation of the National Association of Realtors Code of Ethics, in addition to receiving a penalty up to $5,000 what course may she be asked to take?

a) ethics

b) Principle of Real Estate

c) accounting

d) consumer information

34. Which is an example of steering?

a) a lender only offers balloon loans to a certain group of buyers

b) a realtor tells his clients to sell his home because one of the neighbors rented his house to a section 8 tenant

c) an owner decides not to rent his home to a disabled veteran

d) a sales agent begins showing homes to more African Americans in an affluent area because she feels the neighborhood needs to be more integrated

35. Every year Jim and Opal receive an annual allotment of 300 vacation points through their timeshare program. This type of timeshare program is known as

a) rotation club

b) vacation owner points plan

c) vacation club

d) vacation ownership interest club

36. Of the following, which is vacant land?

a) single-family home

b) retail store

c) warehouse

d) land without buildings

37. Margaret receives a letter from her homeowner association that she needs to replace her roof and garage door. She is very upset because she thought these items were covered by the homeowner's association since her unit is attached to other units. What type of unit does Margaret more than likely own?

a) single family residence

b) cooperative

c) townhome

d) condo

38. Which of the following is included in the bundle of rights with the ownership in fee simple absolute?

a) to dispose by gift

b) to control use within legal limits

c) to quiet enjoyment

d) all of the above

39. A real estate broker refers his client to US Home Warranty Company and in return they send the broker a $125 referral fee. This is a violation of

a) the Comprehensive Environmental Response, Compensation, and Liability Act

b) the Real Estate Settlement Procedures Act

c) Truth in Lending

d) HUD-1

40. Which of the following is NOT a community property state?

a) Texas

b) Arizona

c) New York

d) Wisconsin

41. In a condominium development, which would be considered a "limited" common element?

a) pool

b) elevator

c) parking slots assigned to occupants

d) limited access gates

42. Which of the following is an example of a specific lien?

a) materialmen's

b) writ of attachment

c) income tax

d) estate and inheritance tax

43. One of the most important deadlines in the contract documents is the

a) home inspection

b) option period

c) loan commitment

d) none of the above

44. An HO-6 policy is an insurance policy for a(n)

a) PUD

b) SFR

c) mobile home

d) condo

45. Maintaining upkeep and insurance on the property until closing, obtaining a smoke and carbon monoxide certificate at closing and obtaining certificate 6(d) if the sale is a condominium are _____ responsibilities laid out in the purchase and sale agreement.

a) seller's

b) broker's

c) buyer's agent's

d) buyer's

46. An appraiser will use the _____ approach to reconcile the values of a 3 family rental home.

a) reproduction

b) income

c) cost

d) sales comparison

47. Jane bought her home for $279,000 and now it's worth $333,000. It has _____ in value.

a) appreciated

b) regressed

c) vested

d) diverged

48. Sally received a letter that her home loan with ABC lending was being transferred to Community Bank. This is known as a(n)

a) takeover

b) assumption

c) assignment

d) aggression

49. When a borrower signs a security agreement where he is promising to pay, he is signing a

a) deed of trust

b) promissory note

c) bill of sale

d) offer contract

50. A disadvantage of a bridge loan is:

a) the buyer does not have to sell their current home before they purchase their next home

b) the lender might not require the buyer to make monthly payments

c) the buyer can immediately put their home on the market

d) buyers may be prequalified base on 2 mortgages and they might not meet this requirement

51. Henry's title report suggests that the property he's purchasing is free of legal issues and liens, therefore the property has a(n) _____ title.

a) clear

b) cloudy

c) good

d) efficient

52. In a home loan, which is the collateral?

a) the down payment

b) the equity

c) the property

d) the borrower's liquid assets

53. The date an interest rate changes is known as the

a) payment shock

b) balloon maturity date

c) the adjustment date on an adjustable rate loan

d) none of the above

54. Lisa makes an offer on a home and gives her broker a check to let the seller know she is
serious. These funds are known as

a) security deposit

b) earnest money deposit

c) option period deposit

d) down payment

55. Which best describes an easement?

a) When a tenant who is moving out of the storefront he rented takes his cupcake oven

b) A property owner whose land is adjacent to a river, swims and fishes in the river

c) A neighbor who accesses his barn by legally crossing part of his neighbor's land

d) The state legally takes back private land to widen the highway

56. A subdivision is

a) a neighborhood in a community revitalized area

b) a housing development where tracts of land are turned into individual lots

c) when houses in a neighborhood are the same style and color

d) a neighborhood with a homeowners association board

57. A homebuyer who had limited liquid funds, obtained her home through a non - profit organization, where she helped build her home with her own labor and services. What type of contribution did she make?

a) sweat equity

b) equity deposit

c) money

d) labor

58. Ben, who recently lost his job, is considering transferring ownership of his home back to his lender as he is having great difficulty making the payments and has been unable to sell it. This is known as

a) foreclosure

b) deed-in-lieu

c) short sale

d)adverse possession

59. Stephanie and Max, first time homebuyers in the Commonwealth are currently living on Stephanie's income as a teacher; but Max will be done with residency in 2 more years so they know their income will increase dramatically. In light of this, their loan officer has advised them that they could qualify for a little more house if they took out a loan that increased by no more than 7.5% per year over the next 5 years. What type of loan are they being offered?

a) four-step mortgage

b) fixed rate

c) 2-1 buy down

d) graduated payment

60. According to their lender, a couple must contribute $71,700 in the form of a cashier's check toward the purchase of the $478,000 home they would like to purchase. This amount is known as the

a) earnest money deposit

b) junior mortgage

c) down payment

d) contingency fee

61. For government loans, which statement is true?

a) They are insured by FHA.

b) They are guaranteed by RHS.

c) They are guaranteed by VA.

d) All of the above.

62. Heather conveyed her interest in a property to her brother, Barry's friend, Mike's parents, Mr. and Mrs. Olsen. Who is the grantee?

a) Mike

b) Mr. and Mrs. Olsen

c) Heather

d) Barry

63. Katy and Mickey's home was completely destroyed during the hurricane storm. When they returned to check the damages, they found their basement completely flooded and everything destroyed as the water level reached up to the 2nd floor. Which insurance will more than likely cover the bulk of the damages?

a) hurricane

b) windstorm

c) flood

d) hazard

64.   Which is NOT a liquid asset?

a) money in savings account

b) 401 K

c) parcel of land

d) stocks

65. A homebuyer used a mortgage broker with Finance World to get her home loan. She used the payment coupon provided to her mail her 1st payment to Finance World. Before her 2nd payment was due, she received a letter stating that her loan was being assigned to the Bank of the United States and that the investor Duchess Bank had remained the same. Which is her current lender?

a) Finance World

b) Duchess Bank

c) Bank of the United States

d) Mortgage broker

66. If Justine has power of attorney, she has been granted?

a) limited or full authority to make decisions on behalf of someone else

b) an opportunity to represent someone in court

c) entrance to law school

d) full power to make medical decisions on behalf of someone else

67. The principal is

a) that part of the mortgage payment that reduces the unpaid balance

b) the amount borrowed

c) a and b

d) b only

68. Which best describes an encroachment?

a) You legally drive across part of your neighbor's property to access your property.

b) You continuously use your neighbor's driveway for years and he doesn't stop you.

c) You add a non legal 2nd level to your home which completely blocks your neighbors view to the sea.

d) You allow your horses to drink out of the river which is adjacent to your land.

69. Two sons are joint tenants in a property left to them by their parents. Son A has 1 child and Son B has 4 children. In the event Son B passes, who does the property go to?

a) the property is split equally between the 5 grand children

b) the property goes to Son A and his child

c) the property goes to Son B's children

d) the property goes to Son A only

70. Ansley wants to see a visual representation of when her mortgage will be paid off as well as how much money she will be paying in interest every year. This is known as a(n)

a) loan payment schedule

b) amortization schedule

c) interest rate table

d) rate sheet

71. A bi-weekly payment is one in which

a) the homeowner will make her mortgage payment every 2 weeks

b) the homeowner will make her mortgage payment every other month

c) the homeowner will make a payment 1 time every month, but on the last month of the year 2 payments will be made

d) the homeowner will make half of her mortgage payment every 2 weeks

72. Kelly is told that her ARM loan has an initial interest rate of 5.5% and that as the rate adjusts it can never go above 9%. 9% is the _____ for her loan.

a) buy down

b) APR

c) cap

d) ad valorem

73. Of the following, which is an example of a general lien?

a) lis pendens

b) judgment

c) mechanic's

d) real property tax

74. Henry sells his home to his friend Reese; then Henry gets a letter from his lender demanding full payment. The mortgage included a _____.

a) acceleration clause

b) deed restriction

c) due-on-sale clause

d) covenant of seisin

75. Murray had to go to court to get his property back from his nephew because when he granted him the property he told him that he could not sell alcohol on the premises. What type of estate was this?

a) homestead

b) ordinary with remainder or reversion

c) determinable fee estate

d) fee simple subject to a condition subsequent with right of reentry

76. Which provides the best range of property values on a particular property?

a) competitive market analysis

b) broker price opinions

c) appraisal

d) income approach

77. Jenn and Mike finally found the home of their dreams within their budget of $385,000. They had already been pre-approved for a loan based on 75% loan to value. If the sales price is $380,000 but the appraisal came in at $365,500, what is the max loan the lender will give them for this home?

a) $288,750

b) $380,000

c) $285,000

d) $274,125

78. Which of these liens is NOT involuntary?

a) income tax

b) materialmen's

c) real property tax

d) mortgage

79. What is the Latin word for "pending litigation"?

a) lex scripta

b) lapsus memoriae

c) lis pendens

d) legem terrae

80. In New York, what is true about the passage of property to a surviving spouse?

a) It is done without taxation.

b) It is done with a 5% taxation rate.

c) It is done so with a 1% taxation rate.

d) It is done with a 3% taxation rate.

81. Martha pays her taxes and insurance every month inside her mortgage payment. This is known as a _____ mortgage.

a) equity

b) budget

c) escrow

d) negative amortization

82. A very famous couple chooses a city apartment near all of the amenities they enjoy so they don't have to travel too far out and risk being noticed. Their agent notifies them they did not receive approval because the Board believes they will disrupt the peace and quiet currently enjoyed by all the residents. Which best describes this scenario?

a) The condo association can vote in or out whoever they feel is a good match (or not) for the condo development

b) The Board is violating the Civil Rights Act of 1866

c) celebrities are a protected class and not be discriminated against

d) co ops can deny or approve the sale of shares of stock if they feel someone may jeopardize the quiet enjoyment the residents currently enjoy

83. The realtor tells a couple that because of regression, they may have to list their home at a different price than anticipated. Which best describes what is happening?

a) the neighboring homes haven't been updated and modernized as much as the subject property

b) the home has an outdated floor plan

c) the home is in disrepair

d) a school was recently built around the corner

84. When Broker Jamie takes his clients earnest money deposit and puts it in his personal account to tie him over until his next commission check comes, which fiduciary duty is he not living up to?

a) dedication

b) accounting

c) obedience

d) confidentiality

85. The Homestead Act does NOT protect you from which of the following:

a) credit cards

b) the proceeds from the sale of your home

c) a Medicaid lien from a nursing home stay

d) the proceeds from your insurance claim if your home was damaged by fire

86. The following is which type of description commonly used in New York legal descriptions: North 34 degrees East 200 feet to point.

a) reference

b) bounded

c) strip

d) metes

87. Katy has a voluntary lien on her home. Which represents a voluntary lien?

a) mortgage

b) property tax

c) federal irs

d) mechanic's lien

88. Samantha's condominium unit which recently appraised at $413,000, was recently damaged in a storm. If it was currently assessed at $405,000, what is the minimum amount covered by her HO-6 policy?

a) $81,000

b) $82,600

c) $80,000

d) $84,000

89. If a corporation does not pay its franchise tax, a lien can be placed against the company's property. For a company with an entire net income of $192,000, what would be the franchise tax?

a) 6.85%

b) 7.1%

c) $10,000

d) 4.35%

90. Jane has a document which states she has legal rights of ownership for 1324 Elm St, Any Town, and Any City 45678. This document is known as

a) affidavit

b) quitclaim deed

c) title

d) trustee deed

91. Gerard has a 30 year loan where his interest rate is 5% for 5 years, then increases to 6% for the life of the loan. What type of mortgage does he have?

a) fixed rate mortgage

b) modification

c) two-step mortgage

d) fully amortized

92. The buyers purchasing Geoff's vacation home love his furnishings so much they want to buy all of it. What contract should he use in this type of sale?

a) bill of sale

b) grant deed

c) purchase and sale agreement

d) quitclaim deed

93. Mr. Jethendrux has appointed an executrix to handle his final affairs. Which person could this have been?

a) Kathryn

b) James

c) both a and b

d) neither a nor b

94. Which is the best description of a real estate agent?

a) Anyone, licensed or not, who conducts and/negotiates the sale of real estate

 b) The owner and manager of a real estate firm

c) A person who sells both home warranties and property

d) A person who is licensed who conducts and negotiates the sale of real estate

 95. Ricky's friend Esther is leaving the country. She has a great loan with a 3.5% interest rate and a remaining term of 20 years. Because Ricky would like to take over this loan, he sends her lender all of his income and asset documents. Ricky is trying to get a(n) _____.

a) primary mortgage

b) assumption

c) refinance

d) equity loan

96. A legal document which conveys title to a property is known as a

a) deed

b) preliminary title report

c) purchase and sale agreement

d) promissory note

97. Which is the most common type of bankruptcy?

a) chapter 13

b) chapter 7 no assets

c) chapter 13 no assets

d) chapter 7

98. Someone's credit history report is prepared by a _____.

a) mortgage broker

b) underwriter

c) credit bureau

d) notary public

99. Paula made her mortgage payment 30 days past her due date. Her mortgage is now in

a) arrears

b) default

c) foreclosure

d) bankruptcy

100. What is the age an appraiser uses to describe a property's physical condition?

a) effective age

b) longevity

c) year built

d) average age

Real Estate Sales Exam III Answers

1. b. Multiply the value of the property by 0.02, which equals $5,500. Add $5,500 to the value of the house ($275,000). The appreciated value after one year is $280,500.

2. d. In Massachusetts if you take a real property course in law school, the 24 classroom hours are waived.

3. a. Single-family homes are residential properties, while retail stores are commercial properties. Warehouses are industrial properties and land without buildings, vacant land.

4. b. Single-family homes are residential properties, while retail stores are commercial properties. Warehouses are industrial properties and land without buildings, vacant land.

5. c. A management agreement is between the owner of income property and the property manager which details the scope of work expected by the property manager.

6. a. The Equal Credit Opportunity Act protects against discrimination in lending.

7. c. They are doing the mortgaging, so they are the mortgagor.

8. d. Co ops are transferred as shares of stock in which there is no recording and because of this, individual property taxes are not created for the unit, but rather the Co op or corporation pays a property tax bill for the development and passes along each member's portion to be paid through their monthly maintenance fee.

9. b. The cut trees are moveable so they are personal property.

10. c. A vendee is also known as the purchaser.

11. c. Single-family homes are residential properties, while retail stores are commercial properties. Warehouses are industrial properties and land without buildings, vacant land.

12. d. Both parties are free to renegotiate.

13. c. Equity is the difference between the value and the liens.

14. b. A contingency clause is when a certain act must be accomplished within a given amount of time.

15. a. Of the 6 agent responsibilities, obedience, loyalty, disclosure, confidentiality, accounting and loyalty, the agent showed loyalty to her clients by putting their interest above her own.

16. c. "Taking" is when the municipality takes action against a property owner and through the court land process attempts to gain ownership of the property.

17. d. FHA insures the lender against borrower default.

18. a. With a voidable contract the law gives 1 party an option whether or not to proceed with the agreement.

19. c. MGL chapter 244, Sec 14 states that borrowers have no redemption rights after valid foreclosure.

20. b. Because he has a section 3 homestead and he filed it with the Registry of Deeds he can get $500,000.

21. a. The rectangular survey system.

22. d. In MA order of payment is municipal lien, federal tax lien, state tax lien, condo fees up to 6 months, mechanics lien, and all other liens on order of recording, seller.

23. b. Non-profits are exempt from paying property.

24. b. Realtors are member of the National Association of Realtors and many interior designers are members of the American Society of Interior Designers.

25. d. One mill is equal to one tenth of one penny or one 1/1000 of a dollar and are often used when expressing property tax rates.

26. c. In a right of first refusal the owner gives the holder of the right an opportunity to enter into a transaction with the owner before the owner can enter into a transaction with a 3rd party.

27. a. Subordination agreements change the priority of a mortgage or lien.

28. d. Listing agreement is known as a contract between a broker and seller.

29. b. Depreciation is estimated in the cost approach.

30. c. The contract must stipulate that the agent is responsible for paying their own licensing and professional fees.

31. c. Windstorm insurance is governed by the state.

32. b. The minimum credit score set by FHA in 2010 is 530.

33. a. She may be asked to take an ethics course through the association.

34. d. Steering is the illegal practice of directing potential homebuyers away from or to particular areas.

35. c. Vacation clubs are newer timeshare programs which give members an annual allotment of points.

36. d. Single-family homes are residential properties, while retail stores are commercial properties. Warehouses are industrial properties and land without buildings, vacant land.

37. c. With a townhome purchase, the buyer purchases the individual unit and the ground below it. In addition each unit generally has its own roof and home amenities like garages.

38. d. With the ownership in fee simple absolute, there are a bundle of rights which includes: to quiet enjoyment, to dispose by gift, to sale by deed, or by will, of exclusion, and to control use within legal limits.

39. b. RESPA prohibits kickbacks.

40. c. There are nine community property states: Arizona, California, Idaho, Louisiana, Nevada, New Mexico, Texas, Washington, and Wisconsin.

41. c. Parking spaces assigned to occupants are "limited" to that occupant.

42. a. Specific liens are those against a particular property. Examples include: mortgage, real property tax, and mechanic's.

43. c. The loan commitment deadline is one of the most important deadlines.

44. d. An HO-6 policy, much like a hazard insurance policy for a home, is now required for condominiums by FNMA and FHA.

45. a. The purchase and sales agreements lays out the following seller responsibilities: maintaining upkeep and insurance on the property until closing, obtaining a smoke and carbon monoxide certificate at closing, paying the broker's commission and obtaining certificate 6(d).

46. b. The income approach is used to estimate the value of income producing properties.

47. a. When a home appreciates, it increases in value.

48. c. Assignment is when mortgage ownership is transferred from one company to another.

49. b. A note is a promise to pay.

50. d. Often times bridge loan lenders will prequalify buyers for 2 home loans.

51. a. Clear title is free of liens and legal questions and the legality cannot be challenged.

52. c. Because the borrower can lose the property due to non payment, the property itself is the collateral.

53. c. The adjustment date on an adjustable rate loan is the date an interest rate changes

54. b. The earnest money deposit lets the seller know the buyer is serious.

55. c. An easement is when another other than the owner has right of way legal access

56. b. Developers divide up tracts of land to create individual lots

57. a. When labor or services are provided in lieu of cash, this is known as sweat equity.

58. b. Deed-in-lieu is when the homeowner voluntarily transfers the title back to the lender in exchange for release of lien and payment.

59. d. A graduated payment mortgage is one in which the payment can increase by 7.5% per year over a period of time usually 5 years and then remains the same for the duration on the loan.

60. c. The down payment is generally made in the form of a cashier's check and is the initial amount that the buyer contributes upfront towards the total amount due.

61. d. Government loans are guaranteed by the Veterans Administration and Rural Housing and insured by FHA.

62. b. The individual(s) who receive title to a property is/are the grantee.

63. c. Because the home was damaged the excessive water level and experienced significant flooding, the flood insurance will cover the damages.

64. c. A liquid asset is that which can be easily converted to cash.

65. b. The lender is the actual financial institution that loaned the money.

66. a. Power of attorney grants an individual full or limited authority on behalf of someone else.

67. c. The principal is the amount of money borrowed along with that part of the mortgage payment that reduces the unpaid balance

68. c. An encroachment is an illegal improvement which intrudes another's property.

69. d. Joint tenancy has right of survivorship in which the survivor will now receive the deceased's portion of the property.

70. b. An amortization schedule is a table that how much principal will be applied to each mortgage payment. It also shows the yearly balance as it decreases until it reaches zero.

71. d. With a bi-weekly mortgage payment the homeowner pays half their mortgage payment every 2 weeks; which by the end of the year they will have made 13 payments.

72. c. The limit on ARM loans.

73. b. General liens are claims against all the assets of a person. Examples include: writ of attachment, income tax, and estate and inheritance tax.

74. c. A due on sale clause allows the lender to demand full repayment if the borrower sells the property that served as security for the loan.

75. d. A fee simple subject to a condition subsequent with right of reentry is where the grantor can go to court to get title back to his property if the grantee does not comply with the grantors condition of ownership.

76. a. The competitive market analysis helps the licensed agent/broker to identify a range of values in a given area.

77. d. The lender will lend based on the appraised value which is $365,500.

75% of $365,500 = $274,125.

78. d. Many liens are involuntary, such as judgment, lis pendens, and estate and inheritance tax.

79. c. "Lis pendens" or pending litigation is an example of an involuntary, specific lien.

80. a. When a person becomes deceased, according to federal and New York law, his/her property can pass to the surviving spouse without taxation.

81. b. A budget mortgage is when the lender pulls funds from the borrower's monthly payment and sets it aside in an escrow account in order to make yearly tax and insurance payments.

82. d. While they are bound by fair housing laws and cannot discriminate based on age, gender, ethnicity/race and religion, co ops do have more control than condo association since they transfer share of stock as opposed to real property.

83. a. In this case regression describes the fact that improvements have been made to the subject property that are much greater than the neighboring homes.

84. b. The Fiduciary duty of accounting states that the agent cannot commingle funds.

85. c. A Medicaid lien is a government lien and they are exempt.

86. d. Metes description gives both a bearing and a distance.

87. a. A voluntary lien is created by the lienee's action.

88. b. The HO-6 policy must provide for a minimum of 20% of the appraised value.

89. a. The franchise tax amount of a corporation depends on the company's entire net income (ENI). If the ENI is $290,000 or less, it would be 6.85%.

90. c. Title is a legal document evidencing a person's right or ownership to real property.

91. c. A two-step mortgage generally starts out at a set interest rate then increases after 5 or 7 years and a set rate for the duration of the loan.

92. a. A bill of sale is used in transferring personal property.

93. d. An executrix is a female appointed to administer a will.

94. d. A real estate agent is a licensed person who conducts and negotiates the sale of real estate.

95. b. An assumption is when a buyer assumes the sellers mortgage.

96. a. A deed is a legal document which conveys title to property.

97. b. A chapter 7 no asset is when the filer has no assets to pay the creditors.

98. c. A credit bureau is a 3rd party company which prepares a summary report of an individual's credit history.

99. b. Generally payments 30 days behind on first trust deeds are said to be in default.

100. a. The effective age is a term the appraiser uses to describe a building physical condition.

Real Estate Sales Exam IV

1. The sum of all of Mr. Slayer's personal property and real estate at the time of his death is known as his

a) probate

b) escheat

c) estate

d) will

2. Melody's dad, a cabinet maker, built her a beautiful entertainment unit that he securely attached to the wall 5 years ago. Now that she's married and they want to grow their family they have decided to move. The unit will have to remain in the home because it is a (n)

a) easement

b) trade fixture

c) appurtenance

d) fixture

3. A homeowner's insurance policy

a) is a warranty service contract that covers repair and replacement of home appliances

b) combines hazard insurance and personal liability insurance

c) is hazard insurance

d) all of the above

4. A servicer

a) loans money to purchase a home

b) collects mortgage payments from a borrower

c) conducts title searches

d) insures the loan in case of borrower default

5. A three family home is

a) a dwelling with 1 deed and is for 3 families

b) a commercial property

c) not legal in New York

d) a dwelling with 3 different deeds and is for 3 families

6. Three homeowners live adjacent to a body of water, but their water use rights are based on when they first used or applied for use. This is known as

a) riparian rights

b) littoral rights

c) the doctrine of prior appropriation

d) the doctrine of adverse possession

7. A tenancy that is NOT put in place by operation of law but by the parties expressed intent is

a) tenancy at will

b) tenancy by the entirety

c) community property

d) tenancy in common

8. All are "improvements" except

a) sidewalk

b) street light

c) pizza oven

d) paved road

9. Which is NOT a physical characteristic of land?

a) scarcity

b) non-homogeneity

c) immobility

d) indestructibility

10. Over several years, the Parson's land ownership has increased by means of

a) regression

b) accretion

c) diversion

d) avulsion

11. David allows Mike to store his pickup truck in his driveway for several weeks free of charge. David gave Mike a (n) _____.

a) acknowledgement

b) tenancy right

c) license

d) easement by prescription

12. Marty receives a notice for specific performance of a real estate contract, which is asking for

a) an earnest money deposit

b) conveyance of the property

c) a new contract

d) a deficiency judgment

13. Which is NOT an acceptable means by which a contract can be terminated?

a) sellers decides to get a divorce during transaction

b) destruction of premises

c) mutual agreement of the parties to cancel

d) impossibility of performance

14. Timothy is out of town when his broker tries to inform him that she has a buyer for his home who has made a full price bid and given her (the broker) the $3,000 earnest money deposit. What does the broker have at this point?

a) implied contract

b) executed purchase and sale agreement

c) voidable contract

d) offer

15. Patricia, who fell behind on her mortgage payments, requested assistance from her lender. Her lender helped her by substituting her old mortgage with a newer one in which they lowered her interest rate and extended her term. What term best describes what happened?

a) refinancing

b) novation

c) accelerating

d) none of the above

16. Which of the following statements is TRUE of a listing contract?

a) It obligates the broker to convince the seller to convey the property to the first person to make an offer.

b) It maintains that the broker act as a non-agent with a seller

c) It is an employment contract between the broker and the principal.

d) It is an agreement that lasts indefinitely

17. Which statement represents what an exclusive –agency listing and an exclusive-right-to-sell listing have in common?

a) Both provide for only 1 broker to represent the seller

b) Both are net listings

c) With both, the seller only allows only 1 salesperson to show their property

d) With both, the seller can sell the property without paying a commission

18. Margaret's broker listed and advertised her property, to find Nathan, a ready, willing and able buyer. After reviewing the offer and sleeping on it, Margaret decided to reject the offer, telling her agent she had remorse and no longer wished to sell her home. In this case Margaret

a) will have to pay the buyers for any damages

b) must sell the property

c) owes her broker the commission

d) is within her rights to change her mind

19. Highest and best use is

a) the effective age of a property

b) results in its "highest value"

c) the most marketable value

d) the book value

20. All are significant factors in comparing property with the sales comparison approach EXCEPT:

a) original purchase price

b) financing terms

c) physical appearance and condition

d) sale date

21. PITI stands for

a) payment, insurance, taxes and investment

b) principal, insurance, tariff, interest rate

c) payment, interest rate, taxes, insurance

d) principal, interest rate, taxes and insurance

22. Samantha has a 15 year loan at 4.5% interest rate for 15 years. This is a

a) conventional fixed rate loan

b) fixed rate loan

c) variable loan

d) pay option arm loan

23. You will use which formula to calculate the gross income multiplier (GIM)

a) GIM = annual gross income/sales price

b) GIM = rate x value

c) GIM = sales price/annual gross income

d) GIM = value/rate

24. When a property is pledged for a loan without giving up possession, this is known as

a) substitution

b) acceleration

c) hypothecation

d) alienation

25. Greg is someone who has received training, education and is experienced in estimating real property value. His job title is a(n)

a) loan processor

b) mortgage banker

c) underwriter

d) appraiser

26. Another name for Homeowner Association dues is

a) community property fees

b) common area assessments

c) common law dues

d) apportionments

27. A(n) _____ is when a tenant is lawfully expelled from the property.

a) aversion

 b) eviction

c) conviction

d) avulsion

28. Which is NOT a duty of a recorder?

a) a public official who maintains public real estate records

b) county clerk

c) transcribes real estate transaction

d) collects fees for documents filed

29. Hank and Cheri use a 1003 to

a) apply for a mortgage loan

b) write out a land contract

c) list a property for sale

d) make an offer on a home

30. Once the appraisal was completed, Jet's lender received a CRV or Certificate of Reasonable Value. What type of loan is he getting?

a) Fannie Mae

b) FHA

c) RHS

d) VA

31. _____ and _____ are Government Sponsored Entities.

a) FHA and VA

b) Ginnie Mae and Freddie Mac

c) Fannie Mae and Freddie Mac

d) RHS and Agricultural loans

32. According to Regulation Z Jasmine has _____ to rescind the transaction.

a) 5 days

b) 3 days

c) 4 days

d) 1 day

33. An employer sponsored tax-deferred retirement plan that homebuyers can borrower against is a

a) 401(k)

b) 203(k)

c) 403(b)

d) a and c

34. Jumbo loans refer to loans greater than _____.

a) $417,000

b) $650,000

c) $471,000

d) $617,000

35. The Fair and Accurate Credit Transactions Act of 2003 (FACTA) deals with

a) mortgage fraud

b) commingling of funds

c) prepayment penalties

d) identity theft

36. Which statement about mortgage insurance is NOT true?

a) is also known as private mortgage insurance

b) covers the lender when a homeowner defaults

c) is required when the borrower's down payment is 20% or more

d) is included in the mortgage payment

37. The Barksdale family just learned that the city is planning to build a small commuter airport near their family farm in which the home will sit below the flight path. They were hoping to sell the farm in a year but now fear that their values may be decreased due to

 a) functional obsolescence

b) functional regression

c) economic obsolescence

d) economic regression

38. Last year, 17 year old Jonathan inherited 5 two family homes from his late father. Now 2 years later, Jonathan has decided to sell 1 of them.   If he conveys his interest in the property to a purchaser by signing a deed, the contract will be

a) valid

b) void

c) voidable

d) invalid

39. Valid exclusive listings must include

a) an expiration date

b) a forfeiture clause

c) an automatic renewal clause

d) must allow the listing broker to appoint subagents

40. Meredith wanted Haley to know that her signature was genuine as she was signing a deed transferring ownership of her property to Haley. The declaration that Meredith made before a notary was a (n)

a) sheriff's deed

b) acknowledgment

c) promissory note

d) affidavit

41. Title to real estate can be transferred by involuntary alienation by all of the following except:

a) escheat

b) erosion

c) seisin

d) eminent domain

42. During her closing, Hillary reviewed a legal document which requires that she repay her mortgage loan during a given period of time based on a stated interest rate. This document is known as a

a) mortgage

b) deed of trust

c) lien

d) note

43. Zachary, whose home is set to close in 2 weeks, gets a call from his builder saying that his new home won't be ready for another 3 weeks. Zachary's realtor works out a deal where he can remain in the home 1 week after closing. This is known as a

a) leasehold

b) leaseback

c) lease at will

d) lease purchase

44. A trustee is

a) a fiduciary who controls property for the benefit of another person

b) always the executor of the estate

c) a trustworthy individual

d) an attorney

45. The best type of estate to inherit is

a) a leasehold estate

b) a life estate

c) a fee simple estate

d) a general estate

46. The time and date a document was recorded establish

a) chain of title

b) subrogation

c) escrow

d) priority

47. Rich sells a parcel of land to Tom. Tom quickly records the deed. If Rich tries to sell the same parcel to Kevin, which of the following statements is TRUE?

a) Tom will have to bring a quitclaim deed to court, since Rich is trying to sell the same property.

b) Kevin has been given constructive notice of the prior sale because Tom quickly recorded the deed.

c) Kevin was mailed the actual notice of the prior sale since Tom recorded the deed.

d) none of the above

48. The acquisition of real estate through the payment of money is

a) a sales transaction

b) called a truth in lending transaction

c) a purchase money transaction

d) a deed-in-lieu

49. A property sales price is a

a) debit to the buyer and a credit to the seller

b) credit to the buyer only

c) debit to the seller and credit to the buyer

d) credit to the seller only

50. Wilma collected a security deposit from each of her tenants when they signed their lease agreements. Now that she is selling her property, who should be credit the security deposits?

a) Wilma

b) buyer

c) tenants

d) lender

51. Because Jimmy has the right to control his property, he has a right to do all of the following except:

a) refuse to host a neighborhood block meeting at his home

b) turn away the meter reader from the local utility company

c) put a sign in his front yard that says "no soliciting"

d) host a family barbeque

52. Two properties A and B are separated by a private road. Landowner A owns the road but Landowner B has unrestricted access, as he needs to access the road to reach the main highway. What type of access does Landowner B have?

a) an easement by necessity

b) an encroachment

c) an easement

d) an assessment

53. Mena was so excited as she was purchasing her first home and everything, so far, has gone smoothly. The home inspection came back with minimal issues and her loan was fully approved. But 2 days before her closing date, the home caught on fire and was totally destroyed. Who will more than likely bear the loss?

a) Mena

b) the seller's lender

c) the seller

d) the buyer's lender

54. Contracts for the sale of real property, under the statute of frauds, must be

a) in writing to be enforceable

b) on purchase and sale agreement forms

c) started by a licensed agent

d) executed right away

55. The Martins enter into a sales contract with the Haggardy family in which they will pay the Haggardy family $1500 per month for their family farm. The Martins will pay all insurance premiums, property taxes, and any maintenance and repair costs, but the Haggardy's will maintain title to the property for 20 years. What type of contract do the two families have?

a) lease with option to buy

b) contract for deed

c) contract at will

d) mortgage contract

56. Harry lists his home with Broker Bill. He tells Broker Bill that as long he makes a profit of $203,000 on the sale of his home, Broker Bill can keep the difference as commission. This type of listing is known as

a) an exclusive-agency listing

b) an open listing

c) an exclusive-right-to sell listing

d) net listing

57. The original capital outlay for labor, materials, land and profit is known as

a) the market value

b) the market price

c) Mortgage value

d) cost

58. Kenny, a single man, died and left all of his real estate to his niece, 23 year old Ashley in a will. Title passes to Ashley at what point?

a) when she executes a new deed to all of the properties

b) after she pays all of the property taxes

c) immediately after Kenny's death

d) once she receives a title report that the properties are free and clear

59. How does a condominium differ from a planned unit development (PUD)?

a) a condominium usually has a pool and gym

b) in a PUD, an owner owns the building or unit they live in

c) a PUD has more units

d) all of above are true

60. A rate and term refinance

a) is also known as a no cash out refinance

b) generally covers the previous balance plus the costs associated with obtaining the new mortgage

c) puts cash in the borrowers hands

d) both a and b

61. Existing mortgages are usually bought as a "pool" on the _____.

a) primary market

b) secondary market

c) government market

d) black market

62. Liens and encumbrances shown on the title commitment, other than those listed in the contract, must be removed so that the title can be conveyed free and clear. It is the _____ responsibility to remove these.

a) seller's

b) buyer's

c) lender's

d) title company's

63. The principal amount of the buyer's new mortgage is a

a) debit to the real estate company

b) credit to the real estate company

c) credit to the buyer

d) debit to the seller

64. Jay's lender would like to ensure that he is paying a fair price for the home he is purchasing. In order to determine this, the lender will order a (n)

a) appraisal

b) broker price opinion

c) comparative market analysis

d) chain of title

65. For tax purposes, a (n) _____ *establishes* the value of a property.

a) broker

b) recorder

c) appraiser

d) assessor

66. Which tenancy automatically renews itself at each expiration?

a) tenancy at sufferance

b) tenancy for years

c) tenancy from month to month

d) tenancy at will

67. A valid lease has all of the requirements EXCEPT

a) valuable consideration

b) offer and acceptance

c) capacity to contract

d) county clerk recording

68. Money set aside for the replacement of common property in a condominium or cooperative project is called

a) replacement reserve fund

b) savings fund

c) capital improvements fund

d) contingency fund

69. Judith had to replace her boiler. This type of repair is classified as which type of maintenance?

a) construction

b) corrective

c) preventive

d) routine

70. Which does NOT affect zoning?

a) The principle of conformity enhances value.

b) The city requests that new building conform to specific types of architecture.

c) Values have remained the same because owners have the freedom to develop land as they please.

d) A new city ordinance mandates that the street floors of office building be used for delis and cafes.

71. Happy Family Realty received a lis pendens for their recent listing located at 7892 Oak Street. They now have

a) a notice of special assessment

b) a notice that legal action has been filed which could affect the property

c) a loan commitment letter

d) a home inspection report

72. New agent Barbara was so excited to close her first client that she gave her friend Nicholas $200 for referring the client to her. What Barbara did was

a) give Nicholas what is considered a kickback and is illegal under RESPA

b) legal as it's the cost of doing business

c) as long as Barbara had her attorney draw up an agreement between her and Nicholas, this was legal

d) illegal because she should have given the money to her broker

73. Which is an example of a unilateral contract?

a) a real estate sales contract

b) an agreement which states that you will provide sweat equity as your contribution in having your home built.

c) a contract between a broker and his agent

d) The sales manager says he will offer a 20% bonus if you sell $3.5 million in real estate.

74. The Gramm-Leach Bliley Act (GLBA) requires that companies give consumers privacy notices. Which jurisdiction does this fall under?

a) The Equal Credit Opportunity Act

b) Community Reinvestment Act

c) The Federal Trade Commission

d) The Sherman Anti-Trust Law

75. All are loan payment plans EXCEPT

a) 30 year fixed loan at 5.5% interest rate

b) 2-1 buy down

c) reverse mortgage

d) graduated payment mortgage

76. A primary mortgage loan is funded by

a) a mortgage banker

b) a mortgage broker

c) both a and b

d) neither a nor b

77. What should an owner of an apartment complex do if he has determined that his vacancy rate is less than 4%?

a) Nothing

b) He should lower his advertising budget

c) He should make property improvements

d) He should survey the rental market to determine whether he can raise his rents

78. Jacob and Leslie have a beautiful 2700 square foot home just outside the city, but most of the other homes are about 1800 square foot. Their home value has decreased because of what appraisal principle?

a) regression

b) assemblage

c) diminishing and increasing returns

d) contribution and conformity

79. Under FIRREA appraisers need to be licensed by the _____ in order to appraise real property valued over $1,000,000 in federally related transactions.

a) state

b) federal government

c) county

d) bank

80. In New York, a materialmen's lien is filed within ____ months from the date the materials were supplied.

a) 12

b) 4

c) 6

d) 24

81. A buyer's agent should NOT disclose which of the following to the seller?

a) the relationship between the buyer and the agent

b) agent compensation that will be paid from the broker's commission

c) that the agent may benefit from referring the parties to a subsidiary of the broker's firm

d) that the buyer is anxious to find a place to live

82. The art of weighing the findings and analyzing from 3 approaches to value is known as

a) substitution

b) reconciliation

c) assumption

d) capitalization

83. A prospective buyer is attracted to a property that has a negative cash flow. The following must be TRUE?

a) the depreciable base is large

b) there is no deferred maintenance

c) There is a substantial increase in property value

d) the new buyer will have to make a huge down payment

84. What provision can stop Cary from losing her home to foreclosure if she files for chapter 13 bankruptcy?

a) automatic stay provision

b) automatic stop provision

c) repayment provision

d) payment restructure provision

85. Lisa is frustrated with her homeowners association as they have neglected to fix the walkway where her mother fell. She should

a) stop paying her HOA dues

b) continue to pay her HOA dues because in Massachusetts HOA dues take precedence over all other liens

c) place the money she would normally pay for her dues in an escrow account until the repairs are made

d) fix the walkway with the money she would normally pay her HOA dues and send the HOA a bill

86. What is the name of the common wall in a duplex?

a) party wall

b) perching wall

c) parting wall

d) public wall

87. Raymond's commitment letter which has not expired states his interest rate will be 4.75%. But now his lender tells him that he forgot to lock that rate in and his new rate will be 5.25%. Being that Raymond has met all of the lender requirements, which is true?

a) He will have to pay the new rate of 5.25%

b) the lender will be reprimanded

c) Under New York law the commitment letter may be a binding agreement

d) Raymond will have to pay the discount points to get the 4.75% rate

88. In New York, when transferring a cooperative, can a flip tax be imposed? If so, who pays it?

a) yes; buyer

b) no

c) yes; seller

d) yes; buyer and seller (each pays half)

89. What is the minimum amount of time an "estate for years" can be effect?

a) 30 days

b) 5 years

c) 1 day

d) 2 years

90. Which situation below deals with the Spite Fence Law?

a) A neighbor puts up a 7 foot tall fence tall unattractive fence to get back at his neighbor

b) A neighbor puts up a 5 foot tall fence to keep his small dog in his yard

c) A neighbor puts up a 6 foot tall fence for privacy as he has small children who play in the back yard

d) A neighbor puts up a 5 foot tall fence on part of his neighbor's property

91. "An ownership that arises between a husband and wife when a single instrument transfers property to both of them and says nothing about the type of ownership" is

a) joint tenancy

b) tenancy in common

c) tenancy of sufferance

d) tenancy by the entirety

92. All are public records that may not be found through a title search EXCEPT

a) mistakes in recording legal documents

b) unpaid liens

c) forged deed

d) fraud

93. What type of contract is defined as, "inferred from behavior of the parties"?

a) implied

b) express

c) unilateral

d) bilateral

94. Of the following, which contract is defined as, "parties have agreed to the terms of the contract"?

a) implied

b) unilateral

c) express

d) bilateral

95. Ownership of a property by one person is known as

a) remainder interest

b) entirety

c) severalty

d) reversionary interest

96. The words of conveyance in a deed are in the

a) purchase clause

b) selling clause

c) granting clause

d) heading

97. Which of the following property will have the highest capitalization rate?

a) a modernized school

b) an SFR

c) a convenience store

d) a small shopping center with limited traffic access

98. Open listings are also known as

a) multiple listings

b) nonexclusive agreements

c) exclusive rights to sell

d) net listings

99. Gilbert defaulted on his loan and the lender foreclosed. Which clause requires the lender to look only to the property for satisfaction of debt?

a) exculpatory clause

b) deficiency judgment

c) acceleration clause

d) defeasance clause

100. Grantees are protected by express covenants found in

a) bill of sale deed

b) quit claim deed

c) general warranty deed

d) sheriff's deed

Real Estate Sales Exam IV Answers

1. c. The sum total of an individual's personal and real property at the time of death.

2. d. A fixture is personal property that is attached to the real property.

3. b. A homeowner's insurance policy combines hazard insurance and personal liability insurance

4. b. A servicer collects mortgage payments from a borrower.

5. a. A three family home is a dwelling for 3 families and ownership is evidence by 1 deed.

6. c. The doctrine of prior appropriation is generally in areas of water scarcity. Water rights are assigned priority based on when the right was either first used or applied for.

7. b. Tenancy by entirety is a tenancy a husband and wife can choose that is typically not recognized in community property states.

8. c. A trade fixture is an installed item that the tenant can take with them when they end their lease.

9. a. Scarcity is an economic characteristic of land.

10. b. Accretion is the addition of land when sand or soil is naturally deposited from rivers, streams or lakes.

11. c. Permission was granted for a specified period of time.

12. b. A suit for specific performance, often times, is when there is a defaulting party. In this case non defaulting party is suing to force the defaulting party to carry out the terms of the contract.

13. a. Reasons to discharge a contract include: operation of law, impossibility of performance, mutual agreement of the parties to cancel, substantial performance, partial performance.

14. d. At this point the broker has a signed offer to present to the seller.

15. b. Novation is where the lender substitutes a new obligation for an old one.

16. c. A listing is an employment contract in which the broker provides professional services to the client.

17. a. Both the exclusive-agency and the exclusive-right to-sell listings have only 1 broker.

18. c. Since the broker performed his duties she owes him/her their commission.

19. b. Highest and best value is the most probably use to which a property is used or suited that results in its "highest value"

20. a. Original purchase price is not compared when using the sales comparison approach.

21. d. PITI stands for principal, interest rate, taxes and insurance

22. b. In a fixed rate loan the interest rate stays the same for the duration of the loan.

23. a. Grosss Income Multiplier = annual gross income/ sales price

24. c. When a property is pledged for a loan without giving up possession this is known as hypothecation.

25. d. An appraiser is an individual who is qualified by training, education and experience to estimate value.

26. b. Common area assessments are also known as homeowner association dues.

27. b. Eviction is when a tenant is legally expelled from the property.

28. c. A recorder is a county clerk, who collects fees for documents filed as well as maintains public real property records.

29. a. A 1003 is the loan application form must used by lenders.

30. d. In a VA loan transaction, once the appraisal is done the VA issues a Certificate of Reasonable Value.

31. c. Fannie Mae and Freddie Mac are government sponsored entities' that were chartered by Congress.

32. b. Regulation Z gives most borrowers 3 days to rescind the transaction.

33. d. 403(b) and 401(k) are employer-sponsored investment plans.

34. a. Conventional loan amounts below $471,000 are conforming.

35. d. FACTA was designed to enhance the accuracy of borrower financial information, fight identity theft, and expand consumer access to credit.

36. c. Mortgage insurance is required the LTV is greater than 80%

37. c. Economic obsolescence is when a property loses value due to surrounding factors such as environmental and social forces.

38. a. The conveyance will be valid as his age at the time of conveyance will be 19.

39. a. Listing agreements must have a "from and to" date.

40. b. An acknowledgment is a formal declaration before a public official such as a notary public.

41. c. Involuntary alienation transfers are generally carried out by operation of law.

42. d. A note is a legal document requiring a borrower to repay a mortgage loan during a specified period of time at a stated interest rate.

43. b. A leaseback is where a seller conveys the property to a buyer and the seller leases the property back from the buyer.

44. a. A trustee is a fiduciary who controls property for the benefit of another person.

45. c. A fee simple is an unconditional unlimited estate of inheritance.

46. d. Time and date establish of recording establish priority.

47. b. Constructive notice is based on the legal presumption that an individual may obtain information by diligent inquiry.

48. c. A purchase money transaction is the acquisition of real estate.

49. a. Property sales price results in a credit to the seller and a debit to the buyer.

50. b. The buyer should receive the security deposit credit once the deed is transferred to them.

51. b. Utility company i.e. those companies which own the equipment are generally granted an easement as they have a right to enter and work on the property.

52. a. An easement by necessity is an easement granted by law and court action that is necessary for full enjoyment of the land.

53. c. The purchase and sale agreement states that the seller must maintain insurance on the home. The purchaser can terminate the contract or they can accept the damaged property and an assignment of the proceeds from the insurance company.

54. a. The law goes back to the English common law and can be found in MGL chapter 259, section 1.

55. b. Contract for deed, also known as a land contract, is where the buyer pays installment to the seller for a specified period of time, but the seller maintains title to the property.

56. d. A net listing is based on the net price the seller will receive if the property is sold.

57. d. Cost is the original capital outlay for labor, land, profit and materials.

58. c. A will takes effect after the death of the decedent.

59. b. In a condominium the owner owns the airspace in their unit

60. c. A cash out refinance puts funds into the hands of the borrower.

61. b. The secondary market is where "pools" of existing mortgages are bought and sold.

62. a. The seller must pay off and/or remove any liens before the title can be delivered free and clear.

63. c. The principal amount is the buyer's credit as this is what will be used to purchase the property.

64. a. The lender will order an appraisal which will be done by an appraiser, someone who has been trained and educated and is experienced in estimating value.

65. d. A public official who establishes the value for tax purposes is an assessor.

66. c. Month to month tenancy renews itself at each expiration.

67. d. A lease does not need to be recorded.

68. a. Money set aside for the replacement of common property in a condominium or cooperative project is called a replacement reserve fund.

69. b. Corrective maintenance involves the actual repair of the building's equipment.

70. c. Zoning is a tool for implementing a local plan to prevent incompatible land uses.

71. b. A lis pendens is a legal notice that a legal suit has been filed which could affect the property.

72. a. Per RESPA, kickbacks are illegal.

73. d. A unilateral contract is when a promise is exchanged for performance.

74. c. The GLBA falls under the jurisdiction of the Federal Trade Commission.

75. a. A fixed rate loan is structured for the repayment of borrowed funds.

76. a. A mortgage banker is a firm that can originate, sell and service mortgage loans.

77. d. A vacancy rate lower than 5% generally indicates that rents are too low.

78. c. Improvements can reach a point in which they no longer add value but rather diminish the returns.

79. a. Under FIRREA appraisers need to be licensed by the state in order to appraise real property valued over $1,000,000 in federally related transactions.

80. b. A materialmen's lien is filed with the county clerk. It is done so within 4 months from the date the materials were supplied.

81. d. Confidentiality is an agent responsibility.

82. b. Reconciliation is the art of weighing the findings and analyzing from 3 approaches to value.

83. c. Negative cash flow can be offset by an increase in property value.

84. a. Chapter 13 bankruptcy has an automatic stay provision.

85. b. HOA dues in Massachusetts take precedence over other liens and they can take the homeowner to court and even force a sale.

86. a. The party wall is the common wall shared in a duplex or condominium.

87. c. Under New York law as long as the borrower has met lender requirements and the commitment letter has correct wording, it is a binding agreement.

88. c. A flip tax may be imposed and it is paid by the seller

89. c. Once the fixed term is up, the agreement automatically terminates.

90. a. The Spite Fence Law says that a fence that unnecessarily exceeds 6 feet in height and is maliciously erected for the purpose of annoying the neighbors may be deemed a private nuisance.

91. d. Tenancy by the entirety is when an ownership arises between a husband and wife when a single instrument transfers property to both of them and says nothing about the type of ownership.

92. b. Unpaid liens are generally found in a title search.

93. a. With an implied contract, the parties have not expressly agreed to the contract, but their behaviors indicate their agreement.

94. c. With an express contract, the parties have specifically agreed to the terms.

95. c. Severalty means that all others have been severed or cut off.

96. c. The words of conveyance can be found in the granting clause

97. d. Because traffic is limited, the shopping center will have the greatest risk and therefore the highest cap rate.

98. b. Open listings are also known as nonexclusive agreements

99. a. With an exculpatory clause in place the buyer is not responsible for the debt because it acts as a non recourse loan.

100. c. General warranty deeds contain covenants that warrant the new owner's clear and undisturbed title.

Real Estate Sales Exam V

1. The Edwards family is planning on buying a single family home for $319,750. They need to put down 20% in order to buy the home. How much money does the Edwards family need to put down to secure the house?

a. $68,010
b. $63,950
c. $63,600
d. $61,750

2. Mrs. Ramirez, the local real estate agent, made a profit of $19,500 off a house she just sold. The house closed for $325,000. What was Mrs. Ramirez's commission rate for the sale?

a. 11%
b. 8%
c. 6%
d. 15%

3. Mr. Sanders and his family bought a property ten years ago. It has increased in value by 2% every year that he has owned it. If he bought it for $450,000, what is it worth now?

a. $540,000
b. $465,000
c. $501,000
d. $525,000

4. If you bought your home 20 years for $80,000 and now the value is $225,000, at what percent did the house appreciate each year?
a. 23%
b. 7%
c. 12%

d. 9%

5. Frances put down $68,000 on a $319,000 property. What percent did Frances put down?

a. 21%
b. 35%
c. 18%
d. 12%

6. Real estate often deals with two main types of property. One type is personal property, what is the other type?

a. home owner property
b. real property
c. building property
d. city owned property

7. Which of the following is considered real property?

a. oak tree
b. swing set
c. couch
d. curtains

8. Which of the following is not a physical characteristic of land?

a. immobility
b. indestructibility
c. non-homogeneity
d.situs

9. A physical characteristic of land that states that no two pieces of land are alike is

a. indestructibility
b. non-homogeneity
c. permanence
d. situs

10. How many economic characteristics of land are there?

a. 4

b. 2

c.6

d.9

11. Which of the following is not an economic characteristic of land?

a. scarcity

b. permanence

c. situs

d. immobility

12. An encumbrance is

a. the ability to move personal property from one point to another

b. a type of commercial building

c. a document that shows ownership of personal property

d. a claim or lien on a parcel of real property

13. This type of encumbrance often occurs because of incorrect surveying or marked boundary lines?

a. encroachment

b. liens

c. easement

d. foreclosure

14. Which of the following is not a real estate tax lien?

a. sales tax lien

b. federal tax lien

c. state tax lien

d. property tax lien

15. The grantor index is

a. list of property prices

b. list of realtors

c. an alphabetical list of sellers of the property.

d. list of property purchasers of the property

16. What is considered to be a legal entity that has been incorporated and holds equal right and liability for the owned property through a charter?

a. partnership

b. fee simple estate

c. community property

d. corporation

17. The traditional method of surveying property and measuring factors like precise length of line run, natural materials, surface, and land soil is?

a. government or US public land system

b. rectangular survey system

c. metes and bounds

d. principle meridians

18. Depreciation is

a. when the value increases over time.

b. when the value decreases over a period of time

c. when the value remains constant over time.

d. when the value increases instantly

19. The process that was created to determine whether a seller of a property has saleable interest, any restrictions for a property or any liens and foreclosures is known as

a. owner search

b. title search

c. property search

d. personal search

20. A partnership where only one person is required to be a general partner, but both partners share in profits, debts, and liabilities related to the property is a

a. simple partnership

b. group partnership

c. limited partnership

d. general partnership

21. A property tax lien is

a. when a lien is placed to seize assets on a property or multiple properties

b. when a lien is placed to take unpaid sales tax

c. when a lien is placed to seize unpaid federal taxes

d. when a lien is placed to seize unpaid state taxes

22. If you won a judgment to seize property or payments awarded to you, you will be given a court order called

a. easement

b. encroachment

c. writ of attachment

d. judge's order

23. All of the following are types of estates except

a. non freehold estate

b. life estate

c. freehold estate

d. born estate

24. In the case that an estate should be transferred between parties, it can typically be done the following ways except

a. will

b. word of mouth

c. inheritance

d. deed

25. In regards to real estate, anticipation is

a. the period right before foreclosure

b. the expected value of an owned property and the possible profits when selling it.

c. the final sale price of a property

d. the total taxes that are paid on a property

26. In regards to real estate, progression is

a. an increase in price due to the economy

b. adding an addition to the property

c. buying more land

d. the advantage given to a property because of its desired location

27. In regards to real estate, regression is

a. a price decrease due to the economy

b. taking a property off the market

c. incorrect property lines

d. the disadvantage given to a particular property due to its less desirable location

28. Reasons to have an appraisal done include all of the following except

a. condemnation

b. metes and bounds

c. assessed value

d. insurance reasons

29. Which of the following is correct regarding supply and demand?

a. more for sale properties and less purchasers equals lower prices

b. more for sale properties and more purchasers equals lower prices

c. less properties and more buyers equals lower prices

d. there is always enough supply to meet demand and for prices to remain constant

30. Substitution, in regards to real estate is

a. when a buyer is willing to pay more for a property that is equivalent to another property

b. the advantage a property receives based on its location

c. when a buyer is not willing to pay more for particular property than the price they would pay over an equivalent property

d. when higher priced properties are preferred to lower priced properties

31. There are four elements that help establish the value of a property. Which of the following is not one of them?

a. demand for a particular type of property
b. cleanliness of a property
c. transferability to a new owner of a property
d. Demand for a particular type of property

32. An Offer to Purchase is a type of

a. lease
b. loan
c. mortgage
d. contract

33. A unilateral contract is

a. where only one party has responsibilities to fulfill
b. where two parties have responsibilities to fulfill
c. where there is no agreement
d. where no party has fulfilled the agreement

34. What is a deed?

a. a loan
b. a contract to pay income taxes
c. an offer to buy a property
d. a written document that legally transfers the property title

35. In order for a contract to be valid it should include the following except

a. be posted on the Internet
b. involve competent parties
c. in writing (unless you have a one year or less lease)
d. both parties' signatures

36. When property improvements are performed and they result in a property value increase, it is known as

a. substitution
b. regression
c. progression
d. law of increasing returns

37. When property improvements that are performed do not increase a property's value, it is known as

a. law of decreasing returns
b. supply and demand
c. regression
d. progression

38. The loan value establishes

a. the down payment price
b. the price a home appraises for
c. the maximum loan amount that can be secured based on the property
d. the realtor fees

39. A junior mortgage is

a. a small loan
b. a loan to prepare you for your first mortgage
c. an additional loan to the primary mortgage
d. the process of getting a mortgage

40. An open-end mortgage

a. allows the borrower to have the option to borrow additional funds without having to rewrite the mortgage
b. does not allow any more funds to be borrowed
c. allows the borrower to change the terms of the loan at any time
d. allows the lender to change the terms of the loan at any time.

41. When the property seller is doing the financing for the buyer, it is called

a. blanket mortgage
b. purchase money mortgage
c. balloon loan
d. wraparound mortgage

42. A demand mortgage

a. allows the lender to increase the loan at any time
b. allows the buyer the ability to terminate the loan
c. permits the borrower to make payments whenever they please
d. permits the lender to require the borrower to pay whenever the lender wants.

43. Which of the following is not a type of loan?

a. variable rate mortgage
b. long mortgage
c. open-end mortgage
d. blanket mortgage

44. What is a term loan?

a. a loan that is principal and interest
b. a loan that is principal only
c. a loan that the monthly payments vary
d. a loan that is interest only

45. A loan that is principle and interest, and at the maturity date the loan will be paid in full is a(n)

a. fully amortized loan
b. negative amortization loan
c. equity loan
d. construction loan

46. Which of the following is a type of loan?

a. fully changing loan

b. moving loan

c. constant loan

d. fully amortized loan

47. Legally, it is prohibited to choose to not sell or rent to someone based on all of the following except

a. gender

b. handicap

c. attitude

d. race

48. Which of the following is not a type of lease?

a. up down lease

b. net lease

c. gross lease

d. graduated lease

49. A net lease states that

a. the tenant is responsible for paying for expenses including (property taxes, insurance, maintenance expenses)

b. that the landlord is responsible for paying for expenses including (property taxes, insurance, maintenance expenses)

c. that the landlord and tenant split expenses

d. that the rent can be increased to pay for expenses

50. A gross lease states that

a. the tenant is responsible for paying for expenses including (property taxes, insurance, maintenance expenses)

b. the rent can be increased to pay for expenses at any time

c. the landlord and tenant split expenses

d. the landlord is responsible for paying for expenses including (property taxes, insurance, maintenance expenses)

51. A person is eligible to receive a broker's license if he/she completes a minimum of

a. 10 classroom instruction hours
b. 15 classroom instruction hours
c. 20 classroom instruction hours
d. 30 classroom instruction hours

52. To be eligible for a broker's license, the candidate must be a licensed salesperson and be actively employed by a broker for at least

a. 30 days
b. six months
c. one year
d. three years

53. A correct requirement to be eligible for a broker's license is

a. tenders a surety bond of $10,000 to the Board
b. successfully completes the exam
c. have been employed 6 months by a broker
d. have 20 hours of classroom instruction

54. The exclusive right to sell means

a. multiple brokers receive commission on the sale of the property
b. the property seller does not have to pay a commission to the broker
c. the commission is split between the broker and seller
d. the listing broker receives the commission on the sale of the property, even if another makes the sale

55. MLS stands for

a. multiple liens survey
b. multiple listing service
c. many listers service
d. moveable listings service

56. Agency contracts can be ended by which of the following

a. non-homogeneity

b. change of mind

c. property destruction

d. scarcity

57. An agency contract can be terminated for the following reasons except:

a. revocation

b. bankruptcy of either party

c. time limit expiration

d. change of mind

58. In an agreement between a lessor and lessee, the lessee is responsible to use the property in a proper manner and

a. keep the property clean

b. fix all property damages, regardless of who caused them

c. not invite guests over

d. destroy the property

59. In an agreement between a lessor and lessee, the lessor is responsible for all of the following except

a. having an inhabitable property

b. making rent payments on time

c. allow the lessee to have quiet enjoyment of the property

d. the property does not violate sanitary or building codes

60. The cycle of real estate goes as follows

a. The buyer is qualified, The buyer is shown the property, The property is listed, The agreement between the buyer and seller is signed, The buyer finalizes and secures financing, The closing occurs

b. The property is listed, The buyer is qualified, The buyer is shown the property, The buyer finalizes and secures financing, The closing occurs, The agreement between the buyer and seller is signed

c. The property is listed, The buyer is qualified, The buyer finalizes and secures financing, The buyer is shown the property, The agreement between the buyer and seller is signed, The closing occurs

d. The property is listed, The buyer is qualified, The buyer is shown the property, The agreement between the buyer and seller is signed, The buyer finalizes and secures financing, The closing occurs

61. Which of the following is not a part of the cycle of real estate?

a. an agreement between the buyer and seller is signed
b. the buyer cleans the property
c. the property is listed
d. the buyer is shown the property

62. What is a prime rate?

a. the interest rate given to those with bad credit
b. the highest interest rate allowed to be charged
c. the standard rate given to all borrowers
d. the interest rate charged by banks given to their preferred borrowers

63. There are several important elements to the purchase and sale agreement. Which of the following makes it valid?

a. the names of all parties involved
b. the surrounding properties appraised value
c. information on all upgraded items
d. all previous owners

64. All of the following are valid elements of a purchase and sale agreement except

a. the sale price
b. a land description
c. the contract date
d. the surrounding properties appraised value

65. A deed that includes the communicated or implied words from the grantor about the title's validity is a

a. general warranty deed
b. special warranty deed
c. quit claim deed
d. sheriff's deed

66. A cooperative is owned by

a. employees
b. a corporation
c. two owners
d. one individual

67. Which of the following is not a credit reporting agency?

a. Equifax
b. Expert Credit
c. Experian
d. Transunion

68. Under the Fair and Accurate Credit Transactions Act, consumers can receive a free credit report every

a. 5 years
b. 3 years
c. 6 months
d. 12 months

69. An individual is eligible to get a salesperson license if he/she

a. complete 40 hours of classroom instruction
b. complete 12 hours of classroom instruction
c. complete 20 hours of classroom instruction
d. is at least 18 years old

70. A valid contract means it is

a. legal, binding, and enforceable

b. not legal, binding or enforceable

c. can be ended at any time no matter the reason

d. binding for one party, but not the other

71. A voided contract means

a. must be followed through with

b. legal, binding, and enforceable

c. binding for one party, but not the other

d. not legal, binding or enforceable

72. A voidable contract means it is

a. not legal, binding or enforceable

b. legal, binding, and enforceable

c. binding for one party, but not the other

d. can be terminated at any time no matter the reason

73. What system, also known as the Land Court, is used to register land?

a. Torrens System

b. Register Court

c. Torrent Court

d. Sales System

74. When a property is auctioned off due to foreclosure or a court related action, the title of the property is transferred under this deed.

a. quit claim deed

b. tax deed

c. sheriff's deed

d. gift deed

75. When the title of property is transferred, after being sold at auction, to take care of unpaid taxes it is called a

a. tax deed

b. quit claim deed

c. sheriff's deed

d. gift deed

76. Listing types include all of the following except

a. freedom

b. exclusive agency

c. net

d. open

77. A life estate in reversion is when

a. the life estate has no previous owner

b. the life estate remains with the new owner

c. the life estate is taken by the government

d. the life estate ownership reverts back to its original owner or grantor

78. Which of the following is not considered real property?

a. apple tree

b. potted plant

c. oak tree

d. planted roses

79. Personal property can become real property

a. at no time

b. if it is left on the property prior to the sale

c. if it becomes a permanent fixture of the land

d. all personal property is real property

80. A RV that is parked on the property is considered

a. personal property

b. land property

c. movable property

d. real property

81. A rose plant that has been planted into the ground and has set its roots is considered

a. personal property
b. real property
c. implanted property
d. rooted property

82. Non-homogeneity says that

a. land is easily damageable
b. land cannot be moved
c. all land is the same
d. no two pieces of land are alike

83. Indestructibility of land means

a. it cannot be moved
b. that it cannot be ultimately destroyed
c. that damaged land is useless
d. that the property value is high

84. Immobility of the land means

a. that it is similar to other pieces of land
b. the property is for sale
c. the entire piece of land can be moved
d. it cannot be moved in its entirety

85. Situs is

a. the knowledge of knowing that some owners prefer certain locations
b. a physical characteristic of land
c. an encumbrance
d. means land can be sold to many owners

86. Permanence refers to

a. land being scarce in certain areas

b. the knowledge that some owners prefer certain locations

c. the lasting potential of the land or property

d. the fact that no two pieces of land are alike

87. When land is scarce

a. it is easy to obtain

b. it is normal to own land

c. land prices go up

d. there is an abundance of land

88. Which of the following will not help the economic value of your home?

a. new roof

b. replacing a hole in the wall

c. adding heavy duty curtains

d. fixing dry rot

89. Which of the following will MOST likely add economic value to your home?

a. planter boxes

b. adding a bathroom

c. new roof

d. new curtains

90. If a property has an encumbrance attached to the title it can

a. be difficult to determine the correct owner

b. be easy to find the correct owner

c. make selling the property easy

d. add value to the property

91. An encroachment is when

a. property is auctioned off

b. property is transferred to a relative

c. a structure is up for sale, before being fully paid off

d. a structure or fixture is built on another person's property or land

92. A mechanic's lien is initiated by

a. the government

b. people who have supplied labor or materials to improve the property

c. the lending bank

d. people interested in purchasing the property

93. The process where a lender tries to recover the remaining balance of a loan, after payments have stopped being made, by selling the asses it is known as

a. foreclosure

b. short sale

c. judgment

d. regular sale

94. Liens

a. are always voluntary

b. are always involuntary

c. can be voluntary or involuntary

d. can only be placed on single family home properties

95. Depreciation on a home can occur because of

a. a new roof

b. favorable home improvements

c. property values increasing

d. unfavorable home modifications

96. A fee simple absolute free hold estate gives the owner rights including all of the following except

a. the authority to live in, rent or mortgage the property

b. the authority to sell, destroy, or reassign ownership of the property

c. the authority to construct buildings on the property

d. the authority to not have to pay taxes on the property

97. An estate that states that a person's life interest will last for the life of another person, instead of their own is called

a. life estate in reversion
b. pur autre vie
c. remainderman
d. life estate

98. The remainderman is the person

a. that is given everything left over from inside the property when the original owners move out
b. that transfers the deed from person to person for a small fee
c. who inherits property upon the terminations of the estate from the previous owner
d. who is considered the original owner

99. When the government controls the rights to the property by creating laws or guidelines that have to be followed when owning a parcel of property, it is known as

a. control power
b. police ownership
c. police power
d. property control

100. Eminent domain allows the government to

a. demolish private property will no payment to the owner
b. sale private property without the owner's knowledge
c. take private property for private use
d. take private property for public use

Real Estate Sales Exam V Answers

1. b. Find the answer by taking the cost of the home $319,750 and multiplying it by 20% or .20.

2. c. Divide the profit (commission) Mrs. Ramirez made off the sell by the house sale price. 19,500/325,000= .06

3. a. $450,000 X .02= $9000 increased value each year. Take increased value and multiply it by the amount of years the property has been owned. $9,000 X 10= $90,000 Add the total increased value to sell price.
$450,000 + $90,000= $540,000

4. d. Take $225,000 - $80,000=$145,000 to get the increased value. Then take increased value / purchased price. $145,000/$80,000=1.8 You can find the annual appreciate rate by 1.8/20 years= 9%.

5. a. Take the down payment and divide it by the purchase price. $68,000/ $319,000= .213 or 21%.

6. b. Real property refers to the land and things or items that are permanently attached to it ex. Plant life, houses, etc. Any fixed item that can cause damage to the property when it is moved is real property. Personal property refers to property that is moveable such as furniture, and will not cause any damage to the property.

7. a. Real property cannot be moved without causing damage to the property. Moving an oak tree off of the property would cause severe damage to the land.

8. d. Situs is an economic characteristic of land, not a physical characteristic of land.

9. b. By definition non-homogeneity states that no two pieces of land are alike.

10. a. There are 4 economic characteristics of land. (scarcity, improvements, permanence, situs)

11. d. Immobility is a physical characteristic of land.

12. d. An encumbrance is a claim or lien on a parcel of real property.

13. a. An encroachment is a situation where a structure is built on another person's property. This many times occurs due to incorrect surveying or marked boundary lines.

14. a. The three types of tax liens are: property tax lien, federal tax lien, and state tax lien.

15. c. The grantor index is an alphabetical list of sellers of a property.

16. d. A corporation is a legal entity that has been incorporated and holds equal rights and liability for the property through a charter.

17. b. Rectangular survey system is the traditional method of surveying property and measures factors like precise length of line run, natural materials, surface, and land soil.

18. b. Depreciation is when the value decreases over time. Many things can depreciate in value, including property.

19. b. A title search is done to see if a seller has saleable interest, any restrictions for a property, or any liens or foreclosures.

20. c. A limited partnership is where only one person is required to be a general partner, but both partners share in profits, debts, and liabilities related to the property.

21. a. Property tax lien is a type of lien that is placed to seize assets on a property or multiple properties. This happens when property taxes remain unpaid.

22. c. A court order awarded from a judgment to seize an asset is a writ of attachment.

23. d. Different types of estates include: life estate, non freehold estate, and freehold estate.

24. b. To transfer an estate it in normally done by having a deed, will, or inheritance.

25. b. In real estate anticipation is the expected value of an owned property and the possible profits when selling it. Appraisals can give you a better idea of the value of your property.

26. d. Progression is an advantage that is given to certain properties based on their desired location. This can be for a prominent area in town.

27. d. Regression is the disadvantage given to a particular property due to its less desirable location. This can be due to a dangerous area of town.

28. b. Metes and bounds is not a reason to have an appraisal. It is used to describe real property with geography and land features.

29. a. Supply and demand is based upon need and what is available. If more is available then needed, prices will drop, and vice versa.

30. c. Substitution is the concept that shows that some buyers are not willing to pay more for a property then they would for another equivalent property. If they can find a similar property elsewhere for a better price, they will choose the similar property.

31. b. The four elements to establish the value of a property are: demand, utility, scarcity, and transferability.

32. d. An offer to purchase is a type of contact that is usually has a fill in the blank type set up. It also gives the terms of sale.

33. a. When only one party has responsibilities to complete, it is called a unilateral contact.

34. d. A deed is a written document that transfers a property's title to another. This is a legal document.

35. a. In order for a contract to be considered valid it should have the following: an offer and acceptance, explain the payment, outline the objective, all parties must be competent, be in writing, and signed by both parties.

36. d. The law of increasing returns refers to improvements that are made on a property that increase the property's value. A new roof can increase the value.

37. a. The law of decreasing returns is when upgrades are made to a property, but do not increase its value. Adding another bathroom to the home does not increase its value.

38. c. The loan value establishes the maximum loan total that can be secured by a property.

39. c. A junior mortgage is a second loan. It is a loan that is in addition to a primary mortgage.

40. a. An open end mortgage is designed to give the borrower the option of adding more funds without having to rewrite the mortgage.

41. b. A purchase money mortgage is when the buyer is financed by the property's seller.

42. d. A demand mortgage is a type of mortgage that lets the lender demand payment whenever they feel necessary.

43. b. Some types of loans include open-end mortgages, variable rate mortgages, and blanket mortgages.

44. d. A term loan is a loan that is interest only. At the end of the loan term, the total amount is due.

45. a. A fully amortized loan is principle and interest. At the maturity of the loan date, the loan will be paid in full.

46. d. The only type of loan in the group is a fully amortized loan. A fully amortized loan is principle and interest. At the maturity of the loan date, the loan will be paid in full.

47. c. Attitude is not a protected class. The protected groups include: color, race, religion, ancestry, gender, handicap, and family status.

48. a. Different types of leases include gross lease, net lease, and graduated lease to name a few.

49. a. A net lease is a lease that says the tenant pays for any expenses including property taxes, insurance, and maintenance expenses.

50. d. A gross lease says that the landlord is responsible for paying for expenses including property taxes, insurance, and maintenance expenses.

51. d. Anyone interested in receiving a broker's license must complete a minimum of 30 hours in the classroom.

52. c. A salesperson is eligible to become a broker he if has been actively employed for at least one year by a broker.

53. b. In order to be eligible for a broker's license one must complete 30 hours of classroom instruction, successfully complete the exam, tender a surety bond of $5,000 to the Board, and has been employed by a broker for at least a year.

54. d. The exclusive right to sell means the listing broker receives the commission on the sale of the property. This is true even if that broker does not make the actual sale.

55. b. MLS stands for Multiple Listing Service.

56. c. Agency contracts can be terminated for many reasons including property destruction.

57. d. An agency contract can be ended because of revocation, bankruptcy of either party, or time limit expiration, just to name a few.

58. a. The lessee is responsible to keep the rented property clean, properly use property appliances and fixtures, and do not destroy the property.

59. b. It is not the responsibility of the lessor to make payments. That is the responsibility of the lessee.

60. d. The cycle of real estate is 1. The property is listed 2. The buyer is qualified 3. The buyer is shown the property 4. The agreement between the buyer and seller is signed 5. The buyer finalizes and secures financing 6. The closing occurs

61. b. The cycle of real estate goes as follows and does not include the buyer cleans the property. The property is listed 2. The buyer is qualified 3. The buyer is shown the property 4. The agreement between the buyer and seller is signed 5. The buyer finalizes and secures financing 6. The closing occurs.

62. d. The prime rate is an interest rate that is given to preferred borrowers by the banks.

63. a. The purchase and sale agreement is valid if it has the names of all parties involved, a land description, sale price, the amount of earnest money given by the buyer, the contract date, and buyer and sellers signatures.

64. d. The surrounding properties appraised value is not necessary for a purchase and sale agreement. You need the names of all parties involved, a land description, the sale price, the amount of earnest money given by the buyer, the contract date, and buyer and sellers signatures.

65. a. A general warranty deed states that the spoken or implied words from the grantor, about the title's validity is true.

66. b. A cooperative is owned by a corporation. They are responsible for paying ad valorem taxes.

67. b. The three credit reporting agencies are Equifax, Experian, and Transunion.

68. d. Under the act consumers are able to receive a free credit report from each of the three credit reporting agencies every 12 months.

69. d. To be eligible for a salesperson license, you must be at least 18 years old, completes 75 hours of a qualifying course, and successfully pass the exam.

70. a. A valid contract is legal, binding, and enforceable.

71. d. A voided contract is not legal, binding, or enforceable.

72. c. A voidable contract is binding for one party but not the other.

73. a. The system used to register land is the Torrens System. The title of registered land is searched by the Land Court.

74. c. A sheriff's deed transfers the title of property after being auctioned off because of a foreclosure or another court related action.

75. a. A tax deed is the transfer of the title of property after it is sold at auction to take care of unpaid taxes.

76. a. The following are types of listings: open, net, exclusive agency, and exclusive right to sell.

77. d. A life estate in reversion is when a life estate ownership reverts back to the original owner.

78. b. A potted plant is not considered real property, because it can be moved and taken without damaging the land.

79. c. Personal property can sometimes turn into real property if it becomes a permanent fixture of the land.

80. a. Personal property is any property that can be moved off the land without causing any damage to it.

81. b. If the rose plant is removed from the ground it will cause damage to the property making it real property.

82. d. Non-homogeneity says that no two pieces of land are alike, and is a physical characteristic of land.

83. b. Indestructibility of land means that it cannot ultimately be destroyed. This is because land continues to change over time.

84. d. Immobility of land means that it cannot be moved in its entirety. This makes the land immobile.

85. a. Situs is when you know that some property owners prefer certain locations over others. This can cause property values up or down.

86. c. Permanence refers to the lasting potential of the land or property. Permanence is something that helps property owners feel comfortable, and gives them the knowledge that their property cannot easily be moved or destroyed.

87. c. When land is scarce, the price of land goes up because of the demand and the little availability of it.

88. c. For the economic value of your home to increase you need to make structural upgrades, not added touches like new curtains.

89. c. A new roof will add economic value to your home. It improves the initial foundation of the house, which makes it more valuable.

90. a. Having an encumbrance on a property can make determining the correct owner of the property difficult. Different types of encumbrances that make it difficult are encroachment and easement.

91. d. Encroachment is when a structure of fixture is built on someone else's property. This Is usually because of incorrect surveying.

92. b. A mechanic's lien is initiated by people who have done work on the property, like carpenters, landscapers, etc.

93. a. When a property goes into foreclosure the lender will try to recover the balance of the loan by selling off the property.

94. c. Liens can be voluntary or involuntary depending on the situation. A homeowner can enter into a lien by getting a second mortgage. It can be involuntary when the government puts a lien on your property due to back taxes.

95. d. A home can depreciate in value, if you have done unfavorable home modifications completed on your home. Only positive changes will bring about an increase in property value.

96. d. A fee simple absolute free hold estate gives the owner rights including the authority to live in, rent, mortgage the property, to sell, destroy, or reassign ownership of the property, the authority to construct buildings on the property, the authority to excavate minerals, gas, and oil, and the authority to refuse the use of property by others.

97. b. Pur autre vie literally means for another's life. It is an estate that states that a person's life interest will last for the life of another person, instead of their own.

98. c. The remainderman is a person that inherits property after the termination of the estate from the former owner. This normally happens because the former owner has died.

99. c. Police power creates laws or guidelines that control the rights to the property. Typical examples include zoning laws and fire codes.

100. d. Eminent domain gives the government the right to take private property for public use by a state, municipality, or private person or corporation.

Real Estate Sales Exam VI

1. When the government seizes a property under eminent domain, and fails to pay compensation required by the 5th amendment, it is called

a. condemnation
b. inverse condemnation
c. consequential damage
d. severance damage

2. Consequential damages are

a. accidental damages
b. damages that occurred while moving
c. damages that happen after a contract is completed
d. damages that you can prove occurred because of the failure of one party to meet contractual obligations.

3. Under the Endangered Species Act,

a. it is legal to hunt endangered animals during certain times of the year
b. no land can be seized to preserve species
c. endangered animals are not allowed to be hunted or harmed at any time
d. endangered species are protected for a maximum of 1 year

4. Which of the following is an example of private control?

a. driving requirements
b. police
c. Home Owners Association
d. state laws

5. In regards to water rights, when you attain land due to soil deposited by natural elements it is known as

a. accession
b. alluvion
c. reliction
d. erosion

6. What is it called when water shifts soil from one person's land to another's?

a. avulsion
b. erosion
c. accretion
d. alluvion

7. What is it called when the waters path suddenly changes its course, and a rapid decrease of land results from it?

a. accretion
b. avulsion
c. accession
d. reliction

8. The natural deposit of soil that causes a steady increase in the land is also known as
a. erosion
b. reliction
c. avulsion
d. accretion

9. One of the two, common nationwide water rights is

a. reflection rights
b. marsh rights
c. riparian rights
d. siberian rights

10. Under riparian rights, when dealing with a non-navigable body of water, the property owner's boundary will reach to the water's

a. start point

b. center point

c. most shallow point

d. deepest point

11. When you bring together adjoining parcels under the same ownership for such purposes as commercial or residential development it is known as

a. conformity

b. change

c. anticipation

d. assemblage

12. Why do insurance companies appraise properties?

a. to determine the percent the realtor will receive

b. to determine your loan rate

c. to determine the most it will pay for a loss

d. to determine the property rank in the neighborhood

13. An estate settlement is an appraisal done to

a. verify the value of a deceased person's estate

b. determine the property taxes

c. verify the will

d. determine your loan rate

14. When an appraisal is done to determine the loan value, this means the lender is

a. determining the property taxes that will be paid on the property

b. determining the minimum loan that they will give based on the property

c. determining the maximum loan that they will give based on the property

d. determining how much the property should be sold for

15. Besides the building on the property, the overall property value is also determined by

a. land value

b. water value

c. road value

d. move in value

16. Market data is gathered by comparing the property being appraised with three similar properties that have

a. sold within the past 6 months

b. been on the market for over a year

c. sold within the past three years

d. been foreclosed on

17. Replacement cost is the estimate the appraiser gives that shows

a. how much the original owner spent on upgrades

b. how much a new appraisal will cost

c. how much it will cost to make improvements on the property

d. how much the property will sell for as is

18. There are three types of depreciation that can affect a property's value. Which of the following is not one of them?

a. physical deterioration

b. functional obsolescence

c. economic obsolescence

d. monetary obsolescence

19. Economic obsolescence

a. can be controlled by the owner

b. can be controlled by the buyer

c. cannot be controlled by the owner

d. is always constant

20. The capitalization rate is

a. is the amount a property is purchased for

b. what the owner wishes as a return on an investment

c. the depreciated value of the property

d. the cost to upgrade the property

21. Competitive market analysis uses

a. properties that have been sold

b. only pending properties

c. properties that have been sold as well as those listed and not sold yet

d. different properties throughout the country

22. Comparative market analysis uses

a. only pending properties

b. different properties throughout the country

c. properties that have been sold as well as those listed and not sold yet

d. properties that have been sold

23. The Federal National Mortgage Association (Fannie Mae) purchases

a. home loans below $500,000 only

b only home loans in New York

c. home loans above $500,000 only

d. all types of home loans

24. The Federal Home Loan Mortgage Corporation purchases

a. conventional loans

b. all types of loans

c. home loans below $100,000 only

d. FHA and VA loans

25. Government National Mortgage Association purchases

a. all types of loans

b. home loans below $50,000 only

c. FHA and VA loans

d. conventional loans

26. All of the following are common purchasers of home loans except

a. Fannie Mac
b. Ginnie Mae
c. Freddie Mac
d. Fannie Mae

27. VA-guaranteed loans are back by

a. Freddie Mac
b. Virginia Association of Housing
c. Voluntary Assets group
d. Department of Veteran Affairs

28. Conventional loans

a. are sponsored by Ginnie Mae
b. are backed by the government
c. are not backed by the government
d. are only given out for properties under $100,000

29. A package mortgage

a. puts payments off for an extended period of time
b. has the seller of the property finance it for the buyer
c. allows the lender to require payment at any time
d. uses personal property and real estate as collateral

30. A loan that is offered at a low interest rate in exchange for a portion of the property's equity is a

a. balloon loan
b. shared equity loan
c. variable rate loan
d. negative amortization loan

31. Which act requires financial institutions to safeguard sensitive information of their consumers?

a. Gramm-Leach-Billey Act
b. Home Mortgage Disclosure Act
c. Community Reinvestment Act
d. Fair Credit Reporting Act

32. When selling a property, during the settlement procedures, the seller brings all of the following except

a. payment funds
b. keys
c. deed
d. current property tax certificates

33. When buying a property, during the settlement procedures the buyer should bring all of the following except

a. keys
b. survey
c. insurance policy
d. funds

34. During a settlement procedure, the closing agent should do all of the following except

a. forward the deed to be recorded
b. verify that all signatures are executed correctly
c. issue checks if needed
d. bring all keys, garage openers, etc.

35. A mortgage that merges a new and existing loan together is a

a. purchase money mortgage
b. wraparound mortgage
c. package mortgage
d. junior mortgage

36. This type of loan starts off charging a lower than average fixed rate loan, then after a period of time it dramatically inflates.

a. balloon loan
b. construction loan
c. blanket mortgage
d. demand mortgage

37. When the rate of an adjustable rate mortgage increases, but monthly payments stay the same, it is known as

a. equity loan
b. fully amortized loan
c. term loan
d. negative amortization

38. The Sherman Anti-Trust Act states

a. real estate companies can choose which areas they serve
b. that real estate companies can consciously direct business away from other real estate companies
c. a broker cannot have more than 8 clients at any given time
d. no price fixing

39. This act prohibits home sellers and real estate agencies from racially discriminating against anyone in regards to selling, leasing, or any other activities with real or personal property.

a. Equal Credit Opportunity Act
b. Community Reinvestment Act
c. Federal Fair Housing Act of 1968
d. Federal Civil Rights Act of 1866

40. The Federal Fair Housing Act of 1968 (Title VIII) covers

a. elderly housing that meets particular HUD rules
b. the sale or rental of a property by a religious organization to a person of the same religion for non-commercial purposes
c. making reasonable accommodations for handicapped people
d. rental of properties managed by a private club for purposes other than commercial

41. Which contract type is defined as, "only one party being bound to the terms"?

a. unilateral
b. express
c. bilateral
d. implied

42. What contract type is defined as, "two parties have agreed to the terms of the contract"?

a. implied
b. unilateral
c. express
d. bilateral

43. In cooperatives, buyers of each unit are considered

a. full owners
b. stockholders
c. employees
d. guests

44. A proprietary unit lease, in regards to cooperatives, means

a. the buyer can occupy the property for as long as the corporation owns it
b. the buyer cannot occupy the property while the corporation owns it
c. the buyer does not have to follow the corporation's rules
d. the buyer can live there for a 6 month period

45. In New York, what is the fee for an associate broker license?

a. $50
b. $15
c. $150
d. $10

46. A lease is enforceable once

a. it is signed by the landlord only

b. it is signed by the tenant only

c. it is signed by a third party only

d. it is signed by the landlord and tenant

47. The type of lease that states the tenant will pay a percentage of gross sales as rent as well as a rental base amount is a

a. graduated lease

b. net lease

c. percentage lease

d. ninety-nine year lease

48. When the owner does not want to sell or the tenant want to use its funds on capital improvement, it is known as the

a. ninety-nine year lease

b. percentage lease

c. net lease

d. gross lease

49. The type of lease that offers low rental rates in the start of the agreement, and increases to reach fair market rates is

a. net lease

b. gross lease

c. ninety-nine year lease

d. graduated lease

50. When a buyer is trying to secure financing, they typically go through three steps with the lender after completing an application. Which is not a step done by the lender?

a. review the buyer's credit history

b. have an appraisal done of the property

c. offer a one year trial loan

d. evaluate the buyer's likelihood to pay the loan off

51. On an FHA mortgage, what is the the maximum percentage of the down payment and closing closts that can be gifted?

a. 100
b. 50
c. 75
d. 25

52. A breach of contract is when

a. only one person signs the contract
b. both parties choose to end the contract
c. both parties complete their duties stated in the contract
d. one party in a contract fails to complete their duties stated in the contract

53. If the borrower is not putting a down payment, what is the maximum loan amount he'd qualify for with a VA loan?

a. $289,000
b. $417,000
c. $365,750
d. $521,000

54. The type of deed where the grantor conveys interest that he has in property but does not give word regarding warranty of said property is known as

a. special warranty deed
b. general warranty deed
c. sheriff's deed
d. quit claim deed

55. Lenders that violate Regulation Z can be fined up to

a. $5,000
b. $50,000
c. $15,000
d. $500,000

56. When a seller enters into an agreement to sell with only one broker it is called

a. an open listing
b. exclusive agency
c. a net arrangement
d. right to sell

57. Arrangement that states the homeowner will receive a certain amount from the sale of the property, and anything over that will go to the broker is called a

a. open arrangement
b. net arrangement
c. closed arrangement
d. agency arrangement

58. All of these are activities that require a license to perform when a fee is charged except

a. person acting on own behalf
b. purchases
c. exchanges
d. sales

59. The following activities do not require a license to perform when a fee is charged except

a. public servant executing official duties
b. trustee
c. auctioneer who is licensed
d. loan negotiating

60. A real estate salesperson cannot

a. deal with leases
b. perform negotiations
c. place listings
d. advertise property

61. Adverting requirements

a. allow brokers not to disclose that they are real estate brokers

b. allows for indirectly discriminating against any group

c. do not allow false advertising by brokers

d. allow properties to be advertised under the sales person's name

62. Salespersons

a. must become brokers after one year of employment

b. can negotiate terms of a sale

c. can be self-employed agents

d. cannot be self-employed, but must be hired by a real estate broker

63. Brokers are

a. below real estate salespersons

b. not responsible for their salesperson's actions

c. unable to sell properties

d. responsible for their salesperson's actions

64. All advertisements regarding apartments available for rent should also include this statement

a. "The apartment advertised may no longer be available for rental"

b. "The apartment will remain available until a high bid is placed"

c. "The apartment may become for sale at a later date"

d. "The apartment is available to everyone"

65. Written notification of available apartments should be kept on file for

a. 1 year

b. 3 years

c. 5 years

d. 8 years

66. The Klimt family needed a lot that is at least ¾ of an acre. What is the minimum square footage they need?

a) 21.780 feet

b) 43,560 feet

c) 32, 670 feet

d) 10, 890 feet

67. A primary residence has a cost basis of $330,000. This depreciates 27.5% each year. What is the depreciation over 5 years?

a) $60,000

b) $12,000

c) $ 24,0000

d) $30,000

68.   A residential property has an assessed value of $75,000. The mill rate is 6.7 percent. What would the property tax be based on the values presented?

a) $50,250

b) $8,900

c) $5,700

d) $5,025

69. A couple decides to purchase a home valued at $110,000. They have $33,000 saved for the house. They need to borrow the rest of the money. What would be the loan to value ratio?

a) 77%

b) 70%

c) 75%

d) 11%

70. A homeowner purchased a home for $250,000 with a 30 year FHA loan with an annual MIP of 6%. The payment is $736 a month. The MIP will be cancelled when the amount paid is what?

a) Information not available

b) $195,000

c) $200,000

d) $240,000

71. The real estate agent earns a 7% commission on an $852,000 sale. The agent is not able to find a buyer, but a coworker is able to close the sale. The company has an equal split policy on commissions. What is the total commission amount?

a) $14,910

b) $29,820

c) $59,640

d) $11,225

72. A two-acre lot is priced at $2.10 per square foot. How much is the property selling for?

a) $91,476

b) $182,952

c) $116, 754

d) $154,983

73. A lot recently listed is 520' x 410'. How many acres is it?

a) .489

b) 2.45

c) 4.89

d) 1.22

74. A rental property is valued at $150,000. The net operating income is $30,000. What is the cap rate?

a) 15%

b) 20%

c) 25%

d) 30%

75. A buyer purchased a house valued at $367,000. There is still $100,000 left on the mortgage. What is the home equity?

a) $167,000

b) $100,000

c) $267,000

d) $367,000

76. An income property has a monthly mortgage of $500. The rent is $850. What is the estimated monthly profit when applying for a loan?

a) $137.50

b) $250

c) $150.50

d) $350

77. A property has a circular pool with a 30-foot radius. What is the area of the pool?

a) 314.16 ft

b) 900 ft

c) 262 ft

d) 2,826 ft

78. A loan is $167,000. It is a prime loan plus 3 points, with the prime rate being 6%. What is the mortgage rate?

a) 9%

b) 7%

c) 6%

d) 3%

79. Kendra paid $15,000 towards a house. The remaining loan is $60,000 to be paid over 5 years. The annual interest is $840. What is the interest rate?

a) 2.5%

b) 7%

c) 3%

d) 4%

80. A homeowner needs to add a fence to the property. The property is a rectangle with a length of 1,000 feet and a width of 750 feet. What is the perimeter?

a) 108,000 feet

b) 3,500 feet

c) 750,000 feet

d) 75,000 feet

81. A 40,000 square foot property is selling for $250,000. How much is a square foot?

a) $0.16

b) $62.50

c) $1.60

d) $6.25

82. A house is sold on July 1st. The property taxes for the year are $1,200. The owner lived in the house for 182 days. What is the prorate for the property tax?

a) $750

b) $300

c) $1,200

d) $600

83. The contract price on a house is $650,000 and the adjusted cost basis is $500,000. The federal tax rate is 15% and the state is 9%. What is the capital gain?

a) $325,000

b) $36,000

c) $150,000

d) $22,500

84. A corner plot is a triangular shape. Its dimensions are 1,500 feet with a height of 750 feet. What is the square foot area?

a) 1,125,000 feet

b) 562,500 feet

c) 750 feet

d) 1,500 feet

85. The contract price on a house is $450,000 and the adjusted cost basis is $200,000. The house was purchased by the seller six months ago. The federal capital gains tax rate is 15% and the state is 8%. What is the combined capital gains tax?

a) $57,500

b) $103,500

c) $46,000

d) $37,500

86. The owner of a duplex charges each residence $450 a month and pays a $600 mortgage. The owner charges $25 a month for two parking spaces. What is the gross income?

a) $1,000

b) $950

c) $350

d) $300

87. A family home is sold after 20 years. The house was purchased for $150,000 and sold for $357,000. The state capital gains tax is 7%. What is the capital gains tax?

a) $45,540

b) $4657.5

c) $ 207,000

d) None of the above

88. A lender who violates Regulation Z is facing up to ___ year(s) in prison.

a) 5

b) 1

c) 7

d) 10

89. A 15,000 square foot house in Miranda's neighborhood sold for $80,000. Six months before, an 18,000 square foot house sold for $82,000. She needs to sell her 25,000 square foot house. What is the market value?

a) $5.33 square foot

b) $4.56 square foot

c) Unknown

d) $4.95 square foot

90. A property is sold for $790,000 and there is a $1.00 conveyance tax. What does the buyer pay in conveyance?

a) $790

b) $0.00

c) $7,900

d) $3,800

91. A plot is has a shape of a parallelogram. The base is 400 feet and the height is 700 feet. What is the square footage?

a) 2,800 square feet

b) 1,100 square feet

c) 280,000 square feet

d) 2,300 square feet

92. A two-bedroom home has a value of $173,000. The cap rate is 8%. What is the net operating income?

a) $13,840

b) $21, 625

c) $46,277

d) $14,830

93. A rental property is estimated to generate $12,000 a year. It was purchased at an arm's length transaction for $240,000. What is the GIM?

a) 15

b) 10

c) 12

d) 20

94. The GIM of a rental property is 12. A buyer is interested in the neighboring property, which is estimated to generate $15,000 a year. What is the estimated market value?

a) $180,000

b) $80,000

c) $37,000

d) $150,000

95. A house is valued at $250,000 but purchased for $200,000. The new owner had an 80% LTV ratio that the lender based on the appraised value. What was the down payment?

a) $0.00

b) $100,000

c) $50,000

d) $25,000

96. The selling price of a house is $189,000. The buyer pays 10% down and the seller has 7% carry back. What is the LTV?

a) 75%

b) 73%

c) 77%

d) 83%

97. Angela needs to calculate the replacement cost of a 12,000 square foot residence. The cost per square foot is 156.78. What is the estimated replacement cost?

a) $188,136

b) $156,780

c) $ 94,068

d) $1,881,360

98. Sam is considering buying a lot in a developing neighborhood. The lots are all squares and have 123-foot lengths. What is the square footage of a single lot?

a) 15,129 square feet

b) 492 square feet

c) 7,564 square feet

d) 4,920 square feet

99. A house is purchased at the asking price. The buyer places a 12% down payment with no seller carry back. The mortgage is $87,000. What is the selling price?

a) $10,440

b) $98,863.64

c) $76,560

d) $87,000

100. A family is attempting to purchase a home. They have a stable monthly income of $2,500 and monthly obligation of $450. What is the maximum mortgage payment under the total obligations to income ratio?

a) $900

b) $750

c) $450

d) $1,200

Real Estate Sales Exam VI Answers

1. b. It is known as inverse condemnation when the government seizes property, and does not pay for it. The government is required to pay for any property that is seized under eminent domain.

2. d. Consequential damages are damages that can be proven occurred because of the failure of one party to meet contractual obligations. This is also considered a breach of contract.

3. c. The Endangered Species Act protects all endangered animals. They cannot be hunted, and land maybe seized if it is necessary to protect endangered species.

4. c. A Home Owner's Association is considered private control because home owners are often restricted on what they can do with their own home.

5. a. Accession occurs when you obtain land due to soil deposited by natural elements.

6. d. Alluvion occurs when water shifts the soil from one person's property to another's.

7. b. Avulsion occurs when water suddenly changes course. This change results in an immediate decrease in land.

8. d. Accretion is the natural deposit of soil on to the land. This increase adds an increase to the land.

9. c. The two water rights that are common nationwide are: riparian and littoral rights.

10. b. Riparian rights state that if there is a non-navigable body of water, the boundary of the property will end at the water's center point.

11. d. Assemblage brings together adjoining parcels under the same ownership. This is done, because it can potentially increase the worth of the adjoining parcels.

12. c. Insurance companies do appraisals on properties to determine the maximum amount they will pay in a loss.

13. a. An estate settlement is a type of appraisal that is done to determine the total value of a deceased person's estate.

14. c. The loan value is based on the appraisal. The appraisal will determine the maximum loan that the lender will give out on that property.

15. a. The land value plays a crucial part in determining the overall property value. Without it, you cannot get an accurate appraisal.

16. a. Market data is collected from 3 similar properties that have sold within the past 6 months, and compare their prices of the property being appraised.

17. c. The replacement cost is determined by an appraiser to give an idea on how much it will cost to improve the property.

18. d. The three types of depreciation include: physical deterioration, economic obsolescence, and functional obsolescence.

19. c. Economic obsolescence cannot be controlled by a property owner. They have no control over economic or environmental changes.

20. b. The capitalization rate is what the owner of a property wishes the return on their investment to be.

21. c. Competitive market analysis bases its finding off properties that have been sold. It also uses properties that are listed, but have not been sold yet.

22. d. Comparative market analysis uses properties that have been sold to determine the property appraisal.

23. d. The Federal National Mortgage Association purchases all types of home loans.

24. a. The Federal Home Loan Mortgage Corporation purchases conventional loans

25. c. The Government National Mortgage Association purchases FHA and VA loans

26. a. Common purchasers of home loans include: Fannie Mae, Freddie Mac, and Ginnie Mae.

27. d. VA-guaranteed loans are backed by the Department of Veteran Affairs. In order to be eligible for a loan, the person must be a veteran.

28. c. Conventional loans have no insurance backing from the government. The lender expects the borrower to pay back the loan, or the property will go into foreclosure.

29. d. A package mortgage uses personal property and real estate as collateral for the loan.

30. b. A shared equity loan is offered in order for the lender to have a portion of the property's equity. For this they will offer the borrower a low interest rate.

31. a. The Gramm-Leach-Billey Act requires financial institutions to safeguard any sensitive information of their clients. They also have to explain to them the company's information sharing practices.

32. a. The buyer is responsible for bringing the payment funds, not the seller.

33. a. The seller is responsible for bringing the keys, not the buyer.

34. d. The seller is responsible for bringing the keys to the property to the meeting.

35. b. A wraparound mortgage is when a new and existing loan are merged. The payment is made on both mortgages to the wraparound mortgagee. This group then forwards the payments appropriately.

36. a. A balloon mortgage starts off the loan with a lower then average interest. After a period of time, usually 5,7, or 10 years, the loan "balloons out."

37. d. When the rate of an adjustable rate mortgage increases, but monthly payments stay the same, it is known as negative amortization. The consequences are that the payments are not enough to pay the principal and interest. From here the deficit amount is tacked on to the outstanding principal balance.

38. d. The Sherman Anti-Trust Act prohibits business practices that restrict marketplace competition unfairly. They do not allow price fixing. You cannot offer services in only certain geographical areas, real estate companies cannot consciously direct business away from other real estate offices, and brokers cannot create organizations that unfairly exclude qualified brokers from having access to marketing and sales information.

39. d. The Federal Civil Rights Act of 1866 does not allow individual home sellers and real estate agencies to racially discriminate against anyone when it comes to selling, leasing, or any other activities with real or personal real estate.

40. c. Title VIII protects the handicapped class. It states that there shall be no discrimination against handicapped people by not making reasonable accommodations regarding policies or necessary changes to the premises is prohibited.

41. a. On the contrary, when both parties have agreed to the terms of a contract, a bilateral contract is in effect.

42. d. On the contrary, when only one party has agreed to the terms of a contract, a unilateral contract is in effect.

43. b. In cooperatives, the buyers of each unit are considered stockholders. Once they make the purchase, they are given a stock certificate in the corporation.

44. a. Proprietary unit lease in regards to cooperatives means that they buyer can occupy the property for as long as the corporation owns it.

45. c. A broker's license also requires the $150 fee. To obtain a salesperson's license, a fee in the amount of $50 must be paid.

46. d. A lease becomes enforceable once the landlord and tenant sign it.

47. c. A percentage lease has the tenant pay a percent of gross sales as part of their rent. They also have to pay a rental base amount. This type of lease is normally seen at places like shopping centers.

48. a. A ninety-nine year lease is a lease that is mostly seen in commercial development. It is a lease that is used when the owner does not want to sell or the tenant wants to use its funds on capital improvements.

49. d. A graduated lease offers low rental rates in the start of the agreement, and increases to reach fair market rates. Sometimes this type of lease can increase to rates above fair market rates.

50. c. When a buyer is trying to get a loan for a property, the lender will have an appraisal done of the property, review the buyer's credit, and evaluate their likelihood to pay off the loan.

51. a. This is one of the many advantages of this type of mortgage.

52. d. A breach of contract occurs when one of the parties does not follow through with their end of the contract. The party that did not break the contract can sue for damages.

53. b. Veterans must undergo a thorough screening to ensure they are qualified for the program.

54. d. A quit claim deed is when a grantor shows interest in a property, but does not verbally say that he wants that property.

55. a. A lender who violates Regulation Z can be fined up to $5,000, imprisonment up to a year or both.

56. b. Exclusive agency is when the seller enters into an agreement to sell with one broker. The broker will receive commission if they actively sell the house.

57. b. A net arrangement gives the homeowner a certain amount from the sale of the property, while any profit above that goes to the listing broker. This type is actually illegal in Massachusetts.

58. a. A person needs a license when performing the following activities and charging a fee: sales, exchanges, purchases, rentals/leases, negotiations, offers, listing, options, advertising real property, prospecting, loan negotiating, and apartment search.

59. d. Loan negotiating requires a license when performed for a fee.

60. b. Only brokers can perform negotiations.

61. c. Advertising false or misleading information is against real estate requirements. You cannot advertise the property under the sale person's name and does not allow you to discriminate against any group. Brokers also must state that they are real estate brokers.

62. d. Real estate agents are not allowed to be self-employed. Each real estate agent must be working as an employee or contractor under a broker.

63. d. Since a broker is in charge, they are ultimately in charge of their salespersons actions.

64. a. It is required to put "The apartment advertised may no longer be available for rental" to protect themselves from false advertising

65. b. Written notifications should be kept on file for a minimum of three years. Fee notifications and other notices should also be kept on file for this period of time.

66. c.   1 acre = 43,560

43,560 x .75 = 32, 670 feet

67. a. $60,000. The property is a residence, which has a depreciation of 27.5. I this case it is each year. The annual depreciation is 330,000/27.5, which is 12,000. 12,000 x 5 is $60,000.

68. d.   The mill levy multiplied by the assessed value determines property taxes. $75,000 x .067 is $5,025.

69. b.   The loan to value ratio is the mortgage amount/appraised value. The mortgage amount is 110,000-33,000 = 77,000. 77,000/110,000 = .7 or 70%.

70. a. The information is not available. The MIP for a 30-year loan is cancelled when the amount is 78% and the insurance has been paid for five years.

71. c. The total commission is 7% of the sale price. The total commission is 825,000 x .07 = $59,640.

72. b. An acre is 43,560 square feet. 43, 560 x 2 acres is 87,120. 87,120 feet x $2.10 = $182,952.

73. c. Multiply the lot dimensions 520 x 410 = 213,200 square feet. An acre is 43,560 square feet, which is divided into the square footage. 213,200/ 43,560= 4.89 acres

74. b. The cap rate is the net operating income divided by the property value.

   30,000 x 150,000 = .2

75. c. Equity is the market value of a house minus the remainder of the mortgage.

76. a. Rental income is discounted by 25% when applying for a loan.

   850 x .25 = 212.5   850 – 212.5 = 637.5 – 500 = 137.5

77. d. The area of a circle is πr^2 .

   30^2 x 3.14 = 2,826 ft

78. a. Each point is equal to 1%. This is added to the prime rate. A prime rate of 6% plus 3 points is 9%.

79. b. rate= interest/principle

   5 x 840 = 4,200 total interest

   4,200 /60,000 = .07

80. c. The perimeter is the sum of all four sides.

1,000 + 1,000 + 750 + 750 = 3,500

81. d. The total divided by the square footage shows the price per unit.

250,000/ 40,000 = 6.25

82. d. The percentage is the number of days divided by the days in the year. This answer is multiplied by the total property tax.

182/365 = .498 or .5 x 1200 = 600

83. c. The contract price minus the adjusted cost basis is the capital gain.

650,000 – 500,000 = 150,000

84. b. The area of a triangle is ½ bh.

1,500 x 750 = 1,125,000 /2 = 562,500

85. a. The contract price minus the adjusted cost basis is the capital gain. The capital gain is multiplied by the federal rate and the state rate. Together, they make up the total capital gain tax.

450,000 – 200,000 = 250,000

250,000 x .15 = 37,500

+250,000 x .08 = 20,000

57,500

86. b. The gross income is all income. The costs are used to calculate net income.

450 x 2 = 900 +25 +25 = 950

87. d. The capital gains tax is waived if a home has been owned for 5 years and the capital gain is not too high. A capital gain below 250,000 is not taxed.

88. b. A lender who violates Regulation Z can be fined up to $5,000, imprisonment up to a year or both.

89. c. The houses in this scenario are much smaller than her house. There is not enough information to determine market value.

90. b. The seller pays the conveyance tax.

91. c. The area of a parallelogram is b x h. This gives the square footage

400 x 700 = 280,000

92. a. The net operating income is value x cap rate.

173,000 x .08 = $13,840

93. d. The GIM is the value/gross income.

   240,000/12,000 = 20

94. a. The GIM is multiplied by the income to determine an estimated market value.

   15,000 x 12 = $180,000

95. c. The LTV is typically based on the lower value. 80% of 250,000 is 200,000. This is the selling price, which means there is no down payment if it is based on the higher value.

96. b. The LTV is the percentage of the loan to the value of the house.

   189,000 x .10 = 18,900

   189,000 x .07 = 13,230 +18,900 = 51,030

   189,000 – 51,030 = 137,970/189,000 = .73

97. d. The square footage can be used to create a replacement cost estimate.

   12,000 x 156.78 = $1,881,360

98. a. The square footage of a square is length squared.

   123^2 = 15,129 square feet

99. b. The selling price for the house is

   87,000 x .12 = 10,440. The LTV is 87,000 - 10,440 = 76,560/87,000 = .88 or 88%

   87,000/88% =$98,863.64

100. c. The benchmark for obligations ratio is 36%.

   2500 x .36 = 900 – 450 = $450

Real Estate Sales Exam VII

1. The real estate agent earns a 6% commission on a $452,000 sale. The agent handles both the purchase and sale. What is the commission amount?

a) $14,910

b) $54,240

c) $13,560

d) $27,120

2. A lot is priced at $1,372,140. The price per square foot is $21. How many acres is it?

a) 1

b) 2

c) 1.5

d) 2.5

3. George plans buying a house with a monthly income of $3,400 and obligations of $700. What is the maximum mortgage using the housing expense to income ratio?

a) $252

b) $952

c) $1,224

d) $612

4. Stacy is interested in a commercial property that is appraised at $768,000. The net operating income is estimated to be $150,000. What is the cap rate?

a) 15%

b) 21%

c) 17.5%

d) 19.5%

5. Cynthia has purchased a home that is currently valued at $275,000. Her mortgage is currently $50,000. She needs to know her equity for another loan. What is it?

a) $225,000

b) $325,000

c) $250,000

d) $350,000

6. Thomas is a real estate agent. His clients are looking for a ranch between 3.5 and 7 acres. He needs to limit his search to properties beginning with which square footage in order to meet the minimum requirement?

a) 304,920 feet

b) 43,560 feet

c) 174,240 feet

d) 152,460 feet

7. Helen is considering purchasing a residential property for $769,000. What is the annual rate of depreciation for tax purposes?

a) $38,450

b) $64,083.89

c) $27,963.64

d) $26,896.49

8. Nita lives in a city with a mill rate of 8. Her property is valued at $183,500. What would her property tax be?

a) $36,700

b) $1,468

c) $22,937.5

d) $14,680

9. Tim paid 15% of the selling price of 158,750. Based on this information, what would be the loan to value ratio?

a) 85%

b) 80%

c) 75%

d) 70%

10. Jen purchased a house for $137,800. The commission is 8%. What is the seller's net?

a) $11,024

b) $126,776

c) $137,800

d) $148,824

11. Stella's coworker has a house listed for $432,000, and Stella has interested buyers. The company has an equal split policy on commissions at 7%. What would be her individual commission amount?

a) $14,910

b) $29,820

c) $30,240

d) $15,120

12. A 2.5 acre lot is priced at $850,000. What is the price per square foot?

a) $6.76

b) $7.32

c) $7.81

d) $8.50

13. Sara needs a house large enough for her growing family, and she wants a large yard. A lot says that it is 275' x 380'. How many square feet is it?

a) 104,500

b) 52,250

c) 209,000

d) 1,310

14. Holly purchases a home that requires a $115,000 mortgage with a 12% interest rate. What is the first month's interest?

a) $3,250

b) $13,800

c) $1,150

d) $575

15. Ryan paid a $20,000 down payment on a house purchased for $135,000. The interest rate is 8 percent. What is the first year's interest?

a) $5,550

b) $9,200

c) $6,785

d) $2,875

16. Kyle is considering applying for a loan for an income property. The mortgage for the loan would be $750 a month. The estimated income is $1,500 a month. What is the estimated profit?

a) $325

b) $750

c) $350.50

d) $375

17. Josh is looking at a house with a circular garden that needs a new fence. The diameter of is 7 feet. What is the perimeter for the fence?

a) 21.98 feet

b) 49 feet

c) 10.99 feet

d) 24.5 feet

18. Gina has a mortgage that is $183,000. The prime rate is 7% and there are 4 points added. What is the mortgage rate?

a) 9%

b) 11%

c) 4%

d) 3%

19. Gary purchased an income property for $75,000. He made $12,000 in improvements, and the depreciation is $5,000. What is the adjusted basis?

a) $58,000

b) $77,000

c) $72,000

d) $63,000

20. Fran purchased a property for $95,700. She sold it for $167,000. She added $20,000 in improvements, and the property depreciated $8,000. What is the capital gain for the seller?

a) $71,300

b) $ 115,700

c) $107,700

d) $59,300

21. A property is priced at $106,000. It is 250 feet by 170 feet. How much is it a square foot?

a) $2.52

b) $1.51

c) $1.60

d) $2.60

22. Anna sold her house on February 20. The property taxes for the year are $3,000. She lived in the house for 51 days. What is her prorate for the property tax?

a) $1,500

b) $250

c) $420

d) $588

23. The contract price on a house is $184,000 and the adjusted cost basis is $175,000. The federal tax rate is 15% and there is no state tax. What is the capital gain tax?

a) $9,000

b) $1,350

c) $2,760

d) $2,625

24. A realtor needs to list an unusual house with an elliptical shaped property. R1 is 280 feet and R2 is 410. What is the square footage?

a) 360,655 feet

b) 114,800 feet

c) 21,666 feet

d) 216, 660 feet

25. The contract price on a house is $320,000 and the adjusted cost basis is $200,000. The federal capital gains tax rate is 15% and the state is 4%. What remains of capital gains after the combined capital gains tax?

a) $18,000

b) $120,000

c) $22,800

d) $97,200

26. The owner of a small apartment complex with 10 units charges each residence $510 a month. He pays a $2,500 mortgage. The owner earns $750 a month from a soda machine. What is the monthly net income?

a) $3,350

b) $5,850

c) $5100

d) $ 2,600

27. Kira paid $345,000 for a home and the percentage of commission to the realtor is 7%. What is the dollar amount of the realtor's commission?

a) $24,150

b) $13,450

c) $33,900

d) $11,999

28. What is the percentage of commission if a realtor receives $14,350 on a property with a $287,000 sales price ?

a) 8%

b) 4%

c) 5%

d) 10%

29. A realtor earns a commission of $21,000. The rate is 7%. How much is the sale price?

a) $294,000

b) $147,000

c) $300,000

d) $280,000

30. Ellie sells a house for $295,000 and there is a $1.00 conveyance tax. What does she pay in conveyance?

a) $295

b) $0.00

c) $590

d) $147.50

31. Daniel has a $400,000 mortgage with 8% interest. The mortgage has 30 years and a monthly payment of $1,200. What is the total he will pay in interest?

a) $ 14,400

b) $44,000

c) $32,000

d) $16,000

32. Shaun purchased his house for $88,000. He later sold it for $125,000. What is the rate of appreciation?

a) 23%

b) 42%

c) 32%

d) 24%

33. Stanley listed his house at $307,000, which is 150% his purchase price. How much did he pay for the house originally?

a) $257,468.97

b) $257,000

c) $204,667

d) $204,666.67

34. Emma is interested in a building that has a net operating income of $26,700 and a cap rate of 9%. What is the value of the property?

a) $269,666.70

b) $296,666.67

c) $267,000

d) $267,666.67

35. Carrie paid 20% down for a sale price of $235,000. There is no carry back. What is the LTV?

a) 75%

b) 85%

c) 80%

d) 70%

36. A rental property is purchased for $765,000. Its rate is 11%. Estimate the income.

a) $84,150

b) $69,545.45

c) $76,500.78

d) $77,000

37. Dean is looking at a house with a gabled roof. The gabled end needs to be refurbished. The width of the house is 27 feet and the height is 18 feet. What is the square footage?

a) 729 square feet

b) 486 square feet

c) 364.5 square feet

d) 243 square feet

38. A house is assessed with a 70% ratio. The assessed value is $180,000. What is the market value?

a) $257,142.86

b) $126,000

c) $128,571.43

d) $360,000

39. Renee lives in a state with a $3.20 per $100. Her home is assessed at $169,000. What will her property tax be?

a) $10,816

b) $5,408

c) $54,080

d) $7,610

40. Ron purchased a house for $225,000. He moved in a poor housing market and sold the property for $178,000. What was the rate of depreciation?

a) 17%

b) 20%

c) 21%

d) 12%

41. A company is renting space for $0.75 a cubic foot. James needs a 100 x 150 space. The building is 12 feet high. What is the annual rent?

a) $265,000

b) $150,000

c) $180,000

d) $135,000

42. A rectangular lot is the 220 feet by 198 feet. What is the square footage?

a) .5

b) 1

c) 1.5

d) 2

43. Kevin is calculating a mortgage using the expense to income ratio. He has a monthly income of $2,400 and obligations of $800. What is the maximum mortgage payment?

a) $448

b) $1,600

c) $1,344

d) $672

44. A rental property is appraised at $420,000. The net operating income is estimated to be $70,000. What is the cap rate?

a) 17%

b) 21%

c) 17.5%

d) 21.5%

45. Helen's home is almost paid off. She has $8,000 left on the loan, and the market value is 149,000. What is her equity?

a) $149,000

b) $186,250

c) $141,000

d) $157,000

46. A circular bedroom has a radius of 6 feet. What is the square footage?

a) 131.88 square feet

b) 94.2 square feet

c) 18.84 square feet

d) 113.04 square feet

47. A property is listed at $312,000. If purchased at this price what will be the depreciation the first year?

a) $85,800

b) $14,093.89

c) $11,345.46

d) $26,000

48. Parker's home is valued at $173,800. He lives in a city with 16 mills in effect. What are his property taxes?

a) $3,670.70

b) $2,780.80

c) $27,808.00

d) $2,870.80

49. A house is sold for $215,000, and the buyer pays 18% down. Based on this information, what would be the loan to value ratio?

a) 92%

b) 90%

c) 85%

d) 87%

50. A house is sold for $199,999. The commission rate is 7%. What does the buyer pay in commission?

a) $19,999.00

b) $0.00

c) $13,999.93

d) $14,000

51. Bob has a $204,000 mortgage with a 7% interest rate. How much does he pay in interest the first year?

a) $11,090

b) $1,190

c) $14,280

d) $1,428

52. Wendy has a lot that is 300 feet by 300 feet. The market value for this area is $2.70 per square foot. How much would she ask for the lot?

a) $243,000

b) $90,000

c) $2,430

d) $9,000

53. Kim's house has a 40% assessment ratio. The assessed value is $205,000. What is the market value?

a) $430,500

b) $82,000

c) $256,250

d) $512,500

54. Franklin is considering a 15-year mortgage at 8% interest. The total loan amount is $172,000 and the payments are $1,300. What is the total interest?

a) $62,000

b) $15,600

c) $72,000

d) $31,200

55. Paul paid a $17,000 down payment on a house purchased for $210,000. The interest rate is 9 percent. What is the first month's interest?

a) $16,664.67

b) $1,700

c) $1,388.67

d) $1,567.46

56. An income property has an estimated income of $1,800. The mortgage for the loan would be $950 a month. What is the estimated profit?

a) $1,350

b) $400

c) $450

d) $850

57. Tom needs to build a fence around his property. The lot is 150 feet by 220 feet. What is the perimeter?

a) 1,890 feet

b) 300 feet

c) 440 feet

d) 740 feet

58. The prime rate is 6%. Jonathan only has an additional point when obtaining a mortgage of $150,000. What is his mortgage rate?

a) 9%

b) 7%

c) 5%

d) 8%

59. There is an income property selling for $275,000. The owner made $30,000 in improvements, and the depreciation is $12,000. What is the adjusted basis?

a) $317,000

b) $233,000

c) $305,000

d) $293,000

60. Cassie sold her house for $227,000. She purchased the property for $197,000. She added $60,000 in improvements, and the property depreciated $18,000. What is the capital gain for the buyer?

a) $71,300

b) $12,000

c) $0.00

d) $30,000

61. An empty lot is $192,000. It is 1.5 acres. How much is it per square foot?

a) $2.94

b) $1.98

c) $2.93

d) $2.60

62. The property taxes on Ned's house for the year are $5,000. He sold the house 212 days into the year. What does he pay in prorate?

a) $2,900

b) $5000

c) $2,100

d) $1,450

63. Leslie sells her home for $228,000 and the adjusted cost basis is $220,000. The federal tax rate is 15% and the state tax is 3%. What is the capital gain tax?

a) $1,200

b) $1,440

c) $2,400

d) $8,000

64. A circular shaped patio has a radius of 6 feet. What is the square footage?

a) 56.55 square feet

b) 114 square feet

c) 113.1 square feet

d) 144 square feet

65. Josh has a contract on his property for $245,000 and the adjusted cost basis is $205,750. The federal capital gains tax rate is 15% and no state tax. What is left after paying the capital gains tax?

a) $5,587.50

b) $39,250

c) $44,837.50

d) $33,362.50

66. What is the rate of appreciation on Jake Christopher's home, if he bought it 12 years ago for $573,247.00 and sold it for $ 849,001.00?
a. 32.5%
b. 36.4%
c. 44.7%
d. 48.1%

67. What is the amount of interest paid per year on a loan of $ 36, 150 at an interest rate of 4.46%?
a. $ 1,118.13
b. $ 1,612.29
c. $ 1,309.21
d. $ 1, 491.39

68. The Herrins are considering buying a listed 3 bedroom, 3 bath house. A comparable 3 bedroom, 2 bath house in the same area just sold for $ 142,780. If a bathroom in that area is worth $ 8,000, what is the value of the house the Herrins are considering?
a. $ 134,780
b. $ 125,280

c. 135,280

d. $127,780

69. Mattie McCormick has taken out a home equity loan of $ 33,070. If the rate is 11.99%, what is the monthly payment?

a. $ 231.42

b. $ 330.42

c. $ 354.16

d. $376.90

70. If property taxes are $ 0.005 on the dollar and you pay $ 100 per year, what would your annual taxes be if the taxes were raised to 0.0065 on the dollar?

a. $ 115

b. $ 130

c. $ 145

d. $ 200

71. A condo sold on June 2. The condo fee of $ 278 was paid in full on June 1. What amount is to be credited to the seller and debited from the buyer at the closing?

a. $ 9.27

b. $ 18.54

c. $ 259.56

d. $ 268.83

72. What is the depreciation of a house that originally sold for $ 153,132 and just sold for $117,423 six years later?

a. $ 35,709

b. 23.3%

c. $ 117,423

d. 45.2%

73. If a comparable contemporary 3,200 sq.ft. house just sold for $ 298,000, what is the value of a similar house of 2,952 sq.ft.?

a. $ 93,120

b. $ 320,000

c. $ 298,000

d. $ 274,890

74. If a lot frontage is 95' and has a depth of 225', what fraction of an acre is the lot?

a. 1/2

b. ¼

c. 1/5

d.2/3

75. A broker received a commission of $5,500. How much did the house sell for, if the commission rate is 5%?

a. $ 27,500

b. $ 275,000

c. $ 110,000

d. $ 1.1 million

76. A rectangular lot with frontage of 207' and a depth of 317' is sold for $ 4.25 per sq. ft. If the agent's commission is 6%, how much will he receive?

a. $ 16,732.85

b. $ 3937.14

c. $ 12,539.65

d. $ 4826.87

77. What are the taxes on a $ 452,000 house if the tax rate is 45 mills and the rate of assessment is 72%?

a. $ 10,459

b. $ 12,453.90

c. $ 14,644.80

d. $ 20,340

78. A lot that is 3/8 of an acre is how many square feet?

a. 14,296

b. 15,876

c. 17,355

d. 16,335

79. A list of expenses is presented to be paid by the buyer and the seller. The list includes title insurance for $ 374, appraisal fees for $ 425, and a home inspection fee of $525. The seller agrees to pay for 65% of all costs. How much does the buyer owe?

a. $ 105.26

b. $ 463.40

c. $ 401.95

d. $ 215.88

80. How much interest would be paid on a $20,000 loan at 10% interest for 30 months?

a. $ 2,000

b. $ 6750

c. $ 4500

d. $ 5000

81. What is the principal on a mortgage loan, if the monthly interest payment is $ 5,768 and the interest rate is 7.25%?

a. $ 954,703.45

b. $ 79,558.00

c. $ 95,470.34

d. $ 7955.80

82. A local business owns three parcels of vacant land on Main Street that are valued at $ 56,000, $42,000, and $ 25,000. All three properties are assessed at the same rate of 57%. What is the total assessed value?

a. $ 132,000

b. $ 70,110

c. $ 75,240

d. $ 231,579

83. Bob Williams and his brother bought a building knowing the yearly income is $ 90,000. They expected that would give them a 15% return on investment. What did the building cost?

a. $ 400,000

b. $ 600,000

c. $ 500,000

d. $ 375,000

84. If an unimproved $ 275,000 property depreciates at a rate of 3% a year, what is the property worth after 5 years?

a. $ 233,750

b. $ 147,183

c. $ 205,440

d. $ 175,680

85. A house sold for 155% of its original value. If it sold for $ 755,649.80, what was its original value?

a. $ 506,897.98

b. $ 487,516.00

c. $ 1,171,257.19

d. $ 487,516

86. Doug Fields wants to sell his property for development. If the property is 8,744,000 square feet, how many 1.5 acre lots can he sell?

a. 133

b. 54

c. 106

c. 79

87. A commercial building sold for $1,260,000 and the rate of commission was 7%. If the seller's broker received $ 51,072, what was the commission percentage?

a. 0.57

b. 0.77

c. 0.67

d. 0.87

88. Carl Hall wants to sell his 7 bedroom home on Mockingbird Lane. A similar home in the neighborhood with 6 bedrooms sold for $ 75,000. What is the value of Carl's home?

a. 62,500

b. 87,500

c. 75,000

d. 81,500

89. Mary Ellen decided to pay 4 points on her mortgage. If her mortgage is $ 385,000, how much is she paying for the points?

a. $ 10,125

b. $ 6, 515

c. $ 7,830

d. $ 9,625

90. The first month's interest on a one year loan for $34,000 at 8.2% is $ 234.00. If the monthly payments are $ 2,962.01, including interest, what is the amount of interest paid in the second month?

a. $ 234.60

b. $ 215.78

c. $ 220.98

d. $ 235.90

91. What is the principal on a loan that has an interest rate of 5.57% and a monthly interest

payment of $ 763.98?

a. $ 176,987.32

b. $ 154,982.53

c. $ 142,583.62

d. $ 164,591.74

92. Kevin Moss will pay $ 5,000 in interest on a 2 year, $ 75,000 loan. What is the interest rate being charged?

a. 0.368%

b. 5 ¼%

c. 3 1/3%

d. 4 ½%

93. A vacation home was valued new at $ 1,357,990. Using straight line depreciation to depreciate it over 25 years, what would be the depreciation each year?

a. $ 96,255

b. $ 108,639

c. $ 54,319

d. $ 45,216

94. If land in a development goes for $ 48,575 an acre, how much would a 142,614 square foot lot sell for?

a. $ 146,160

b. $ 155,430

c. $ 176,160

d. $ 164,210

95. If a house depreciates at a rate of 3.75% for 4 years and was worth $ 132,800 originally, what is it worth today?

a. $ 112,800

b. $ 157,720

c. $ 110,870

d. $ 106,420

96. A lot contains 139,392 square feet. If land in the development sells for $ 45,675 an acre, how much would the lot sell for?

a. $ 146,160

b. $ 192,115

c. $ 176,160

d. $ 168, 245

97. What is the annual interest if the loan amount is $80,000 and interest rate, 6%?

a. $1,200

b. $3,600

c. $5,200

d. $4,800

98. Darlene Cox will pay $ 10,000 in interest on a 2 year loan of $ 75,000. What is the interest rate on the loan?

a. 5 ¼%

b. 4 ½%

c. 0.06%

d. 0.278%

99. The assessed value of the Reynolds' home is $340,000, or 8.5% of the market value. Their yearly property taxes are approximately $4,760. How much does this add to their monthly mortgage payment?

a. $ 3.96

b. $ 39.96

c. $ 396.67

d. $ 432.98

100. What is the cost of the concrete needed to pave the Miller's driveway if it is 70' long by 14' wide and 6" deep? The concrete costs $ 150 per cubic yard.

a. $ 2,100

b. $ 1,904

c. $ 2,265

d. $ 2,178

Real Estate Sales Exam VII Answers

1. d. The agent gets the complete commission.

    452,000 x .06 = $27,120

2. c. The price is 1,372,140. Divide by cost per square foot to show the square footage.

    1,372,140/21 = 65,340/43,560 = 1.5

3. b. The benchmark for the housing expense to income ratio is 28%.

    3,400 x .28 = 952

4. d. The cap rate is the net operating income divided by the property value.

    150,000/768,000 = .195

5. a. Equity is the market value of a house minus the remainder of the mortgage.

275,000 − 50,000 = $225,000

6. d. There are 43,560 square feet in an acre.

    43,560 x 3.5= 152,460

7. c. Residential properties have a 27.5 depreciation rate, meaning it depreciates for 27 years.

    769,000/27.5 = 27,963.64 annually

8. b. The mill levy multiplied by the assessed value determines property taxes.

    183,500 x .008 = $1,468

9.a. The loan to value ratio is the mortgage amount/appraised value. First find the mortgage.

    158,750 x .15 = 23,812.5

    The mortgage is 158,750 − 23,812.5 = 134,937.5. This is divided by the value.

    134,937.5 / 158,750 = .85

10.b. The purchase price minus the commission is the net.

    137,800 x .08 = 11,024

    137,800 − 11,024 = 126,776

11.d. The commission is the sale price times the commission rate divided by two.

    432,000 x .07 = $30,240

    30,240 / 2 = $15,120

12.c. Calculate the square feet. Then divide the cost by square footage.

    43,560x .2.5 = 108,900

    850,000 /108,900 = $7.81

13.a. Calculate the square feet of a rectangle by multiplying the length and width.

    275 x 380 = 104,500

14.c. Determine the interest rate for the year by multiplying the mortgage and rate. Divide this by 12 to find the first month.

115,000 x .12 = 13,800/12 = $1,150

15.b. First determine the mortgage. Multiply the interest rate by the mortgage to determine the first year's interest.

135,000 - 20,000 = 115,000 x .08 = 9,200

16.d. The income property includes a 25% discount on income. Then subtract the mortgage.

1,500 x .25 = 375

1,500 – 375 = 1,125 – 750 = 375

17.a. The perimeter of a circle is d(π).

7 x .3.14 = 21.98

18.b. Each point is equal to 1%. This is added to the prime rate. 7% + 4% = 11%

19.c. The adjusted basis is takes depreciation and improvements into account. It is used to calculate capital gains.

75,000 + 12,000 = 77,000 – 5,000 = 72,000

20.d. First, find the adjusted basis. Subtract the adjusted basis from the sale price.

95,700 + 20,000 = 115,700 – 8,000 = 107,700

167,000 – 107,700 = 59,300

21.a. First, find the square footage. Then, divide it into the price.

250 x 170 =42,000

106,000/42,000 = $2.52

22.c. The percentage is the number of days divided by the days in the year. This answer is multiplied by the total property tax.

51/365 = .14 x 3,000 = 420

23.b. The capital gain is multiplied by the federal rate to create the capital gain tax. First calculate the capital gain.

184,000 – 175,000 = 9,000 x .15 = 1,350

24.a. The formula for an ellipses is $\pi r1 r2$

3.14 x 280 x 41 = 360,654.99

25. d. The contract price minus the adjusted cost basis is the capital gain. The capital gain is multiplied by the federal rate and the state rate. Subtract the tax from gains to find the remainder.

320,000 – 200,000 = 120,000 x .15 = 18,000

120,000 x .04 = 4,800 +18,000 = 22,800

120,000 – 22,800 = 97,200

26.a. The net is the gross income minus the cost.

510 x 10 = 5100 +750 = 5,850 – 2,500 = $3,350

27. a. Real estate commission is calculated by multiplying the sales price by the percentage of commission. $345,000 x 0.07 = $24,150

28. c. $287,000(x) = $14,350

29. c. Divide the commission percentage into the commission to find the sale price.

21,000 / .07 = $300,000

30. a. Conveyance tax rate is based on $1,000 of the price.

295,000/1,000 = $295

31. c. The total interest is the amount paid minus the original loan amount.

1,200 x 12 = 14,400 a year x 30 years = 432,000 – 400,000 = $32,000

32. b. The rate of appreciation requires finding the change in value, which is the new value minus the old. Then, divide the change in value by the original value.

125,000 – 88,000 = 37,000

37,000/88,000 = .42

33. d. Divide the current price by the percent to find the original value.

307,000/1.50 = $204,666.67

34. b. The value of a property is the net operating income divided by the cap rate.

26,700/.09 = $296,666.67

35. c. The LTV is the percentage of the loan to the value of the house. First find the amount of the loan.

235,000 x .20 = 47,000

235,000 – 47,000 = 188,000/ 235,000 =.8

36. a. The income is value x rate

      765,000 x .11 = $84,150

37. d. The area of a triangle is ½(b)(h)

      27 x 18 x .5 = 243

38. a. The market value is the assessed value/assessment ratio.

      180,000/.70 = $257,142.86

39. b. The tax rate x value is the property tax.

      169,000 x .032 = $5,408

40. c. The rate of appreciation requires finding the change in value, which is the new value minus the old. Then, divide the change in value by the original value.

      225,000 – 178,000 = 47,000

      47,000/225,000 = .208 = .21

41. d. A cubic foot is volume. It found by multiplying length x width x height.

      100 x 150 x 12 = 180,000 x .75 = $135,000

42. b. First, find the area. Then divide the answer by the 43,560.

      220 x 198 = 43,560/43.560 = 1

43. d. The benchmark for the housing expense to income ratio is 28%.

      2,400 x .28 = $672

44. a. The cap rate is the net operating income divided by the property value.

      70,000/420,000 = 1666 = 17%

45. c. Equity is the market value of a house minus the remainder of the mortgage.

      149,000 – 8,000 = $141,000

46. d. The area of a circle is r^2 (π)

      6 x 6 x 3.14 = 113.04

47. c. Residential properties have a 27.5 depreciation rate, meaning it depreciates for 27 years. Divide the value by the rate.

312,000/ 27.5 = $11,345.46

48. b. The mill taxes a 10th of a penny on dollar amounts. Value x mill rate = property tax

173,800 x .016 = $2,780.80

49. a. The loan to value ratio is the mortgage amount/appraised value. First, find the mortgage. Then, divide it by the appraised value.

137,800 x .08 = 11,024

137,800 – 11,024 = 126,776/137,800 = .92

50. b. The seller is responsible for paying the commission.

51. c. loan x interest rate = annual interest

204,000 x .07 = $14,280

52. a. The area of a square is l^2. Find the square footage and multiply it by the cost.

30 x 30 = 90,000 x 2.7 = $243,000

53. d. The market value is the assessed value/ratio.

205,000/.40 = $512,500

54 a. The total interest is the sum total of payments minus the loan amount.

1,300 x 12 = 15,600 x 15 = $234,000 – 172,000 = $62,000

55. c. First determine the mortgage. Multiply the interest rate by the mortgage to determine the first year's interest and then divide by 12.

210,000 – 1700 = 208,300 x .08 = 16,664/12 = $1388.67

56. b. The income property includes a 25% discount on income for estimate. Then subtract the mortgage.

1,800 x .25 = 450

1,800 – 450 = 1,350 – 950 = $400

57. d. The perimeter of a rectangle is the sum of all the sides.

150 x 2 = 300

220 x 2 = 440 + 300 = 740

58. b. Each point is equal to 1%. This is added to the prime rate.

6 + 1 = 7

59. d. The adjusted basis is takes depreciation and improvements into account. It is used to calculate capital gains. Add improvements and subtract depreciation.

275,000 + 30,000 = 305,000 – 12,000 = $293,000

60. c. Capital gain goes to the seller.

61. a. Find the square footage and divide it into the sale price.

43,560 x 1.5 = 65,340

192,000/65,340 = 2.938 = $2.94

62. a. The percentage is the number of days divided by the days in the year. This answer is multiplied by the total property tax.

212/365 = .58 x 5,000 = $2,900

63. b. The capital gain is multiplied by the federal rate and state rate to create the capital gain tax. First, calculate the capital gain.

228,000 – 220,000 = 8,000

8,000 x .15 = 1,200

8,000 x .03 = 240 + 1,200 = $1,440

64. c. The area of a circle is $r^2(\pi)$.

6 x 6 x 3.14 = 113.1

65. d. The contract price minus the adjusted cost basis is the capital gain. The capital gain is multiplied by the federal rate to find the tax. Subtract the tax from gains to find the remainder.

245,000 – 205,750 = 39,250 x .15 = 5,587.50

39,250 – 5,587.5 = $33,362.50

66. d. To determine the rate of appreciation, subtract the original purchase price from the current sales price. Divide this amount by the original sales price.
$849,001-$573,247=$275,754
$275,754 divided by $573,247=0.481 or 48.1%
67. d. Multiply the loan amount $34,050 by interest rate 0.0438=$1,491.39

68. c. Subtract the worth of one bedroom ($7500) from the sales price of the comparable home ($142,780)=$135,280

69. b. Multiply the home equity loan amount by the interest rate.
$33,070 x 0.1199=$3965.09
Divide $3965.09 by 12=$330.42

70. b. To determine the annual taxes, divide $100 by 0.005=$20,000. Multiply $20,000 by 0.0065=$130

71. d. To determine the amount to be credited to the seller, divide $278 (condo fees paid) by 30 (days in the month)=$9.27. Multiply $9.27 x 29=$268.83

72. a. To determine the depreciation, subtract the current sales price from the original price.
$153,132 - $117,423=$35,709

73. d. To determine the value of the similar house, divide the sales price of the contemporary house by the number of square feet in the house. $298,000 divided by 3,200=$93.12.
$93.12 x 2,952=$274,890

74. a. The fraction of the acre is determined by multiplying the lot dimensions (95' x 225')=21,375
21,375 divided by 43,560 (number of feet in an acre)=0.49 or ½ acre

75. c. Divide the amount of commission ($5,500) by the rate of commission (5%)=$110,000

76. a. To determine the amount of commission to be received, multiply the lot dimensions (207' x 317')=65,619 sq. feet
Multiply 65,619 x $4.25=$278,880.75
Multiply $278,880.75 x 0.06=$16,732.85

77. c. To determine the taxes, multiply $452,000 x 0.72 (assessment rate)=$325,440. Multiply $325,440 x 0.045 (millage rate)=$14,644.80

78. d. To determine the number of square feet, divide 3 by 8=0.375. Multiply 0.375 by 43,560 (number of feet in an acre)=16,335

79. b. To determine the amount the buyer owes, add up all expenses and multiply this total by 0.65 (percentage of all costs) $1324 x 0.65=$463.40

80. d. Multiply the loan amount ($20,000) by the interest rate (10%)=$200,000. Multiply $200,000 by 2.5 years=$5,000

81. a. Multiply the interest payment ($5,768) by 12=$69,216. Divide $69,216 by the interest rate (7.25%) converted to the decimal 0.075=$954,703.45

82. b. To determine the total assessed value, total all three assessments. Multiply the total by the assessment rate (57%) converted to a decimal (0.57)=$70,110.

83. b. To determine the cost of the building, divide the yearly income ($90,000) by the return on investment converted to a decimal (0.15).

84. a. To determine the worth of the property, multiply the property value ($275,000) by the depreciation rate converted to a decimal (0.03)=$8250. Multiply this figure ($8250)by the number of years (5)=$41,250. Subtract $41,250 from the property value ($275,000)=$233,750.

85. d. to determine the original value of the house, divide the sales price by the percentage converted to 1.55.
$755,649.80=$487,516

86. a. Divide the square footage of the property by the number of square feet in one acre (43,560) to get the total number of acres. Divide this number by 1.5.

87. a. Multiply the sales price by the rate of commission. Divide the total amount of commission by the amount received by the seller's broker.

88. b. Divide the sales price of the similar home by 6 to get the value of each bedroom. Multiply that figure by 7 to get the value of Carl's home.

89. d. Divide the loan amount by the number of points.

90. b. Subtract the amount of interest from the monthly payment. Subtract that figure from the loan amount. Multiply this figure by the interest rate and multiply that figure by 1/12.

91. d. Divide the monthly interest by the interest rate converted to a decimal (.05570) Multiply that figure by 1/12.

92. c. Multiply $75,000 by 2=$150,000. Divide the amount of interest paid ($5000) by $150,000.

93. a. Divide the value of the home ($1,357,990) by 25 to determine the yearly depreciation.

94. b. Divide the number of square feet by the number of square feet in one acre. Multiply this figure by the per acre price.

95. a. Multiply the original value of the house ($132,800) by 0.0375 x 4=$19,920. Subtract $19,920 from $132,800=$112,800.

96. a. To determine the selling price of the lot, divide the square footage of the lot by the number of

square feet in an acre. Multiply this figure by the selling price per acre.

97. d. Annual interest is calculated by multiplying the loan amount by the interest rate. $80,000 x 6%.

98. c. To determine the interest rate, divide the amount of interest paid by 2 times the loan amount.

99. c. Divide $ 4,760 by 12=$396.67

100. b. Multiply the driveway dimensions and multiply this figure by 0.15 to get the total number of cubic feet. Divide this figure by 27 cu.ft. Multiply this number by the cost of the concrete.

Real Estate Sales Exam VIII

1. Charlie Canfield has a contract to sell a lot on Elm Street. He will receive 4% for the first $ 25,000 and 6.5% for every dollar over that. What was the selling price of the property is his commission was $1,800?

a. $ 14,000

b. $ 39,000

c. $ 37, 307

d. $ 25, 104

2. A local department store property was sold and had an 8% rate of appreciation per year for 12 years. It was originally bought for $ 713,480. What was the latest sale price?

a. $ 1,265,439

b. $ 627,648

c. $ 515,126

d. $ 1, 398,420

3. Felix Munoz decided to pay 4 points on his mortgage. If the mortgage is $ 326,000, how much is he paying for points?

a. $ 10,620

b. $ 1,043

c. $ 13,040

d. $ 107.42

4. Jean Garvey has a contract with a local real estate agency that pays her 65% of its 45% of all commissions she generates. If Jean sold 3 houses for a combined total of $ 834,000 and both had 6% commissions to be split between broker and salesperson, how much was her commission check at the end of the month?

a. $ 1,386.45

b. $ 13,646.70

c. $ 2,133.00

d. $ 47,200

5. If a house sold for 175% of its original value of $ 316,880, what was its selling price?

a. $ 554,540

b. $ 712,750

c. $ 316,182

d. $ 295,100

6. A house depreciates at 3.56% a year for five years and was worth $ 154,600 at the beginning of that period. What is it worth today?

a. $ 145,389

b. $ 127,082

c. $ 234,765

d. $ 109,856

7. Bob Carter bought a house for $ 95,000. Eighteen years later, it is now valued at $ 330,000. What is the amount of appreciation and the rate of appreciation?

a. $ 235,000, 2.4%

b. $ 315,787, 2.8%

c. $ 127,654, 1.9%

d. $ 301,625, 2.5%

8. Luigi's Pizza Palace was bought 8 years ago for $ 160,000. The property was sold for $ 145,000. What was the depreciation per year?

a. 0.058

b. 0.078

c. 0.093

d. 0.035

9. What is the value of a 6 year old property that is 3,205 square feet and has a replacement cost of $65 per square foot, a land value of $ 52,000 and a depreciation rate of 3%?

a. $ 125,000

b. $ 212,458

c. $ 179,512

d. $ 222,831

10. The Dobsons are looking to buy a 4 bedroom house on Douglas Ave. A similar house on the same street with 5 bedrooms just sold for $82,500. What is the value of the house that the Dobsons want to buy?

a. $ 72,500

b. $ 65,000

c. $ 66,000

d. $ 81,000

11. What monthly income should a building costing $ 670,000 produce, if the annual rate of return is to be 14%?

a. $ 9,125

b. $ 7,816

c. $ 8150

d. $ 7250

12. An apartment building with 30 apartments renting at $ 1,400 each has just been sold. If the buyers have told to expect a 12% rate of return, what was the selling price?

a. $ 4,200,000

b. $ 3,915,000

c. $ 4,150,000

d. $ 2,636,000

13. Dean Metzger has a 7 acre property he wants to subdivide into as many 1,000 square feet lots as possible. How many lots can he sell?

a. 175

b. 256

c. 304

d. 108

14. Melissa Ross has purchased a property that is ½ of an acre. How many square feet is in the lot?

a. 32,670

b. 21,780

c. 58,080

d. 5,808

15. Bakersville wants to install brick sidewalks in the downtown area. The cost per square foot to install the sidewalks is $ 26. The city has $ 325,000 to spend on the sidewalks. How many square feet of sidewalk can the city purchase?

a. 7,935

b. 1,500

c. 50

d. 12,500

16. What is the area of a triangular lot that has a depth of 515' and a frontage of 475'?

a. 162

b. 35,174

c. 122,312

d. 23,414

17. A subdivideable 260 acre lot has an asking price of 0.58 per square foot. What is the listing price?

a. $ 5,094,134

b. $ 6,568,848

c. $ 5,128,036

d. $ 1,156,004

18. If land in a development sells for $27,425 an acre, how much would it cost to buy a lot measuring 242,580 square feet?

a. $ 140,716.24

b. $ 423,737.62

c. $ 150,837.50

d. $ 1,407,565.00

19. Bill Cooper bought his home in 1987 for $ 82,726 and sold it in 2010 for $ 108,565. What was the amount of appreciation?

a. $ 28,981

b. $ 15,122

c. $ 11,219

d. $ 25,839

20. Sarah Williams' house has just been sold for $ 157,200. The saleswoman and the broker split the commission. The commission was 5.75%. The broker receives 60% of the commission,

how much of the commission did the saleswoman receive?

a. $ 9039

b. $ 6,875

c. $ 3,616

d. $ 5,238

21. An 80% of value loan was made on a building with an appraised value of $132,000. The annual rate of interest is 4.38%. How much interest will be paid in 6 months?

a. $ 2312.64

b. $ 2890.80

c. $ 4,127.28

d. $ 3,504.10

22. A colonial style home in Oneida has just been sold for $ 411,260. It has 5 bedrooms and 3.5 bathrooms and is 2,540 square feet. A similar colonial in Oneida with 5 bedrooms and 3.5 bathrooms and 2,430 square feet is for sale. What is its value?

a. $ 465,380

b. $ 393,449

c. $ 479,424

d. $ 265,549

23. A 55,000 square foot office building was recently sold for $ 873,500. If the monthly income is expected to be 0.375 per square foot, what is the expected rate of return?

a. 3.5%

b. 2.1%

c. 3.2%

d. 2.8%

24. Sue Stone has exclusive rights to sell the Woodlands development for Johnson Realty. She

earns 6% commission on the first $100,000 and 7% on every dollar over $ 100,000. What was her total commission check for April when she sold houses worth $ 73,000, $ 97,000, and $ 83,000?

a. $ 15,340

b. $ 16,710

c. $ 14,250

d. $ 11,126

25. Joe Gonzales' home was assessed at $ 2,206,000. The previous tax rate was 4.50 per $100. The current tax rate is 6.50 per $100. What is the difference in his monthly tax bill?

a. $ 44,120

b. $ 36,508

c. $ 41,915

d. $ 38,604

26. If real estate taxes of $ 6,270 are paid in full on January 1 and the house closes on August 1, who is owed what?

a. The buyer is owed $ 3637.50

b. The buyer is owed $ 2612.50

c. The seller is owed $2612.50

d. The seller is owed $ 3657.50

27. Riverside Bank will make a loan of 3% on 70% of the value of a property that has depreciated 4% a year for 5 years. If the original price of the property was $ 184,950, how much is the bank going to lend to its customer?

a. $ 110,045.25

b. $ 126,843.50

c. $ 147,960.00

d. $ 172,207.50

28. Taxes are due in full on June 1. There is a 1% late penalty for each month the taxes are late. How much in total will the Jamisons pay on their $ 923,400 house that is assessed at a rate of 58% and a total tax rate of 29 mills, if they pay in full on August 17th?

a. $ 26, 883.11

b. $ 22, 546.91

c. $ 12, 354.87

d. $ 15, 842.18

29. What is the commission on the sale of a house that sold for $ 583,720, if the salesperson receives a 4.25% commission?

a. $ 21,179.35

b. $ 22,895.60

c. $ 15,045.10

d. $ 25,226.96

30. A parcel of land can be broken into a rectangle and a triangle. The rectangle has a depth of 97' and a frontage of 375'. The triangle shares the depth and has frontage of 84'. What is the total square footage of the land?

a. 40,539

b. 32,942.5

c. 34,987

d. 30,615.5

31. What income is needed from an office building with a value of $636,487, if a return of 15.2% is expected?

a. $ 32,947

b. $ 48,103

c. $ 37,555

d. $ 96,746

32. What is the amount of interest paid over the course of a $ 724,920 mortgage at 6% with monthly payments of $ 9,243.98?

a. $ 90,053

b. $ 105,126

c. $ 170,282

d. $ 152,345

33. The cost to install stone on a façade is $26 per sq.ft. What is the total cost to cover the front of a building that measure 36'wide by 28' high?

a. $ 16,900

b. $ 26,208

c. $ 19,210

d. $ 21,504

34. Mary Cox wants to buy a home with 3 bedrooms and 2.5 baths with 2550 sq.ft. A comparable house on the same street recently sold for $375,600. It has 4 bedrooms and 2 baths with 2500 sq.ft. What is the value of the house Mary wants to buy if the bedrooms are worth $ 15,000 and the bathrooms are worth $7500?

a. $ 356,838

b. $ 301,805

c. $ 392,111

d. $ 387,040

35. What amount of interest does the Republic Bank receive at the end of 3 years on a $ 273,000 loan at 5.5 interest?

a. $ 15,626

b. $ 39,919

c. $ 50,749

d. $ 45,045

36. Jake's annual salary is $ 65,000. His mortgage payment (PITI) is $395 per month. Jake has additional debt of $109 per month. What is Jake's front and back end DTI (debt to income) ratio?

a. .04, 0.25

b. .03, 0.16

c. .07, 0.19

d. .09, 0.20

37. What is the total amount of interest on a $ 265,000, 20 year loan with a monthly payment of $ 2004.05?

a. $ 96,108.75

b. $ 10,315.26

c. $ 970,504.00

d. $ 215,972.00

38. A square parcel of land originally sold for $ 2.55 per sq.ft. It now sells for $ 4.25 per sq.ft. How much has the parcel appreciated if it has a frontage of 752 feet?

a. $ 664,706.90

b. $ 961,356.80

c. $ 575,100.00

d. $ 682,763.90

39. A triplex sold for $ 468,000. If the property generates $ 42,500 a year in income, what is the rate of return?

a. 10.3%

b. 9.6%

c. 9.8%

d. 8.7%

40. Condo fees of $ 308.56 a month are due on the first of every month. If Evelyn Bates sells her condo on April 16th to John Clark, how much does John owe Evelyn?

a. $ 97.64

b. $ 154.20

c. $ 107.18

d. $ 129.02

41. Bob Wallace decides to buy a house for $ 330,000. He pays $ 9000 in earnest money and applies for a 75% loan. How much more money does he need to make up the purchase price of the house?

a. $ 51,603

b. $ 30,590

c. $ 73,500

d. $ 61,201

42. How many 100 ft. by 100 ft. lots can be developed from a 3 acre land parcel?

a. 8

b. 11

c. 41

d. 13

43. A lot sold for $ 250 a front foot. If the lot was 96 ft. deep with an area of 6,336 sq.ft, how much did the lot sell for?

a. $ 11,770

b. $ 14,055

c. $ 16,500

d. $ 21,600

44. Melinda sells her property for $ 88,000, which was a 22% loss from her original purchase price. What was the original purchase price?

a. $ 112,820.51

b. $ 68,640.00

c. $ 107,360.00

d. $ 100,000.00

45. A tract of land measures 500 ft. by 5280 ft. How many acres are in the lot?

a. 300

b. 60.60

c. 1, 584,000

d. 748

46. Peter Murphy sold his home for $ 248,500 and made a 42% profit. How much did he pay for the home?

a. $ 175,000

b. $ 210,000

c. $ 143,000

d. $ 153,000

47. A condo sells for $ 125,600 and the buyer gets a loan with a 90% loan to value ratio. What will the seller's closing costs be if they are paying an 8% commission, 3 points for the buyer, and $ 2100 in additional closing costs?

a. $15,464.25

b. $15, 539.00

c. $ 14, 501.62

d. $ 13,768.95

48. Tanya sold her townhouse for $ 484,437.50. She had owned it for 7 years and originally paid $ 575,000.00 for it. What was the annual rate of depreciation?

a. 3 ¾%

b. 2 ¾%

c. 2 ¼%

d. 4 ½%

49. Stacy Monroe sold Bill Parker's home for him. After paying Stacy a commission of 7 ½% of the sale price, Bill ended up with $ 184,907.50. What was the sales price?

a. $ 199,900

b. $ 185,241

c. $ 105,100

d. $ 172,631

50. Waldrip, Crawford, and Lively are partners in the ownership of a property worth $ 440,000. The property produces a 21% return per year in income collected monthly. Waldrip owns a 37% share of the building. How much is Waldrip's monthly income from the property?

a. $ 3915

b. $ 2888

c. $ 3239

d. $ 2849

51. Mr. Jenkins just sold a building for $ 643,000 that he had originally bought 8 years earlier for $875,000. What was the percentage rate of his loss? What was the annual rate of depreciation he sustained?

a. 45.6%, 4.8%

b. 34.8%, 4.9%

c. 30.5%, 2.8%

d. 40.9%, 3.1%

52. An 8 year old building was worth $ 100,000 after depreciating at a rate of 3% per year. What was its original value?

a. $ 415,000

b. $ 250,000

c. $ 325,000

d. $ 175,000

53. Ford's mortgage loan for $ 200,000 carries an annual interest rate of 6%. Monthly rates are $ 1200.00. How much will the principal be reduced by the second monthly payment?

a. $ 315

b. $ 441

c. $ 173

d. $ 201

54. Harriet bought a home for $ 420,000. Four years later she sold it for $599,000. What is the average annual rate of appreciation?

a. 10.65%

b. 12.13%

c. 8.91%

d. 11.17%

55. Chuck Peavy bought 11 lots for $ 21,000 each. He kept 4 and sold the remaining lots for a total of $28,000 more than he originally paid for all of them. What was the average sale price of each lot that he sold?

a. $ 49,000

b. $ 27,000

c. $ 33,000

d. $ 37,000

56. A salesperson receives 60% of total commission on a sale for $315,000. The salesperson received $ 15,120.00. What was the rate of commission?

a. 0.06

b. 0.09

c. 0.08

d. 0.10

57. Rent for a 90ft. by 60ft office is $ 6300 per month. What is the annual rent per sq.ft.?

a. $14

b. $11

c. $ 7.56

d. $ 140

58. Jack works for a broker. He receives 42% of all commissions he brings in. Jack sells a home for $ 140,700 at a commission of 6 ½%. What is the broker's share of the proceeds?

a. $ 3841

b. $ 5304

c. $ 9146

d. $ 1407

59. Nate buys a new home costing $ 188,000. Land value is 15% of the total price. The house contains 1733 sq.ft. What is the cost per sq.ft. of the house alone (not including the land)?

a. $ 16.44

b. $ 92.21

c. $ 9146

d. $ 1407

60. Jerry bought a lot for $ 20,000 in 1993 and spent $ 130,000 to build a house on it in 1995. The house has increased 40% in value and the lot has increased 800%. What is the combined value of the house and lot today?

a. $ 180,000

b. $ 182,000

c. $ 210,000

d. $ 362,000

61. How many square feet are there in 1 ¼ acres?

a. 10,890

b. 54,450

c. 44,649

d. 152,460

62. A broker listed a house for $ 350,000 at 6% commission. The eventual sales price was $ 315,000. How much less was the broker's commission than it would have been if the house had sold at the listing price?

a. $ 210

b. $ 20,100

c. $ 18,900

d. $ 35,000

63. A property is assessed at $ 180,000 and the millage rate is 32.5. What is the tax on the property?

a. $ 58.50

b. $ 595.00

c. $ 5850.00

d. $ 58,500.00

64. Sandra borrowed $ 7500 for 4 years, paying interest every quarter. The total amount of interest that she paid was $2700. What was the annual interest rate?

a. 9%

b. 10%

c. 27%

d. 36%

65. Matt Finley sold a parcel of land for $ 172,750. He made a profit of 47%. What was the purchase price?

a. $ 82,755

b. $ 115,000

c. $ 93,736.50

d. $ 117,517

66. Steve wants to buy a house for $325,000. A 20% down payment is required by the bank. How much will Steve's down payment be?

a. $ 50,000

b. $ 42,000

c. $ 75,000

d. $ 65,000

67. Stan must get at least $ 75,000 from the sale of his home. He assumes his cost will be 8% of the sales price. What is the minimum sales price Stand should accept?

a. $ 80,525

b. $ 81,521

c. $ 76,254

d. $ 73,415

68. When a house on Blair Street sells, half of the 6% commission will go to David Blake, the real estate broker. David will give 20% of the commission to Paul, the listing agent. The other half of the commission goes to the selling agent's brokerage, who gives 40% to the selling agent. The sales price of the house is $ 292,000. How much will David, the listing agent, the selling brokerage, and the selling agent receive?

a. $ 7008, $ 1752, $ 5266, $3504

b. $ 2569, $ 2994, $ 6109, $ 4205

c. $ 6808, $ 3541, $ 5100, $ 5604

d. $ 4215, $ 1068, $ 5204, $ 3662

69. Rental income for a property is $ 1700 per month. If the closing date is June 20th, how much rent is owed the buyer at closing?

a. $ 602.40

b. $ 566.66

c. $ 438.52

d. $ 715.85

70. A house sells for $120,000. The borrower obtains an 80% loan. If the bank charges 2 points at closing, how much in points must the borrower pay?

a. $ 1920

b. $ 3500

c. $ 1625

d. $ 1432

71. Mike bought a townhouse three years ago for $ 312,000.00. If the area depreciated at 5% per year, what is the value of the house today?

a. $ 12,500

b. $ 46,500

c. $ 265,200

d. $ 237,450

72. A seller's agent sells a property for $ 825,000 and makes a commission of 6%, which is split 70/30 with his broker. How much does the agent receive?

a. $ 14,850

b. $ 39,000

c. $ 34,650

d. $ 27,604

73. A broker receives a commission check of $ 8550.00. The commission rate is 5.5%. What was the sales price of the home?

a. $ 540

b. $ 175,000

c. $ 540,000

d. $ 150,000

74. Donald bought his home four years ago for $ 190,000. He sold it last month for $295,000. What is the annual rate of appreciation?

a. 57%

b. 100%

c. 0.13%

d. 1.5%

75. Ben sold his condo on August 15th. The property is subject to an HOA fee of $455 per month, which Ben prepaid for the month of August. How much will the buyer owe Ben in HOA fees?

a. $ 11.50

b. $ 179.64

c. $ 220.05

d. $ 215.14

76. A real estate agent sells a property for $ 465,000 and receives a commission check of $24,535. What was the rate of commission?

a. 19%

b. 18%

c. 5.5%

d. 4.5%

77. How many 7,000 sq. ft. lots can be developed from a 10 acre parcel of land?

a. 41

b. 53

c. 62

d. 74

78. How much is the PI payment on a 7.25%, $ 200,000 mortgage amortized over 30 years using an amortization factor of 6.62%?

a. $ 200

b. $ 1,324

c. $ 550

d. $ 1,234

79. A five year old house with 2,100 sq.ft. has a replacement cost of $65/sq.ft. The land is valued at $125,000 and the depreciation is 2% per year. What is the value of the property?

a. $ 247,850

b. $ 346,790

c. $ 13,501

d. $ 130,200

80. A lot that is 5/6th of an acre is how many square feet?

a. 36,299

b. 25,693

c. 45,780

d. 23,541

81. What is the first month's interest on a one year loan for $ 34,000 at 8.28%?

a. $ 2,346

b. $ 281.52

c. $ 2,815.20

d. $ 234.60

82. The Coopers bought a beachfront property that is 3/4 of an acre and the beachfront frontage is 110'. Assuming that the property is rectangular, what is the depth of the property?

a. 296

b. 332

c. 298

d. 297

83. What is the area of a triangular lot with a depth of 369 ft. and a frontage of 214 ft.?

a. 162

b. 72,232

c. 144,504

d. 39,483

84. If land in a development sells for $25,595 an acre, how much would it cost to buy a lot that measures 239,580 sq. ft.?

a. $ 407,739.98

b. $ 1,407,725.00

c. $ 140,772.50

d. $ 142,774.50

85. What is the listing price for a subdivideable 225 acre lot, if the asking price is $0.52 per sq. ft.?

a. $ 5,096,520

b. $ 509,652.00

c. $ 100.67

d. $ 5,256.36

86. The listing salesperson on a sale receives $ 2300 commission. The seller pays an 8%

commission, which is divided between the brokers. The listing broker pays the selling broker 40% of the total commission, and pays the salesperson 52% of his (the listing broker's) share. What is the sale price of the house?

a. $ 92,147.43

b. $ 138,221.15

c. $ 69,920.00

d. None of the above

87. If a home was bought for $ 140,000 and sold for 10% more, and a 10% commission was paid as well as other closing costs, what would be the net amount of proceeds?

a. $ 140,000.00

b. $ 169,400.00

c. $ 141,414.13

d. $ 138,600.00

88. A condo was sold for $98,000 which was a 14% loss from its original purchase price, how much did the buyer pay for the condo?

a. $ 113,953.48

b. $ 111,720.00

c. $ 84,280.00

d. $ 128,947.36

89. How much interest is there on a 15 year loan of $ 72,000 at 13.36%?

a. $ 14,428.80

b. $ 13, 768.09

c. $ 15,456.32

d. $ 10,478.89

90. What are the taxes on a $ 180,000 house if properties are assessed at 40% of market value, and the tax rate is $2.80 per hundred dollars of assessed value?

a. $ 257.14

b. $ 2016.00

c. $ 5040.00

d. None of the above

91. If a house sells for $ 124,900, and the buyer gets a loan with a 90% loan-to-value ratio, what will the seller's closing costs be if they are paying an 8% commission, 3 points for the buyer, and $ 2100 in additional closing costs?

a. $ 15,464.30

b. $ 15,839.00

c. $ 15,026.52

d. $ 14,465.10

92. The interest payment on a loan this month is $ 420.00. The interest rate on the loan is 8%. What is the current balance of the loan?

a. $ 5250.00

b. $ 40,320.00

c. $ 52,500.00

d. $ 63,000.00

93. If the taxes on a property are $ 1400, the market value of the property is $90,000, and the property is assessed at 45% of its market value, what is the tax rate in mills?

a. 7

b. 28.93

c. 34.57

d. 70

94. A tract of land measures 400 ft. by 5280 ft. How many acres is this equivalent to?

a. 48.48

b. 300

c. 792

d. 1,584,000

95. A townhouse sold for $ 387,300. It has a yearly rental income of $ 17,000. What is the rate of return?

a. 0.02

b. 0.04

c. 0.06

d. 0.05

96. An 8.4 acre lot is for sale at $225,000. What is the price per foot?

a. 0.84

b. 0.61

c. 0.47

d. 0.52

97. Monthly rental on a property is $825.00. The Gross Rent Multiplier is 175, what is the estimated value of the property?

a. $ 356,878

b. $ 237,123

c. $ 144,375

d. $ 765.93

98. Jeff and Carol are considering the purchase of a 3 bedroom, 2 bath house on Franklin St. A similar house on the same street with 4 bedrooms just sold for $96,500. What is the value of the house that Jeff and Carol want to buy?

a. $ 72,375

b. $ 68,908

c. $ 89,000

d. $ 59,098

99. A building costs $587,000. What monthly income should it produce, if the annual rate of return is to be 16%?

a. $ 6,438

b. $ 8,712

c. $ 5,479

d. $ 7,826

100. Bernie borrows $12,000. He pays $210 each quarter in interest. What is the annual interest rate on the loan?

a.0.15

b. 2.4

c. 0.7

d. 1.9

Real Estate Sales Exam VIII Answers

1. c. To determine the sales price of the lot, multiply $25,000 by the percentage rate for the first $25,000 (0.004). Subtract this figure from the total amount of the commission check. Divide that figure by the percentage rate above $25,000 (6.5%). Add this figure to the $25,000.

2. d. To determine the latest sale price, multiply the original purchase price by the rate of appreciation. Multiply this figure by the number of years. Add this figure to the original purchase price.

3. c. To determine how much is being paid for the points, multiply the mortgage amount by the number of points converted to a decimal (0.04).

4. b. To determine the amount of the commission check received at the end of the month, multiply the combined total of houses sold by the commission rate of 6%. Multiply that figure by 45%, converted to a decimal (0.045). Multiply that figure by 65%, converted to a decimal (0.065).

5. a. To determine the selling price, multiply the original value of the house by the percentage of its original value, converted to a decimal. (1.75)

6. b. To determine worth of the house today, multiply the depreciation percentage by five years to get the rate of depreciation. Multiply the original worth of the home by the rate of depreciation. Subtract this figure from the original value of the home.

7. a. To determine the amount of depreciation, subtract the original price of the house from its current value. To determine the rate of depreciation, divide the amount of depreciation by the original price of the home. Convert the figure to a decimal.

8. c. To determine the amount of depreciation per year, subtract the sales price from the original purchase price. Divide this figure by the original purchase price.

9. d. To determine the value of the property, multiply the square footage by the replacement cost per square foot to get the total replacement cost. Multiply this figure by the depreciation rate to get the amount of depreciation per year. Multiply the amount of depreciation per year by 6 years to get the

amount of depreciation for that period. Add the replacement cost amount to the land value and subtract the 6 year depreciation amount.

10. c. To determine the value of the house to be purchased, divide the sales price of the similar home by 5 to get the value of one bedroom. Multiply this figure by the number of bedrooms in the house to be purchased.

11. b. To determine the monthly income, multiply the cost of the building by the annual rate of return. Divide this figure by 12.

12. a. To determine the selling price, multiply the number of apartments by the rental rate to get the total income. Multiply this figure by 12 to get the total annual income. Divide the total annual income by the rate of return.

13. c. To determine how many lots can be sold, multiply the square feet in one acre by 7. Divide this figure by 1,000.

14. b. To determine the number of square feet in the lot, multiply the number of square feet in an acre by 0.50.

15. d. To determine the number of square feet of sidewalk to be purchased, divide the amount of purchase money by the square foot cost.

16. c. To determine the area of the lot, multiply the depth of the lot by ½. Multiply that figure by the frontage amount.

17. b. To determine the listing price, multiply the amount of square footage in one acre by the price per square foot. Multiply this figure by the size of the lot.

18. c. To determine the cost to buy the lot, divide the square foot amount of the lot by the number of square feet in one acre. Multiply the sales price per acre by the number of acres in the lot.

19. d. To determine the amount of appreciation, subtract the original purchase price from the current sales price.

20. c. To determine the amount of commission received by the saleswoman, multiply the sales price by the commission rate. Multiply this figure by 40%.

21. a. To determine the amount of interest to be paid in six months, multiply the appraised value by 80% (.08). Multiply this figure by the annual rate of interest (0.0438). Multiply this figure by .05.

22. b. To determine the value of the home, divide the sales price of the original home ($ 411,260) by the number of square feet in the home. Multiply this figure by the number of square feet in the house that is for sale.

23. d. To determine the expected rate of return, multiply the square footage in the building by 0.375. Multiply this figure by 12. Divide this figure by the sales price.

24. b. To determine the total commission amount, add the amounts of the homes sold. Subtract $100,000 from this total. Multiply $100,000 by 6%. Multiply $153,000 by 7%. Add these figures together.

25. a. To determine the difference in the tax bill, multiply the assessment amount by the previous rate. Multiply the assessment amount by the current rate. Subtract the previous tax amount from the **current** tax amount.

26. c. To determine who is owed what, divide the amount of taxes by 12. Multiply this figure by 5.

27. a. To determine the amount the bank will loan, multiply the original property value by the loan percentage. Multiply that figure by the years of depreciation. Subtract that figure from the original purchase price of the home. That figure is multiplied by the loan value, converted to a decimal (.02).

28. d. To determine the tax total, multiply the price of the house by the assessment rate. Multiply this figure by the number of mills, converted to a decimal. This figure is multiplied by the late penalty percentage, converted to a decimal.

29. b. To determine the commission on the sale, multiply the sales price by the commission rate, converted to a decimal.

30. a. The total square footage is determined by multiplying the frontage of the rectangular portion by its depth. Multiply the depth by the frontage of the triangle and then multiply this figure by ½. Add the amount of square footage in the rectangle to the amount of square footage in the triangle.

31. d. To determine the amount of income needed, multiply the property value by the percentage of return.

32. c. To determine the amount of interest paid over the course of the loan, multiply the monthly payment amount by 60. Subtract this figure from the amount of the loan.

33. b. To determine the cost of installation, multiply the width by the depth of the building. Multiply that figure by the cost per square foot.

34. a. Subtract the square footage of the comparable home from the square footage of the house Mary wants to buy. Divide the sale price of the comparable house by its square footage. Multiply that figure by 50 (difference between the square footage of the houses). Subtract that figure from the sales price of the house. Add the value of bathrooms (7,500 x0.5) and subtract 7,512.

35. d. To determine the amount of interest to be received, multiply the total loan amount by the interest rate and divide that figure by the number of years.

36. c. The front and back end DTI ratios can be determined by adding up the total monthly debt. Divide the annual salary by 12. To get the front end ratio, divide the mortgage payment by one month's income. To determine the back end ratio, divide the total debt by $7,500.

37. d. The total amount of interest can be determined by:

$2004.05 x 12 x 20=$480,972. $480,972-$265,000=$215,972

38. b. The amount of appreciation can be determined by: $4.25-$2.55=$1.70; 752 x
752=565,504;565,504 x 6%=$961,356.80

39. c. The rate of return can be determined by dividing income from the property by the sales price.

40. b. The amount John owes Evelyn can be determined by: $308.56 divided by 30=$10.28. $10.28 x
15=$154.20.

41. c. To determine the amount of money needed to purchase the home, complete the following steps.

Subtract $9,000 from $330,000= $321,000. The loan is 75% of $330,000 ($330,000 x 0.75=$247,500).
Subtract $247,500 from $321,000=$73,500.

42. d. A 100 ft. x 100 ft. lot contains 10,000 sq. ft. The three acre plots contain 130,680 sq.ft (43,560 x 3).
Divide 130,680 by 10,000=13.068 or 13 full lots.

43. c. To determine how much the lot sold for, divide 6,336 by 96=66 ft. At $ 250 a front foot, the lot
would sell for 66 x$250=$16,500.

44. a. To determine the original purchase price, consider the full purchase price as being 100% of that
amount, of which she lost 22% when she resold it. She now has 78% of the original amount. Multiply the
original price by 78% to get the new amount, which is $88,000. Divide $88,000 by 78% which equals
$112,820.51.

45. b. To determine the equivalent acres, multiply 5,280 ft. by 500=2,640,000. Divide 2,640,000 by
43,560 (ft. in an acre)=60.60 acres

46. a. $248,500 is 142% of the purchase price. Divide $248,500 by 1.42=$175,000

47. d. Anne's $1,171.80 was 12% of Connie's commission which was $1,171.80 divided by 0.12=$9,765. If
the sales price was $139,500, the rate of commission was $ 9,765 divided by $139,500=0.07 or 7%.

48. c. Subtract $484,437.50 from $575,000=$90,562.50. Next, determine what percentage this figure is
of $575,500. $90,562.50 divided by $575,000=15 3/4%.
15 3/4% divided by 7=2 1/4%.

49. a. If Parker paid a 7 1/2% commission, this $184,907.50 represents 92 1/2% of the sales price.
(100%-7 1/2%=92 1/2%). Divide $184,907.50 by 0.925=$ 199,900.

50. d. .021 x $440,000= $92,400 annual income. $ 92,400 divided by 12=$7,700 monthly income to the
building. Waldrip gets 37% of $7,700=$2849.

51. b. The total amount of the loss is determined by subtracting $643,000 from $875,000=$232,000. This
is 26% of $875,000. ($232,000 divided by $875,000=0.265). Profit and loss are calculated based on the
purchase price originally paid. Since the depreciation occurred over an 8 year period, the annual

depreciation rate is 0.265 divided by 8=3.3%

52. b. After depreciating for 8 years at 3% per year, the building lost 24% of its original value (8 x 0.03). This means that it is now worth the remaining 76% of its original value. If that sum is $190,000, then the original value is $190,000 divided by 0.76=$250,000.

53. d. 6% of $200,000=$12,000. Interest for a single month would be $12,000 divided by 12=$1,000. Therefore, of the $1200 first payment, $1,000 goes to interest, leaving $200 to reduce the principal. This means that Ford will pay interest on $199,800 the second month. Figuring the same way, we get a monthly interest charge of $999.00 for the second month on the amount; this will leave $201 by which the second monthly payment will reduce the principal.

54. a. The total appreciation is $599,000-$420,000=$179,000. Total percentage of appreciation is $179,000 divided by $420,000=42.619. The average over 4 years is 42.619 divided by 4=10.65%.

55. d. 11 lots x $21,000=$231,000. 7 lots for a total of $28,000 more than that ($231,000 + $28,000=$259,000). The average sales price is $259,000 divided by 7=$37,000.

56. c. The amount of the commission check ($15,120) divided by 6%=$25,200 total commission. $25,200 divided by the sale price ($315,000)=0.08=8%.

57. a. Area= 90ft.x60'=5400 sq.ft. $6300 x 12=$75,600 per year. $75,600 divided by 5400 sq.ft=$14.00

58. b. First, find the total commission amount. 0.065 x $140,700=$9145.50. The broker keeps 58% of the proceeds. 0.58 x $9145.50=$5304.39.

59. b. The cost per square foot is determined by finding the value of the home alone. The land is 15% of the total value, which means that the house is 85% of the total. The house is then worth - 0.85 x $188,000=$159,800. If the house has 1,733 sq.ft, the cost per square foot is $92.21.

60. d. The lot value has increased by 800%. The lot was worth 100% of its value in1993, so if it has gone up 800%, then today, it is worth 900%, or 9 times its value. 9 x $20,000=180,000-lot value today. Since the house is worth 40% more, today it is worth140% of its original value. 1.4 x $130,000= $182,000 house value today. House and lot together are worth - $180,000 + 182,000=$362,000.

61. b. One acre=43,560 sq. ft. 1 1/4 x 43,560=54,450 sq. ft.

62. b. Determine the commission on $350,000 and $315,000. 0.06 x $350,000= $210,000; 0.06 x $315,000=$189,900. Subtract $189,900 from $210,000=$20,100.

63. c. To determine the tax, multiply the millage rate (32.5) converted to a decimal (0.0325) by $180,000=$5,850.

64. a. To determine the annual interest rate, divide $2700 by 4 years = $675 per year. Divide $ 675 by $7500=0.09=9%.

65.b. If Matt made a profit of 43%, then he sold the land for 143% of its purchase price. $164, 450 divided by 1.43=$115,000.

66. d. To determine the amount of the down payment, multiply the loan amount by the percentage of the down payment.

67. b. To determine the minimum sales price to be accepted, subtract 8% from 100%=92%. Divide $75,000 by 92%, converted to a decimal (0.92)=$81,521.

68. a. Selling Price - $292,000
    Total Commission - $17,500.
    First 50% of the commission goes to listing agent=$ 8760. 80% of the $8760 goes to listing broker=$7008. 20% of the $8760 goes to the
    listing agent=$1752.

    Second 50% of the commission goes to the selling brokerage=$8760. 60% of the $8760 goes to the selling broker=$5,266. 40% of the $8760 goes to the
    selling agent=$3504

69. b. Divide rent amount by 30 to get rent per day=$56.66. Multiply daily rent by 10 (days in June that buyer rents property) $56.66 X 10=$566.66

70. a. To determine the amount in points to be paid, multiply the property price by the percentage of loan received. Multiply the product by the number of points. This equal the points amount in dollars.

71. c. Calculate the annual depreciation ($312,000 x .05=$15,600). Calculate depreciation over 3 years ($15,600 x 3=$46,800). Calculate value - $312,000 - $46,800=$265,200.

72. c. Multiply the sales price of the property ($825,000) by 6%=$49,500. Multiply $49,500 by 7%=$34,650.

73. D. Divide commission amount by rate of commission

74. c. Subtract $190,000 from $295,000=$105,000 to get total appreciation. Divide $105,000 by $190,000=0.55 to get percentage of appreciation. Divide 0.55 by 4=0.13.

75. c. Buyer owes Ben for one month of HOA fees. $455 divided by 31=$14.67. Buyer owes for 15 days. $14.67 x 15= $220.05

76. a. Divide the sales price by amount of commission received.

77. c. Multiply 10 acres by 43,560 (number of sq.ft in one acre)=435,600. Divide 435,600 by 7,000=62 lots.

78. b. Multiply the Mortgage Amortization Factor by loan amount. 6.62 x 200=$1,324.

79. a. Replacement cost - 65 x 2100=$136,500

Annual Depreciation - $136,500 x .02=$2,730

Depreciation over by 5 years - $2,730 x 5=$13,650

Value=Replacement cost + Land Value-Depreciation =$247,850

80. a. Divide 5 by 6=0.833. 0.833 x 43,560=36,299

81. d. Multiply $ 34,000 by 0.0828 x 1/12=$234.60

82. d. Multiply 43,560 by 3/4=32,670. Divide 32,670 by 110=297'

83. d. To determine the area, use the following formula. 1/2 x 369 x214=39,483.

84. c. Divide 239,580 by 43,560=5.5 5.5 x $25,595=$140.772.50

85. a. 43,560 x 0.52=$22,651.20 price per acre. 22,651.20 x 225 acres=$5,096,520

86. a. First, if the selling broker gets 40%, then the listing broker gets 60%. Then, going forward, sales price x 8% x 60% x 52%=$2300. Then, $2300 divided by the salesperson's 52% will give us the broker's commission=$4,423,.08. $4,423.08 divided by 60% will give us the total commission of $7371.79. $7173.79 divided by 8% will give us the sale price of $92,147.43.

87. d. $140,000 x 10%=$14,000. $140,000 plus $14,000=$154,000. $154,000 x 10%=$15,400. $154,000 - $15,400=$138,600

88 a. If 14% was lost, that means you only have 86% of what you originally had. Divide $98,000 by 86%=$113, 953.48.

89. a. Multiply the loan amount by the interest rate converted to a decimal. $72,000 x 0.01336=961.92 x 15=$14,428.80.

90. b. Multiply $180,000 by 40%=72,000 of assessed value. Since the rate is in dollars per hundred, divide by 100 to get 720. 720 times the rate of $2.80=$2016.

91. a. The loan is 90% of the sale price, so $124,900 x 90%=$112,410. One point is 1% of the loan amount or $1124.10, so 3 points would be $3372.30. The commission is based on the sales price, so $124,900 x 8% = $9992. $3373.30 + 9992+$2100=$15,464.30.

92. d. Interest rates are based on 1 year. Need to multiply the monthly interest by 12 to get 1 year's worth of interest, or $5,040. $5,040 divided by the rate of 8%=$63,000

93. c. $90,000 x 45=$40,500 assessed value. The tax of $1400 divided by $40,500 gives a rate of .03457 or 34.57 mills.

94. a. Multiply 400 x 5280=2,112,000 ft. Divide 2,112,000 by 43,560= 48.48

95. b. Divide the amount of rental income by the sales price. $17,000 divided by $387,300.

96. b. Divide the sale price by 8.4=$26,785.71 divided by 43,560=0.61

97. c. Multiply the rental income by the Gross Rent Multiplier-$144,375.

98. a. Divide the sales price by the number of bedrooms in the similar house (4) =$ 24,125. Multiply $24,125 by 3 (number of bedrooms)=$72,375

99. d. Multiply the building cost by the annual rate of return. Divide $ 93,920 by 12=$7,826

100. c. Multiply interest payment per quarter by 4. Divide this amount by $12,000=0.07 or 7%

Real Estate Sales Exam IX

1. A buyer's agent earned a $ 2,400 commission on a sale. If the total commission paid on the deal was 5.5%, what was the sales price of the house?

a. $ 480,000

b. $ 43,636

c. $ 87,272

d. $ 26,400

2. After paying a 6% commission, Fran received net proceeds of 456,786.00 on the sale of her home. What was the sales price?

a. $ 488,541

b. $ 678,906

c. $ 712,456

d. $ 623,590

3. Sales agent Ray Ross has a 60/40 split with his broker. He just sold a home for $ 220,000 which paid a 3% commission. How much money did Ray make?

a. $ 3960

b. $ 2640

c. $ 6600

d. $ 3300

4. The sales price of a home was $ 180,000. The sellers paid a 4% commission to the broker. They then paid 1% of the price for fees and another $500 in miscellaneous fees. What were the net proceeds to the seller?

a. $ 172,800

b. $ 170,500

c. $ 171,000

d. $ 170,572

5. The Blackwells accepted an offer approximately 10% below their listing price of $275,000. They paid a 5% commission to their broker. What was the amount of commission made by the sales agent?

a. $ 12,375

b. $ 233,100

c. $ 13,000

d. $ 12,400

6. A broker negotiated a 4% commission fee based on net proceeds. The home sold for $ 325,000 and expenses to sell the home totaled $24,000. What was the commission amount paid?

a. $ 12,960

b. $ 12,040

c. $ 13,000

d. $ 12,400

7. The Acme Insurance Company recently sold its property for $ 4,534,203. If the property was purchased 15 years ago for $ 737,222, what is the annual rate of appreciation?

a. 45%

b. 34%

c. 21%

d. 16%

8. If a home depreciates at a rate of 4.25% a year for 6 years and it was worth $ 305,000 at the beginning of that period, what is it worth today?

a. $ 226,750

b. $ 201,756

c. $ 155,444

d. $ 253,198

9. What is the principal on a mortgage loan, if the monthly interest payment is $7,349 and the interest rate is 8.56%?

a. $ 957,108

b. $ 700,249

c. $ 1,030,233

d. $ 889,125

10. What is the interest on 65% of a $ 400,000 loan with a 12% interest rate for the first year?

a. $ 22,000

b. $ 31,489

c. $ 39,000

d. $ 26,450

11. A house is listed for $250,000 with an agreed upon 6.5% rate of commission. The owner receives an offer for $ 225,000, and after negotiations, sells for $ 235,000. How much commission will the selling and listing broker each receive?

a.$ 7,104.50

b. $ 7,637.50

c. $ 6,940.00

d. $ 6,550.14

12. How much income must be generated from a $ 2,415,720 building if a 14% return on investment is required?

a. $ 278,156

b. $ 311,588

c. $ 338,200

d. $ 251,125

13. A duplex sold for $ 175,000. It has a yearly rental income of $ 18,000. What is its rate of return?

a. 0.10

b. 0.11

c. 0.6

d. 0.13

14. What is the replacement cost of a building if the final value is $ 215,750, the land value is $10,200, and depreciation is $5,101.00?

a. $ 208,021

b. $ 207,588

c. $ 165,345

d. $ 210,651

15. If the interest for 3 months on a loan of $ 95,000 was $ 2,700, what is the rate of interest on the loan per year?

a. 0.7

b. 0.1

c. 0.4

d. 0.3

16. A lot sold for $ 980 a front foot. If the lot was 132 ft. deep and had an area of 6,468 sq. ft., how much did the lot sell for?

a. $ 64,680

b. $ 57,710

c. $ 48,000

d. $ 39,000

17. A 2.6 acre lot sold for $ 188,000. What was the price per foot?

a. $ 1.19

b. $ 1.55

c. $ 1.66

d. $ 1.82

18. Eli buys a townhouse costing $ 232,800. The loan requires a 15% down payment, an origination fee of 0.75%, 2.25 point discount, and a 0.5% PITI fee. How much money does Eli need for these expenses?

a. $ 23,250

b. $ 28,995.75

c. $ 41,791.88

d. $ 43,012.50

19. A 1.6 acre lot sold for $ 25,100. What was the price per square foot?

a. $ 3.61

b. $ 0.36

c. $ 1.88

d. $ 2.28

20. Marie buys a condo from Ray for $ 77,900. She gets a VA loan for 90% of the purchase price. The loan discount paid by Ray is 2.5 points. The broker's commission on the sale is 6% and the interest rate on the loan is 9.75%. What is the amount of the discount?

a. $ 1,264.20

b. $ 2,102.40

c. $ 1, 752.75

d. $ 6,947.50

21. A rectangular lot with a frontage of 207 feet and a depth of 317 feet is sold for $ 4.25 per sq. ft. If the agent's commission rate is 6%, how much will the agent receive from the sale?

a. $ 16,732.85

b. $ 20,593.34

c. $ 45,236.23

d. $ 18,741.36

22. The market value of a house is $ 82,000. If the property is assessed at 35% of market value and the annual tax rate is 46 mills, how much is the tax?

a. $ 1205.40

b. $ 2102.40

c. $ 3956.21

d. $ 1357.29

23. The annual net operating income from an apartment building is $11,000. If a capitalization rate of 11% is used, what is the market value of the building?

a. $ 126,000

b. $ 176,000

c. $ 100,000

d. $ 242,000

24. To earn 12% on an investment, what should be paid for a property that earns $6,000 per month and has operating expenses of $1,250.00 per month?

a. $ 475,000

b. $ 150,000

c. $ 229,166

d. $ 333,333

25. A 100 unit apartment complex includes 40 one bedroom units that rent for $950.00 and 60 two bedroom units that rent for $ 1,150 monthly. The vacancy rate is 5% and miscellaneous income is $ 5,000 annually. Operating expenses amount to $ 400,000. The mortgage loan requires payments of $ 630,000 annually. What is the potential gross income of the complex?

a. $ 10,289

b. $ 112,000

c. $ 107,000

d. $ 1,284,000

26. If the monthly rental for a property is $ 575 and the Gross Rent Multiplier is $ 127, what is its estimated value?

a. $ 74,750

b. $ 75,000

c. $ 72,945

d. $ 73,000

27. What is the value of a property that rents for $ 750 per month, using a gross rent multiplier of 110, if the expenses of the property are $ 125 per month?

a. $ 75,125

b. $ 82,500

c. $ 68,750

d. $ 73,592

28. A 7 year old home is currently valued at $72,000. What was its original value if it has appreciated by 60% since it was built?

a. $ 115,200

b. $ 38,751

c. $ 45,000

d. None of the above

29. A parcel of land sold for $ 115,000. If it appreciated at 12% per year, and the seller held it for 4 years, how much did the seller pay for the land? (disregard taxes, selling costs)

a. $ 56,000

b. $ 102,000

c. $ 81,400

d. $ 73,000

30. A 30 year old building with an effective age of 20 years has a total life expectancy of 50 years. How much depreciation has occurred?

a. 10%

b. 30%

c. 40%

d. 60%

31. A building contains 25 one bedroom units and 75 two bedroom units. The one bedroom units rent for $ 550.00 per month and the two bedrooms rent for $ 675.00 per month. The vacancy rate is 7% and the operating expenses are estimated at 40% of the effective gross income. There is $ 1000 annual income from vending machines. What is the net operating income?

a. $ 431,655

b. $ 286,940

c. $ 408,219

d. $ 756,333

32. Land purchased for $100,000 cash appreciates at a rate of 15%, compounded annually. About how much is the land worth after 5 years? (Disregard taxes, insurance, and selling expenses)

a. $ 115,000

b. $ 200,000

c. $ 15,000

d. $ 75,000

33. A house on Elm Street has a swimming pool and a garage. The appraiser estimates that a pool adds $ 20,000 to the value of the house and a garage contributes $ 15,000. A similar home, with a garage but no pool, in the neighborhood recently sold for $ 300,000. What is the value of the comparable home?

a. $ 300,000

b. $ 345,000

c. $ 320,000

d. $ 315,000

34. A fully leased commercial property produces $ 20,000 per month in rent. It has a vacancy rate of 9% and a capitalization rate of 12%. What is the market value of the property?

a. $ 1,666,666

b. $ 2,000,000

c. $ 1,525,702

d. $ 218,400

35. Leah bought a half acre lot at $ 10 per square foot and built a house 50' x 50' for $ 75 per square foot. What was her total cost?

a. $ 238,110

b. $ 405,300

c. $ 650,000

d. $ 245,801

36. Sam, a real estate salesperson, is associated with Peter, a broker. Sam lists a home for sale for $ 320,000 with a 6% commission due at closing. Three weeks later, the owner accepts an offer of $ 300,000 brought in by Sam. Peter's practice is that 45% of the commission goes to the brokerage and the rest to the sales person. How much will Sam make on the sale?

a. $ 18,000

b. $ 10,500

c. $ 9500

d. $ 9900

37. A seller has agreed to pay 2 points to the lender to help the buyers obtain a mortgage loan. The house was listed for $ 320,000 and is being sold for $300,000. The buyers will pay 20% down and borrow the rest. How much will the seller owe to the lender for points?

a. $ 4,800

b. $ 6,900

c. $ 5,120

d. $ 2,100

38. The listing broker receives a commission of 6% on the first $ 250,000 of the sales price and 4% on any amount above $ 250,000. If the property sells for
$450,000, what is the total commission?

a. $ 15,000

b. $ 27,000

c. $ 29,000

d. $ 23,000

39. The lender's underwriting criteria specifies a maximum house expense to income ratio of 28%. If the applicant proves annual earnings of $ 75,000 in the previous years and that salary is continuing, what is the maximum monthly PITI?

a. $ 2,600

b. $ 1,750

c. $ 5,123

d. $ 6,350

40. Roger's home cost $ 449,000. He financed the purchase with a 90% loan. The discount was 3 points. The interest on the loan was 7% per year and the term of the loan was 25 years. How much interest would be payable with the first payment?

a. $ 3,570

b. $ 1,726

c. $2,619.75

d. $ 3,109.65

41. Candy Cook receives a commission check of $ 7,200.00 and wonders what house sale it is for. The broker knows that she receives 5.5% commission on every house the brokerage lists, so how much did the house for which she received the commission sell for?

a. $ 130,909.09

b. $ 158,202.03

c. $ 175,915.05

d. $ 125,512.06

42. An agent sells a house for a list price of $ 1,567,000 and receives a commission of $ 117,525.00. What is the commission rate?

a. 6.2%

b. 5.9%

c. 7.5%

d. 9.1%

43. Mandy sells units in a condo building and receives a 6% commission on the first $150,000 of sales per month and a 2% commission on all sales exceeding that. In July, she sold condos for $ 95,000, $ 105,000, and $ 87,000. What is her total commission for the month?

a. $ 12,309

b. $ 22,444

c. $ 15,395

d. $ 11,740

44. For tax purposes, Tom Fletcher's $230,000 house is assessed at 63%. What is the assessed value of the house?

a. $ 485,586

b. $ 344,900

c. $ 403,005

d. $ 321,609

45. If the local tax rate is 33 mills and the assessment rate is 48%, what would be the amount of taxes owed on a house worth $365,095?

a.$ 7878.40

b. $ 2015.25

c. $ 5783.10

d. $ 6225.04

46. If a house depreciates at a rate of 3.50 a year for 6 years and was worth $ 168,700 at the beginning of that period, what is it worth today?

a. $ 150,500

b. $ 89,214

c. $ 143,605

d. $ 125,313

47. Using straight line depreciation, a house that is valued at $ 790,400 and has a useful life of 35 years is worth how much after 8 years?

a. $ 609,737.15

b. $ 309,781.00

c. $ 545,455.00

d. $ 631,110.25

48. A 9 year old building was worth $ 170,000.00, after depreciating at a rate of 4% per year. What was its original value?

a. $ 202,800

b. $ 154,000

c. $ 265,625

d. $ 178,415

49. Hal bought a home for $ 576,000. Six years later, he sold it for $700,000. What was the annual rate of appreciation?

a. 28.2%

b. 30.45%

c. 14.36%

d. 35.87%

50. Tony receives 60% of the total commission on a sale of $495,000. He received $ 17,250.00. What was the rate of commission?

a. 3.2%

b. 5%

c. 4.7%

d. 7.2%

51. How many square feet are there in 6 1/4 acres?

a. 152,325

b. 272,250

c. 44,650

d. 10,820

52. If a property is assessed at $280,000 and the millage rate is 34.5, what is the amount of tax on the property?

a. $ 9660

b. $ 5850

c. $ 7340

d. $ 6598

53. Craig sold a parcel of land for $ 426,150. He made a profit of 58%. What was the purchase price?

a. $ 348,048.05

b. $ 225,900.10

c. $ 269,715.18

d. $ 173,417.29

54. Velma borrowed $ 6250 for 7 years, paying interest every quarter. The total amount of interest she paid was $3500. What was the annual interest rate?

a. 6%

b. 8%

c. 5%

d. 3%

55. The property tax rate is 71 mills, based upon 30% of the market value of the property. Bob Davis paid $ 170,000 for a home. What will the tax be on his home?

a. $ 3621

b. $ 4108

c. $ 2596

d. $ 3885

56. Marilyn paid 7% commission on the sale of her home. She received net proceeds of $ 348,510.50 on the sale. What was the sale price?

a. $ 372,738.50

b. $ 370,108.50

c. $ 299,995.10

d. $ 286,444.56

57. What percent of a square mile is 350 acres?

a. 27.5%

b. 41.3%

c. 39%

d. 54%

58. Carrie Anderson sold a property for $ 116,000. If the broker received 50% of the commission and Carrie's 60% share of that amount was $ 2, 504.00, what was the commission rate charged on the sale?

a. 9%

b. 7.6%

c. 7.2%

d. 5%

59. What percent of a square mile is a lot 1085 ft. by 900 ft.?

a. 3.5%

b. 7.9%

c. 5.4%

d. 6.1%

60. A lot is 1356 ft. by 690 ft. How many acres does it contain?

a. 21.47

b. 15.22

c. 9.19

d. 10.48

61. To earn a 15% annual cash return on a cash investment, what should be paid for a property that earns $ 4,000 per month and has operating expenses of $ 1850 per month?

a. $ 275,000

b. $ 333,481

c. $ 172,000

d. $ 150,000

62. After paying a commission of 8% and additional expenses of $ 800.00, the seller netted $ 229,300. What was the seller's gross selling price?

a. $ 175,616

b. $ 250,108

c. $ 386,222

d. None of the above

63. What is the total interest paid on a $ 200,000, 30 year mortgage with an interest rate of 8% and a $ 1,467.53 monthly payment?

a. $ 328,310.80

b. $ 528,310.80

c. $ 228,410.75

d. $ 426,000.00

64. If an unimproved $ 335,000 property depreciates at a rate of 3% per year, what is the property worth after 6 years?

a. $ 148,505

b. $ 274,700

c. $ 342,001

d. $ 417,560

65. The replacement cost of a 3 year old building is $ 422,790. What is the value for the total property if the land is worth $ 125,000 and the rate of depreciation is 5%?

a. $ 560,790

b. $ 375,507

c. $ 517,195

d. $ 484,371.50

66. Broker Carol Weaver lists a property for $58,000. The commission rate is 6.5%. Another offer is made through another broker for $53,000 and is accepted. What is Carol's commission as the listing broker?

   a. $ 1630.25
   b. $ 1525.16
   c. $ 1722.50
   d. $ 2415.10

67. What would be the total amount of interest paid on a $ 265,000 30 year loan with a monthly payment of $ 1,323.89?
   a. $ 354,125.16
   b. $ 105,256.43
   c. $ 211,600.46
   d. $ 265,414.50

68. James will have to pay a three point discount in order to get an $ 85,000 mortgage loan. What is the discount amount?

a. $ 1650.00

b. $ 2174.00

c. $ 1912.00

d. $ 2550.00

69. The Lansfords have combined two building lots to build a new home. If the combined assessed value of the lots is $ 150,000.00 and the assessment rate is 62%, how much is the new lot worth, rounded to the nearest dollar?

a. $ 241,935.00

b. $ 200,912.00

c. $ 239,847.00

d. $ 270,943.00

70. You take out a loan for $25,000.00 and pay $ 6000.00/year in interest. What is the interest rate?

a. 3.6%

b. 2.4%

c. 3.8%

d. 2.7%

71. Bill and Mara Peterson are in the process of filing their taxes. For the current year, they have paid $7,500 in mortgage interest. They've also paid $976 in property taxes. Since they are in the 15% tax bracket, what will they save in taxes? (Round to the nearest dollar)

a. $848

b. $1,200

c. $652

d. $1,635

72. After setting a list price for the sale of a client's home, the agent and homeowner decide the price should be reduced by $\frac{1}{4}$. If the original list price is $234,987, what will the new price be? (Round to the nearest dollar)

a. $209,876

b. $176,240

c. $197,378

d. $200,500

73. The main living area in the home is 12 feet x 20 feet. What is the area of that room?

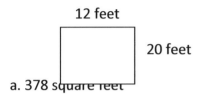

12 feet

20 feet

a. 378 square feet

b. 960 square feet

c. 240 square feet

d. 509 square feet

74. How many acres make up a quarter section of land and if each acre is sold at $1,245, what would be the total sale price?

a. 140; $167,390

b. 160; $239,098

c. 140; $188,354

d. 160; $199,200

75. Burt is a homeowner who has a $246,376 current balance mortgage. His interest rate is 7.25% and monthly payment, $1,625.42. After he makes the next three payments, what will his balance be?

a. $245.962.81

b. $246,239.10

c. $246,101.37

d. $245,843.65

76. Millie Richards purchased a home for $398,764. She put down 27% and requires a loan for the remaining amount. What is the remaining amount of the purchase price.

a. $107,666.28

b. $291,097.72

c. $156,987.09

d. $245,876.34

77. How much will the homeowner pay for 347 square feet if 2400 square feet cost $172,800?

a. $20,674

b. $72

c. $24,984

d. $39,076

78. Gill Persons borrowed $39,876 and pays $3,200/ year in interest. What interest rate is Gill being charged?

a. 9.2%

b. 6.5%

c. 4%

d. 8%

79. Paul Jones has purchased a total of 3600 square feet of land that is 60 feet wide. What is the length of this land?

a. 60 feet

b. 43 feet

c. 89 feet

d. 54 feet

80. Land that measures 6876 square feet and 120 feet in length, measures _____ feet in width.

a. 32.9

b. 57.3

c. 91.7

d. 62.4

81. The broker made a commission on a $452,375 home sale. If the total commission amount is $31,666, what is the broker's commission rate?

a. 3%

b. 5%

c. 7%

d. 9%

82. What is the loan-to-value ratio if the loan amount is $123,000 and value $175,000?

a. 60%

b. 30%

c. 70%

d. 10%

83. What are the annual taxes of a property of the assessed value of the property is $312,000 and tax rate is $1.50 per $100?

a. $2240

b. $3790

c. $1200

d. $4680

84. The annual depreciation of a building is $5,432. What is the total depreciation of an 8 year old building?

a. $47,484

b. $43,456

c. $49,759

d. $41,288

85. The replacement cost of a building is $76,000. The total depreciation of that building is $20,987. What is the current value of the building?

a. $58,000

b. $52,367

c. $55,013

d. $56,909

86. Valerie owns a home that has two mortgages. The balance of the first mortgage is $150,000. The second mortgage balance is $15,000. Valerie has equity of $35,000 in her home. What is the value of her home?

a. $300,000

b. $128,000

c. $190,000

d. $200,000

87. Geraldo is applying for a $120,000 FHA mortgage loan. In order to qualify, he must pay a 3-point discount. What is the discount amount?

a. $3,600

b. $4,500

c. $1,200

d. $2,500

88. Mrs. Snow said her taxes are $2,700 and property assessment $184,000. What is the tax rate percentage?

a. 3.56%

b. 1.46%

c. 2.12%

d. 1.89%

89. Bill has 4,598 square feet of land that is 45 feet wide. What is the land's length?

a. 246 feet

b. 311 feet

c. 102 feet

d. 290 feet

90. Gil Irving borrowed $47,000. He is paying $850 / year in interest. What is the interest rate he is being charged?

a. 2.5%

b. 6.5%

c. 4.7%

d. 1.8%

91. The broker made a commission on a $988,543 home sale. If the total commission amount is $29,656, what is the broker's commission rate?

a. 8%

b. 12%

c. 4%

d. 3%

92. A homeowner who sells his house for $187,000 is required to pay a tax stamp. The tax stamp rate is $2 / $500 of the home's sale price. How much will the seller pay in tax stamps?

a. $748

b. $823

c. $911

d. $456

93. A homeowner sells her property for $409,654 and has to pay a tax stamp in the amount of $1639. If the tax stamp is per $500 of the home sale price, what is the tax stamp rate (per $500)?

a. $7.00

b. $4.50

c. $2.00

d. $6.50

94. The annual depreciation of a building is $4,187. What is the total depreciation of a 20 year old building?

a. $112,876

b. $65,385

c. $83,740

d. $90,215

95. The replacement cost of a building is $128,000. The total depreciation of that building is $36,402. What is the current value of the building?

a. $23,876

b. $37,498

c. $72,366

d. $91,598

96. Chip owns a home that has three mortgages. The balance of the first mortgage is $250,000. The second mortgage balance is $45,000. The third mortgage balance is $15,000. Chip has equity of $65,000 in his home. What is the value of his home?

a. $375,000

b. $45,000

c. $65,000

d. $215,000

97. Paula is applying for a $75,000 FHA mortgage loan. In order to qualify, she must pay a 2-point discount. What is the discount amount?

a. $3,200

b. $1,500

c. $5,354

d. $4,502

98. Mr. Glass said his taxes are $3,540 and property assessment $322,000. What is the tax rate percentage?

a. 4.12%

b. 3.23%

c. 1.09%

d. 2.53%

99. Carl has 6,345 square feet of land that is 37 feet wide. What is the land's length?

a. 454 feet

b. 387 feet

c. 299 feet

d. 171 feet

100. Barbara Ring borrowed $56,000. She is paying $1,354 / year in interest. What is the interest rate she is being charged?

a. 2.4%

b. 3.9%

c. 6.2%

d. 4.5%

Real Estate Sales Exam IX Answers

1. b. Divide the amount of commission by the commission rate=$43,636

2. a. If Fran paid a 6 1/2% commission, then the $456,786 she has left represents the remaining 93 1/2% of the sales price. $456,786 divided by 0.935=$488,541.

3. b. Multiply $220,000 by 0.03=$6600 x 40%=$2640

4. b. Multiply $180,000 by .04%; multiply 180,000 by .01%. Add these totals and the $500=$9500. Subtract $9500 from $180,000=$170,500.

5. a. Multiply $275,000 by 10%=$27,500. Subtract $27,500 from $275,00=$247,500. Multiply this figure by 5%=$12,375

6. b. Subtract $24,000 from the sale price of the house=$301,000. Multiply $301,000 by 4%=$12,040.

7. b. Subtract the original purchase price ($737,222) from the sale price ($4,534,203) = $3,796,981. Divide $3,796,981 by $737,222 = 5.1; 5.1 divided by 15 = 0.34=34%

8. a. Value Now=Original Price – Depreciation. However, to determine this, the rate of depreciation at the end of the 6 years must be found. Value x Rate for 1 year x Period of Years=Rate of Depreciation. 0.0425 x 6=0.25; $305,000 x 0.25=$76,250 (depreciation over 6 years)
Value Now = $305,000 - $76,250 = $ 226,750.

9. c. Multiply the monthly payment by 12 and divide by 0.0856. $7349 x 12 divided by 0.0856 = $1,030,233.

10. d. Multiply the loan amount ($400,000) x 0.65 = $260,000. Multiply $260,000 x .01 = $26,000.

11. b. Commission = Gross Selling Price x Rate of Commission. $235,000 x 6.5% or 0.065=$15,275. $15,275 divided by 2 = $7,637.50.

12. c. Multiply $2,415,720 x 0.14 = $338,200

13. a. Divide $18,000 by $175,000 = 0.10=10%

14. d. From the final value of $215,750, subtract the land value $10,200 and add the amount of depreciation. $215,750 - $10,200 + $5,101=$210,651

15. b. Three months = 3/12=0.25. Divide the interest for three months ($2700) by ($95,000 x 0.25=

$23,750) = 0.1 or 10.

16. c. The number of front feet in the lot must be determined. Divide 6,468 by 132=49 to get the number of front feet. Multiply 49 x $ 980=$48,020=$48,000 rounded

17. c. Divide the sale price ($ 188,000) by 2.6 (lot size)= $ 72,307.69 per acre. Divide $ 72,307.69 by 43,560 (feet in an acre)=1.659 or 1.66 rounded.

18. c. Must calculate the down payment, origination fee, discount, and the PMI fee. Add all of these totals to determine the amount of money needed. Down payment - 15% - $ 232,500 x 0.15=$ 34,875. The origination fee, discount, and PMI fee are calculated as part of the loan amount (not the sales price). The loan will be the sales price less the down payment - $232,500-34,873=$ 197,625. Origination fee (0.75%) is $ 197.625 x 0.0075=$ 1,482.19 rounded. The discount (2.25%) is $197,625 x 0.0225=$ 4,446.55. PMI fee (0.5% or 1/2) is $ 197,625 x 0.005= $988.13. Add $ 34,875 + $ 1,482.19 + $ 4,446.56 + $ 988.13=$ 41,791.88.

19. b. 1.6 x 43,560=69,636 sq.ft. $ 25,100 x 69,636=0.36

20. c. The discount is based on the loan amount. The loan is 90% of $ 77,900 or 0.9 x 77,900=$ 70,100. The discount is 2.5 points or 2.5%. 1025 x $ 70,110=
$ 1,752.75.

21. c. Multiply the frontage (207 ft.) x the depth (317 ft.)=65,619 sq. ft. Multiply 65,619 x $ 4.25= $278,880.75. Multiply 278,880.75 x 0.06=$ 16,732.85.

22. a. The assessed value is 35% of $ 82,000. 0.35 x $ 82,000=$ 28,700. 42 mills is 4.2%. 0.042 x $ 28,700=$1,205.40.

23. c. Value=Net Operating Income divided by the capitalization rate. $ 11,000 x 0.11=$ 100,000

24. a. Subtract operating expenses ($ 1250 per month) from earned income ($ 6,000)=$ 4750. Annual NOI is $ 4,750 x 12=$ 57,000. $ 57,000 divided by 12=
$ 475,000.

25. d. Multiply monthly rents. 40 x $ 950=$ 38,000; 60 x $ 1150=$ 69,000. Add $ 38,000 + $ 69,000=$ 107,000. $ 107,000 x 12=$ 1,284,000.

26. d. Value=Rental Amount x Gross Rent Multiplier- $ 575 x 127=$ 73,025 or $73,000 rounded.

27. b. When using Gross Rent Multiplier, disregard the expense amount. Use the monthly rent of $ 750. Value=rent x Gross Rent Multiplier. $750 x 110=$82,500

28 c. The residence is now worth 160% of what it was worth since it was built. $ 72,000 divided by 1.6=$ 45,000.

29. d. The purchase price will be $ 115,000 divided by (1.12)4=1.12x1.12x1.12x1.12=1.574. $ 115,000 divided by 1.574=$ 73,084=$ 73,000 (rounded)

30. c. Effective depreciation is figured for 20 out of a total of 50 years. 20 divided by 50=0.4=40%

31. d. Net Operating Income is determined by amount of effective gross income less the operating expenses, which are 40% of the effective gross. Net operating income is 60% of effective gross. $ 719,425 x 0.6= $431,655.

32. b. Value of the land will be (1.15)5=2.011. 2.011 x $ 100,000= $201,100 rounded to $ 200,000.

33. c. The comparable home sold for $ 300,000 without a garage. Add $20,000 for the garage= $ 320,000

34. d. $ 20,000 monthly rent x 12=$ 240,000 annually. Subtract the vacancy rate of 9%= $ 21,600 from the annual rent=$218,400.

35. B. Lot=43,560(sq.ft. in one acre) x $ 10 x 1/2=$ 217,800. The house=50 x 50=2500 x $ 75=187,500. Add $ 217,800 + $ 187,500= $ 405,300.

36. d. Multiply sales price of home ($ 300,000) by 6%= $ 18,000. Multiply 18,000 by 55%=$9,900.

37. a. Multiply the mortgage loan amount ($ 300,000) x (1.00-20=.80)=$ 240.000. Multiply $ 240,000 x .02= $ 4,800.

38. d. Multiply $ 250,000 x 6%=$ 15,000. Multiply $200,000 x 4%=$ 8,000. $ 15,000 + $8,000=$ 23,000.

39. b. Multiply the annual earnings ($75,000) by 28% (housing expense to income ratio)=$ 21,000. Divide $ 21,000 by 12 months=$ 1750.

40. c. Interest for the first month will be 1/12 of annual interest on the full loan amount, since none of it will have been paid by during the first month of the loan. 0.07 x $449,000=$ 31,437 annual interest. $ 31,437 divided by 12=$2619.75 interest for the first month.

41. a. When looking for the gross selling price, use: Gross Selling Price=Commission divided by Rate of Commission. $ 7200 divided by 5.5=$130,909.09.

42. c. Rate of Commission=Commission divided by Gross Selling Price. $ 117,525 divided by $1,567,000=0.075 or 7.5%

43. d. First, total the amounts of all the sales= $150,000.Subtract $150,000 from $ 287,000=$ 137,000. Multiply $ 150,000 x 0.06=$ 9,000. Multiply $ 137,000 by 0.06=$ 2,740. Add $ 9,000+ $ 2,740=$ 11,740.

44. b. Assessed value=Actual Value x Assessment Rate. $ 230,000 x 63% (0.63)=$ 344,900.

45. c. Multiply house value ($ 365,095) x 48%= $ 175,245.60. Multiply $ 175,245.60 x 0.033=$ 5783.60

46. d. Value Now=Original Price - Depreciation. First, find the rate of depreciation at the end of six years. Value x Rate for 1 year x Period of Years=Rate of Depreciation. 0.350 x 6=0.21. $ 168,700 x 0.21=$ 33,327. $ 168,700- $ 38,327=$ 125,313.

47. a. $ 790,400 divided by 35 years= $22,582.85. $22,582.85 x 8 years=$ 180,662.85. Subtract $

180,662.85 from $ 790,400=$609,737.15

48. c. After depreciating for 9 years at 4% per year, the building has lost 36% of its original value. (9 x 0.04=0.36). This means that it is now worth the remaining 64% of its original value. If that sum is $170,000, then the original value is $170,000 divided by 0.64=$ 265,625.00.

49. d. Total appreciation is $ 700,000- $576,000=$ 124,000. The total percentage of appreciation is $ 124,000 divided by $ 576,000=21.527% over 6 years is 21.527 divided by 6=35.87% annual rate of appreciation.

50. b. Tony's $17,250 was 60% of the total commission, so $ 17,250 divided by 6%= $287,500. $ 285,500 divided by $ 495,000=0.05% commission rate

51. b. One acre contains 43,560 sq.ft. 6 1/4 x 43,560=272,250

52. a. The millage rate of 34.5 is 34.5%, so tax on $ 280,000= $ 9660.

53. c. If Craig made a profit of 58%, then he sold the land for 158% of its purchase price. $ 426,150 divided by 1.58=$ 269,715.18.

54. b. Velma paid $ 3500 in interest over 7 years. This comes to $500 per year (3500 divided by 7). The annual interest rate is $ 500 divided by $ 6250=0.08=8%

55. d. Taxable value= $ 170,000 x 0.30=$ 51,000. Since 74 mills is the same as a tax rate of 7.1%, the tax is 0.071 x $ 51,000=$ 3885.

56. a. If Marilyn paid 7% commission, then the $ 348,570.50 she has left represents the remaining 93 1/2 % of the sales price. $348,510.50 divided by 0.935=$372,738.50.

57. d. One square mile contains 640 acres. 350 acres divided by 640=0.54=54%

58. b. First, find the amount of total commission. Carrie's share of $ 2650.00 was 60% of the total the firm received. $ 2650 divided by .06=$ 4416 for the firm's share, which was 50% of the total. ($ 4416 divided by .05=$ 8832. $8832 divided by $ 116,000= (0.76=7.6%)

59. a. 1,085 ft. x 900 ft.=976,500 sq. ft. in the lot. Because 1 sq. mile contains 5,280 ft x 5280=27,875,400 sq.ft. 976,500 sq.ft. divided by 27,875,400=0.035=3.5%

60. a. The area is 1356 x 690=935,640 sq. ft. 935,640 divided by 43,560 (number of feet in an acre)=21.47

61. c. Subtract the amount of expenses per month ($ 1850) from the amount of income ($ 4,000)= $ 2150.00. Multiply $ 2150.00 by 12= $25,800 per year. $ 25,800 divided by 0.15 (annual return)=$ 172,000.

62. b. The gross selling price= ($ 229,300 + $ 800= $ 230,100) $ 230,100 divided by 0.92= $ 250,108.

63. a. The monthly payment - $ 1467.53 x 12 x 30= $ 528,310.80. Subtract loan amount ($ 200,000 from

$ 528,310.80= $ 328,310.80.

64. b. Value x Rate x Number of Years=Value over time - $ 335,000 x 0.03= $ 10,050 x 6= $ 60,300. Subtract $ 60,300 from $ 335,000=$ 274,700.

65. d. Replacement Cost x Rate of Depreciation=Depreciation. $ 422,790 x 0.05= $ 21,139.50. $ 21,139.50 x 3=$ 63,418.50.
    Replacement Cost ($ 422, 790) + Land value ($125,000) - Depreciation ($ 63,418.50)= $484,371.50.

66. c. To determine the commission amount, multiply the sale price by the commission rate.

67. c. To determine the total amount of interest paid on the loan, multiply the monthly payment by 12 and then multiply that figure by 30. Take that amount and subtract it form the total amount of the loan.

68. d. To determine the discount amount, convert the number of points to a decimal (.03). Multiply the amount of the loan by the number of points converted to a decimal (.03).

69. a. To determine the worth of the new lot, divide the assessed value of the lots ($ 150,000.00) by the assessment rate (62% converted to a decimal .062). Round that figure to the nearest dollar.

70. b. To determine the interest rate, divide the amount of interest paid by the total amount of the loan.

71. a. The taxpayers will save $848. The calculation for tax savings is the amount paid in interest = the amount paid in property taxes x the tax rate. ($7,500 + $976) x .10 = $848.

72. b. The first step to determining the new list price is to convert $\frac{1}{4}$ to a decimal, which would be .25. Next, multiply .25 times the old list price ($234,987). Subtract this amount from $234,987. $234,987 - $58,747. = $176,240.

73. c. To determine the area of a rectangle or square, multiply the length x width. 20 feet x 12 feet = 240 square feet.

74. d. There are 160 acres in a quarter section of land. Calculate the total sale price by multiplying the number of acres and the price per acre. 160 x $1,245 = $199,200.

75. a. $246,376 x .0725 ÷ 12 = $1,488.52 monthly interest; $1,625.42 - $1488.52 = $136.90 principal; $246,376 - $136.90 = $246,239.10; $246,239.10 x .0725 ÷ 12 = $1,487.69 monthly interest; $1625.42 - $1,487.69 = $137.73 principal; $246,239.10 - $137.73 = $246,101.37; $246,101.37 x .0725 ÷ 12 = $1,486.86 monthly interest; $1625.42 - $1,486.86 = $138.56 principal; $246,101.37 - $138.56 = $245,962.81

76. b. $398,764 x .27 = $107,666.28; $398,764 - $107,666.28 = $291,097.72

77. c. $\frac{172,800}{2400}$ = $72 per square foot; $72 x 347 = $24,984

78. d. 3,200 = 39,876(x)(1)

3200 = 39876x

$$\frac{3200}{39876} = \frac{x}{39876}$$

.080 = x

x = 8%

79. a. 3600 = (x) (60)

$$\frac{3600}{60} = \frac{(x)(60)}{(60)}$$

$$x = \frac{\frac{3600}{60}}{}$$

x = 60 feet

80. b. 6876 = (120) (x)

$$\frac{6876}{120} = \frac{(x)(120)}{(120)}$$

$$x = \frac{\frac{6876}{120}}{}$$

x = 57.3

81. c. $\frac{452,375}{452,375} = \frac{31,666}{452,375}$

x = 0.069

Change to a decimal and round to the nearest whole percent.

0.069 = 7%

82. c. Calculate the loan to value ratio by dividing the loan amount by the value of the property.

83. d. Since the tax rate is $1.50 per $100, divide $1.50 by $100. Multiply the answer by the assessed value ($312,000). This equals $4680.

84. b. annual depreciation x age of the building = total depreciation. $5,432 x 8 = $43,456

85. c. replacement cost – depreciation = current value. $76,000 - $20,987 = $55,013.

86. d. add the mortgages and equity of Valerie's home to determine its value.

$150,000 + $15,000 + $35,000 = $200,000

87. a. (.03) (120,000) = $3,600.

88. b. $\dfrac{2,700}{184,000}$ = .0146 The rate is 1.46%.

89. c. 4598÷45 = 102 feet (rounded)

90. d. I = principal x rate x time. $850 = $47,000(x)(1). $850 ÷ $47,000 = .018, which is 1.8%.

91. d. $\dfrac{988,543}{988,543} = \dfrac{29656}{988,543}$

x = 0.029

Change to a decimal and round to the nearest whole percent.

0.029 = 3% (rounded)

92. a. There are 374 ($500s) in $187,000. Therefore, you multiply the stamp amount per $500, which is $2 times 374.

$2 x 374 = $748

93. c. $\dfrac{\$409,654}{\$500}$ = $819.31

$1639 = (x)($819.31)

$\dfrac{\$1639}{\$819.31} = \dfrac{(x)(\$819.31)}{(\$819.31)}$

2.00 = x

The tax stamp rate is $2.00 per $500.

94. c. annual depreciation x age of the building = total depreciation. $4,187 x 20 = $83,740

95. d. replacement cost − depreciation = current value. $128,000 - $36,402 = $91,598.

96. a. add the mortgages and equity of Chip's home to determine its value.

$250,000 + $45,000 + $15,000 + $65,000 = $375,000

97. b. (.02) (75,000) = $1,500.

98. c. $\dfrac{3,540}{322,000}$ = .0109 The rate is 1.09%.

99. d. 4598÷45 = 171 feet (rounded)

100. a. I = principal x rate x time. $1,354 = $56,000(x)(1). $1,354 ÷ $56,000 = .024, which is 2.4%.

Real Estate Sales Exam X

1. Eleanor Mitchell has inherited a quarter section of land on the death of her father. If she sells the entire quarter section at $1500 per acre, how much will she make?

    a) $150,000
    b) $240,000
    c) $210,000
    d) $300,000

2. The Johnsons have purchased two plots of land. One plot is 80 feet by 30 feet. The other is 50 feet by 40 feet. What is the total area of the land, and how much did the land cost them in total if they paid $125 per square foot?

    a) 4400 square feet; $550,000
    b) 200 square feet; $250,000
    c) 9900 square feet; $1,237,500
    d) 5200 square feet; $650,000

3. The Robinsons purchase a duplex that has a total area of 3000 square feet. Each unit in the duplex is of equal area. They decide to live in one unit and rent the other out to tenants. If they charge $3.25 per square foot per month for the rental property, how much does the rental unit rent for? How much rental income (gross) will they earn in one year, assuming the duplex is occupied for the entire period?

a)$4875 per month; $585,000 per year

b) $9750 per month; $117,000 per year

c) $4875 per month; $58,500 per year

d) $4875 per month; $75,000 per year

4. The Robinsons purchase a duplex that has a total area of 3000 square feet. Each unit in the duplex is of equal area. They decide to live in one unit and rent the other out to tenants. Their mortgage for the property is $627,000. They have a 25 year mortgage at 4% interest. The Robinsons want the income from the rental unit to pay the mortgage on the whole property. How much must they charge per square foot, per month, in rent to make the required amount of money? Round to the nearest dollar.

a) $1.50 per square foot

b) $3.00 per square foot

c) $1.40 per square foot

d) $2.25 per square foot

5. A homeowner sells her property for $740,000. She pays her agent 7% commission. How much does the homeowner make from the sale of this property?

a) $733,000

b) $688,200

c) $222,000

d)$634,700

6. A homeowner sells her property for $740,000. She pays her agent 7% commission. How much does the agent make from the sale of this property?

a) $222,000

b) $5,180

c) $51,800

d) $22,000

7. A homeowner sells her property for $740,000. She pays her agent 7% commission. She also has an outstanding mortgage on the property for $534,000. How much does the homeowner make from the sale of this property?

    a) $733,000

    b) $206,000

    c) $191,600

    d) $88,800

8. Helen owns a house on which she has three mortgages. The amount of the first mortgage is $213,500. The second mortgage is worth $35,000, and the third is worth $14,000. There is $42,500 worth of equity in the home. How much is Helen's home worth?

    a) $42,500

    b) $262,500

    c) $220,000

    d) $305,000

9. An agent sold three houses last year. The first sold for $425,000 and she made a 6% commission on the sale. The second sold for $110,000 and she made 4% commission on the sale. The third sold for $225,500 and she made 6% on the sale. How much total commission did this agent earn from these three sales?

    a) $43,430

    b) $121,680

    c) $40,000

    d) $120,000

10. Last year, Adam paid $1500 in property taxes. His property is assessed at $42,000. What is his annual tax rate? Round to the nearest $1/10^{th}$ percent.

    a) 28%

    b) 4%

c) 3.6%

d) 15%

11. Lauren lives in Center County. The tax rate in Center County is $6.25 per hundred acres. Lauren shares that last year she paid $3100 in property taxes. What is her property assessment?

a) $49,600

b) $4960

c) $193.70

d) $19,375

12. A developer is building a circular pond on a commercial property. The radius of the pond is 10 feet. What is the total area of the pond?

a) 100 square feet

b) 31.4 square feet

c) 62.8 square feet

d) 314 square feet

13. An agent helps a homeowner sell a property for $224,500. The agent earns $15,715 on the sale. What percentage of the total sale price is her commission?

a) 10%

b) 7%

c) 6%

d) 15%

14. Leo is applying for a mortgage of $115,000. He must pay a 3 point discount. What is the amount of the discount?

a) $112,000

b) $5,000

c) $3,000

d) $3450

15. Kendra and Hugh purchase a triangular lot to build a new shop. The lot is 60 feet by 85 feet. What is the total area of the lot?

a) 5100 square feet

b) 145 square feet

c) 290 square feet

d) 510 square feet

16. Kendra and Hugh purchase a triangular lot to build a new shop. The lot is 60 feet by 85 feet. If they pay $0.65 per square foot for the property, how much is the total sale price of the lot?

a) $350

b) $5100

c) $3315

d) $33,150

17. Sharon buys a duplex for $200,000. The duplex is 3200 square feet in area. How much did Sharon pay per square foot for the property?

a) $62.50

b) $125

c) $6.25

d) $.62

18. Richard's property was assessed at $65,000. He paid $2400 in property taxes last year. What is his tax rate?

a) .04%

b) 3.69%

c) 27%

d) .3%

19. The Lelands are purchasing a home that costs $130,000. They are putting down a 5% cash down payment, and they will apply for a mortgage to cover the remaining amount. What will be their mortgage amount, before interest?

a) $125,000

b) $104,000

c) $123,500

d) $6500

20.The Lelands are purchasing a home that costs $130,000. They are putting down a 5% cash down payment, and they will apply for a mortgage to cover the remaining amount. How much will their down payment be?

a) $123,500

b) $65,000

c) $13,000

d) $6500

21. The Lelands are purchasing a home that costs $130,000. They are putting down a 5% cash down payment, and they will apply for a mortgage to cover the remaining amount. They are offered a mortgage with 9% interest. What will be the total amount of their loan?

a) $141,700

b) $134,615

c) $247,000

d) $241,150

22. Sarah owns two properties in Clay County, where the tax rate I $4.75 per hundred square feet. One property is 2000 square feet while the other is 3750 square feet. What is Sarah's total tax bill? Round to the nearest dime.

a) $273.10

b) $2731.50

c) $27.31

d) $95

23. Roland owns one property in Clay County, where the tax rate is $4.75 per hundred   square feet. The property is 3200 square feet. He owns another property in neighboring Stone County, where the tax rate is $3.80 per hundred square feet. That property is 2400 square feet. What is Roland's **total** tax liability for the year?

a) $47,880

b) $476.50

c) $243.20

d) $2432

24. An agent makes an 8% commission on the sale of a $532,000 home. How much money does he make on this transaction?

a) $66,500

b)$425,600

c) $42,560

d) $4,256

25. An agent and a homeowner are working together to determine the list price of a house. The homeowner still owes $115,000 on her mortgage. The agent will make a 6% commission on the sale of the house. If the house is listed for $200,000, how much will the homeowner make on the sale?

a) $0 – the homeowner will lose money on this sale

b) $85,000

c) $127,000

d) $73,000

26. Alice purchases a rectangular piece of land that is 4400 square feet. It is 60 feet wide. How long is the property? Round to the nearest foot.

a) 60 feet

b) 73 feet

c) 80 feet

d) 70 feet

27. An agent and a homeowner are working together to set a listing price for a house. The homeowner would like to make at least $40,000 on the sale. The agent will earn 6% commission for the sale. The homeowner has an outstanding mortgage on the property for $85,000. What is the **lowest** price for which the property can be listed if the homeowner is to make at least $40,000?

a) $100,000

b) $125,000

c) $250,000

d) $135,000

28. Tax stamps in Silver City are $2.00/$500 of a home's sale price. If a homeowner sells his home for $550,000, how much does he owe the city for tax stamps?

a) $2200

b) $1925

c) $17,500

d) $192.50

29. A developer is building a large reflecting pool in the center of a shopping center. She wants the pool to be 15 feet across. What will be the area of the pool when it is completed? Round to the nearest tenth.

a) 706.5 square feet

b) 47.1 square feet

c) 176.6 square feet

d) 25 square feet

30. If 50 square feet of hardwood flooring cost $25.00, how much do 2 square feet cost?

a) $0.50

b) $1.00

c) $0.35

d) $1.25

31. Last year, the Allens paid $1475 in property taxes. Their property is assessed at $75,000. What is their tax rate?

a) 19%

b) .01%

c) 1.96%

d) 5%

32. Leslie wants to fence her backyard. The yard is a rectangle that is 12 feet long and 15 feet wide. How much fencing will she need to fully enclose the yard?

a) 180 feet

b) 27 feet

c) 80 feet

d) 54 feet

33. Leslie wants to fence her backyard. The yard is a rectangle that is 12 feet long and 15 feet wide. The fencing she has chosen is $1.30 per foot. What will the total cost of enclosing the yard be?

a) $234

b) $70.20

c) $35.10

d) $104.50

34. Leslie wants to put a swimming pool in her backyard. The yard is 12 feet long and 15 feet wide. She wants to install a round pool. A pool with all but which of the following diameters will fit in Leslie's backyard?

a) 9 ft

b) 16 ft

c) 8 ft

d) 10 ft

35. Jose has purchased a duplex. He wants to live in half and rent half out. He decides to run a length of fence up the center of the backyard, dividing the yard into two equal halves. The yard is 10 feet wide and 13 feet long. It is already fully fenced. What will be the area of each of the new, smaller yards once he installs the new length of fence?

a) 65 square feet

b) 130 square feet

c) 32.5 square feet

d) 70 square feet

36. The Jones' have purchased a home. They have a mortgage for $155,500 at a 75% loan to value ratio. What is the original value of the home? Round to the nearest dollar.

a) $135,500

b) $272,125

c) $176,233

d) $194,375

37. Samuel lives in Grey County, where the property tax rate is $5.13 per assessed hundred. Last year, he paid $2400 in property taxes. What is the assessed value of Samuel's property? Round to the nearest dollar.

a) $476,836

b) $12,000

c) $4,768

d) $46,784

38. Angela has bought a property with a triangular backyard. The yard is 30 feet long at the base. The side of the yard that is perpendicular to the base is 25 feet. What is the total area of Angela's backyard?

a) 750 square feet

b) 55 square feet

c) 110 square feet

d) 150 square feet

39. Richard buys a property that has a perfectly square backyard. The yard is 35 feet long. He wishes to fence the yard. How many feet of fencing will he need to purchase to enclose the yard?

a) 70 feet

b) 140 feet

c) 1225 feet

d) 35 feet

40. Richard buys a property that has a perfectly square backyard. The yard is 35 feet long. What is the area of the yard?

a) 70 square feet

b) 140 square feet

c) 1225 square feet

d) 3500 square feet

41. Richard buys a property that has a perfectly square backyard. The yard is 35 feet long. The property also holds a house that is perfectly square and 35 feet long. What is the total area of Richard's property?

a) 1225 square feet

b) 3000 square feet

c) 4900 square feet

d) 2450 square feet

42. Richard buys a property that has a perfectly square backyard. The yard is 35 feet long. The property also holds a house that is perfectly square and 35 feet long. If he pays $12.45 per square foot for the property, how much does he pay in total? Round to the nearest dime.

a) $30,502.50

b) $15, 251.30

c) $61,005.00

d) $37,350.00

43. Marianne owns a quarter section of unimproved pasture land. If she breaks it up into 40-acre lots to sell, how many lots will she have?

a) 5

b) 4

c) 8

d) 2

44. Marianne owns a quarter section of unimproved pasture land. If she breaks it up into 40-acre lots to sell, and sells each lot for $27 per acre, how much will she make in total?

a) $1080

b) $2160

c) $4320

d) $3240

45. Marianne owns a quarter section of unimproved pasture land. If she breaks it up into 40-acre lots to sell, and sells each lot for $27 per acre, how much will she make for each lot?

a) $4320

b) $3240

c) $800

d) $1080

46. Julie and Diane are purchasing a house that is listed at $215,450. If they put down a 15% down payment, how much will that down payment be? Round to the nearest dollar.

a) $32,318

b) $14636

c) $3232

d) $5000

47. Julie and Diane are purchasing a house that is listed at $215,450. If they put down a 15% down payment, how much will their mortgage be? Round to the nearest dollar.

a) $247,768

b) $183,132

c) $350,000

d) $315,450

48. Julie and Diane are purchasing a house that is listed at $215,450. They put down a 15% down payment. If they get a mortgage at 16%, how much will their mortgage be? Round to the nearest dollar.

a) $249,922

b) $215,450

c) $212,433

d) $115,450

49. Julie and Diane purchase a house that is listed at $215,450. If the seller had an outstanding mortgage on the home for $75,000 and paid her agent a 6% commission on the sale, how much does the seller make on the sale of the home?

a) $140,450

b) $132,023

c) $202,450

d) $127,523

50. Benjamin and Samantha are trying to choose which house to build. They have the blueprints for two houses that will cost the same amount per square foot to build. The first house is 75 feet by 60 feet and will cost $157,500 to build. The second house is 80 feet by 72 feet. How much will it cost to build the second house?

a) $201,600

b) $157,500

c) $258,000

d) $200,500

51. Benjamin and Samantha are trying to choose which house to build. They have the blueprints for two houses that will cost the same amount per square foot to build. The first house is 75 feet by 60 feet and will cost $157,500 to build. The second house is 80 feet by 72 feet. What is the cost per square foot of building these houses?

a) $50

b) $35

c) $30

d) $45

52. Louis has just bought an investment property that generates a yearly gross income of $325,000. If his operating costs are 60% of his earnings, how much does it cost Louis to operate the property?

a) $75,000

b) $200,000

c) $195,000

d) $175,000

53. Louis has just bought an investment property that generates a yearly gross income of $325,000. If his operating costs are 60% of his earnings, how much does Louis earn from the property?

a) $195,000

b) $300,000

c) $25,000

d) $130,000

54. Louis has just bought an investment property that generates a yearly gross income of $325,000. If his operating costs are 60% of his earnings, and Louis wants his return to be at least 20% of his investment, what is the most Louis can pay for the property?

a) $650,000

b) $500,000

c) $325,000

d) $800,000

55. The replacement cost of a building is $72,800. Its total depreciation is $18,500. What is the value of the building?

a) $91,300

b) $54,300

c) $72,800

d) $60,000

56. The annual depreciation of a building is $4100. If the building is 30 years old, what is its total depreciation?

a) $136,000

b) $123,000

c) $200,000

d) $120,000

57. The total replacement cost of a 20 year old building is $95,000. If the building still has 25 years of useful life left, how much can be charged to annual depreciation?

a) $19,000

b) $47,000

c) $3800

d) $5000

58. If a building has a 5% depreciation rate, how many years of useful life does it have?

a) 100

b) 25

c) 20

d) 50

59. If a building has 25 years of useful life, what is its depreciation rate?

a) 5%

b) 3%

c) 10%

d) 4%

60. The Hendersons are purchasing a home that is listed for $140,000. If they make a 3% down payment, what will be the total value of their mortgage?

a) $4200

b) $135,800

c) $139,700

d) $98,000

61. The Hendersons are purchasing a home that is listed for $140,000. If they make a 3% down payment, and get a mortgage rate of 14%, what will be the total value of their mortgage?

a) $135,800

b) $159,600

c) $144,200

d)$154,812

62. Mariella rents out the top unit of a duplex. Her unit is 30 feet by 35 feet. If she pays $1.50 per square foot in rent each month, how much is her monthly rent for the unit?

a) $1575

b) $1500

c) $2000

d) $1050

63. The Smyths recently put a round swimming pool in their backyard. The pool is 16 feet across. They wish to put a fence around the pool for safety reasons. How much fencing will they need? Round to the nearest foot.

a) 16 feet

b) 51 feet

c) 32 feet

d) 201 feet

64. The Smyths recently put a round swimming pool in their backyard. The pool is 16 feet across. What is the total area of the pool? Round to the nearest foot.

a) 51 square feet

b) 32 square feet

c) 201 square feet

d) 100 square feet

65. The Lindos purchased two adjoining lots. Both lots are rectangular. One lot is 30 feet long and 15 feet wide, while the other is 40 feet long and 20 feet wide. What is the total area of the Lindos' new property?

a) 210 square feet

b) 2450 square feet

c) 2250 square feet

d) 1250 square feet

66. The Lindos purchased two adjoining lots. Both lots are rectangular. One lot is 30 feet long and 15 feet wide, while the other is 40 feet long and 20 feet wide. The purchase price for the first property was $5.50 per square foot. The purchase price for the second property was $4.75 per square foot. How much did the Lindos pay for this property in total?

a) $6,275

b) $25,132

c) $62,750

d) $5,213

67. Harlen owns a piece of property in Greyson County. The tax rate in Greyson county is $4.25 per $100 assessed. His property is assessed at $50,000. What is his tax liability?

a) $21,250

b) $2125

c) $212.50

d) $4250

68. The Smyths recently put a round swimming pool in their backyard. The pool is 16 feet across. They wish to put a fence around the pool for safety reasons. If they choose fencing that costs $3.25 per foot, how much will it cost to fence the pool? Round to the nearest dollar.

a) $325

b) $1600

c) $166

d) $250

69. A broker makes a home sale for $242,000. Her commission is $19,360. What is her commission rate?

a) 6%

b) 7%

c) 10%

d) 8%

70. A broker makes a home sale for $557,500. If her commission rate is 6%, how much does she make on this sale?

a) $33,450

b) $35,000

c) $3,345

d) $134,000

71. A homeowner lists his home for $117,600. If he pays his agent a 7% commission, how much will he make on the sale if the home sells for the listed price?

a) $8232

b) $109,368

c) $115,000

d) $110,600

72. Jesse and James have purchased an investment property. Their operating costs on the property are $162,400. If the operating costs are 55% of their gross income, what is the gross income of the property? Round to the nearest dollar.

a) $893,000

b) $332,800

c) $295,273

d) $775,255

73. The replacement cost of a building is $150,600. The depreciation on the building is $35,700. What is the current value of the building?

a) $186,300

b) $150,600

c) $115,000

d) $114,900

74. The annual depreciation of a building is $2775. If the building is 13 years old, what is its total depreciation?

a) $36,075

b) $21,347

c) $4700

d) $47,000

75. It has been determined that the replacement cost of a 30 year old building is $67,000. The building still has 15 years of useful life in it. How much can be charged to annual depreciation? Round to the nearest dollar.

a) $5,050

b) $4,467

c) $15,750

d) $4,500

76. If a building has an annual depreciation rate of $1460, what is its total depreciation   after 24 years of use?

a) $5,840

b) $24,000

c) $35,040

d) $40,050

77. If a building depreciates at a rate of 4% per year, how many years will it take to reach 100% depreciation?

a) 10

b) 100

c) 75

d) 25

78. An agent sells one home for $372,500. She makes a commission of 7% on this sale. She sells another property for $115,000 and makes a 6% commission on that sale. How much does she make in total from these two sales?

a) $32,975

b) $63,375

c) $18,025

d) $53,775

79. Kara buys a cottage for $70,000. If she pays $24 per square foot for the cottage, what is the total area of the cottage? Round to the nearest foot.

a) 3000 square feet

b) 2917 square feet

c) 7000 square feet

d) 10,000 square feet

80. William is considering a house that is listed at $326,700. If he wants to put 10% down on the property, how much will his down payment be?

a) $10,000

b) $15,000

c) $32,670

d) $52,775

81. The Carringtons purchase a four-plex. The building has a total area of 6400 square feet. If the building is divided into equal sized units, what is the area of each unit?

a) 600 square feet

b) 1200 square feet

c) 800 square feet

d) 1600 square feet

82. The Nelsons purchase a four-plex. The building has a total area of 6400 square feet. The building is divided into equal sized units. If the Nelsons charge $2.50 per square foot, per unit, in rent, how much do they make from each unit per month.

a) $4000

b) $1600

c) $16,000

d) $6400

83. The McGregors purchase a four-plex. The building has a total area of 6400 square feet. The building is divided into equal sized units. If the McGregors charge $2.50 per square foot, per unit, in rent, how much do they make each month from the total property?

a) $4000

b) $16,000

c) $1600

d) $10,000

84. The Halsteads purchase a four-plex. The building has a total area of 6400 square feet. The building is divided into equal sized units. They charge $2.50 per square foot, per unit, in rent. If their operating costs are $500 per unit, per month, how much do they make each month from each unit?

a) $14,000

b) $1100

c) $3500

d) $4500

85. The Harrisons purchase a four-plex. The building has a total area of 6400 square feet. The building is divided into equal sized units. They charge $2.50 per square foot, per unit, in rent. If their operating costs are $500 per unit, per month, how much do they make each month from the entire property?

a) $3500

b) $16,000

c) $6000

d) $14,000

86. Gregory sells his house for $325,000. He sells the house without the help of an agent or broker. He still has an outstanding mortgage on the property for $162,500. How much does Gregory make from this sale?

a) $162,500

b) $325,000

c) $487,500

d) $344,500

87. Bill sells his house for $325,000. He sells the house with the help of an agent whom he pays a 7% commission. He still has an outstanding mortgage on the property for $162,500. How much does Bill make from this sale?

a) $162,500

b) $139,750

c) $22,750

d) $318,000

88. Gary sells his house for $325,000. He sells the house with the help of an agent whom he pays a 7% commission.. He still has an outstanding mortgage on the property for $162,500. How much does the agent make from this sale?

a) $162,500

b) $139,750

c) $22,750

d) $318,000

89. Victor sells his house for $325,000. He sells the house with the help of an agent whom he pays a 7% commission.. He still has an outstanding mortgage on the property for $162,500. If

Victor lives in a county that has a tax stamp rate of $2.00 per $500, what is his tax liability? Round to the nearest dime.

a) $22,750

b) $889.20

c) $780

d) $1300

90. Monica owns a parcel of land. Her tax bill is $1,150. If her tax rate is $2.50 per acre, how many acres is her property?

a) 460 acres

b) 1150 acres

c) 750 acres

d) 115 acres

91. Mr. Perkins owns a quarter section of land. In his will, he wants to bequeath equal portions of the land to all four of his children. How many acres will each child get in the will?

a) 25 acres

b) 40 acres

c) 80 acres

d) 100 acres

92. Mr. Williamson owns three quarter sections of land. If the property tax rate is $0.75/acre, what is his tax liability?

a) $120

b) $75

c) $360

d) $480

93. Mr. Hutchins owns three quarter sections of land. If he sells two of them for $8.15 per acre, how much does he make from the sale?

a) $2608

b) $3912

c) $10,050

d) $2500

94. Katherine buys an investment property that makes annual revenue of $605,750.If her operating costs are 60% of her income, what is her annual operating cost? Round to the nearest dollar.

a) $60,500

b) $363,450

c) $36,345

d) $242,300

95. Bertha buys an investment property that makes annual revenue of $605,750.If her operating costs are 60% of her income, what is her annual net income? Round to the nearest dollar.

a) $60,500

b) $363,450

c) $36,345

d) $242,300

96. Sharla buys an investment property that makes $435,000. If her operating costs are $239,250, what percentage of her total income do operating costs represent?

a) 55%

b) 60%

c) 65%

d) 40%

97. Tara buys an investment property that makes $435,000. She wants to keep her operating costs at 45% or lower. If she is to do, her operating costs can be no higher than which of the following amounts?

a) $195,750

b) $100,750

c) $190,000

d) $165,500

98. Robert buys a rectangular plot of land that is 100 ft long and 42 feet wide. What is the total area of the property?

a) 142 square feet

b) 4200 square feet

c) 42,000 square feet

d) 14,200 square feet

99. Daniel buys a rectangular plot of land that is 100 ft long and 42 feet wide. If he pays $5 per square foot, how much does he pay for the property?

a) $542

b) $4200

c) $21,000

d) $210,000

100. Alex buys a rectangular plot of land that is 100 ft long and 42 feet wide. He makes some improvements to the land. It is assessed at $44,0000. The land is now worth how much per square foot? Round to the nearest dollar.

a) $100

b) $25

c) $5

d) $10

Real Estate Sales Exam X Answers

1. b. Ms. Mitchell will make $240,000 from the sale of her quarter section. There are 160 acres in a quarter section of land. The calculation for the total sale price of the quarter section is the number of acres (160) multiplied by the per-acre sale price ($1500). 160 x 1500 = $240,000.

2. a. The Johnsons have purchased 4400 square feet of land, at a total cost of $550,000. To determine the area of the land, perform the calculation (80)x(30) + (50)x(40) = A. 2400+ 2000 = A. A = 4400 square feet. To determine total cost, perform the calculation 4400 x $125 = $550,000.

3. c. The Robinsons have purchased a property that is divided into 2 units of 1500 square feet each. At $3.25 per square foot, the rental unit rents for $4875 per month (3.25) x (1500) = 4875. If the unit occupied for the full 12 months, they will earn $58, 500 in rental income: (4875)x(12) = 4875.

4. a. $1.50 per square foot. With interest, the Robinsons' total mortgage on the property is $652,080: (625,000)x(.04) = 25080; (25080)+(625,000) =$652,080. Their yearly mortgage payment is $26, 083.20:

(652,080)/(25) = 26,083.20. Their monthly mortgage payment is $2173.60: (26083.20)/(12) = 2173.60. The rental property is 1500 square feet (3000/2 = 1500). For the Robinsons to make the required amount of money to pay the mortgage out of rental income, they must charge $1.50 per square foot on the rental property: (1.50)x (1500)= 2250.

5. b. The homeowner makes $688,200 after paying the commission to the agent. The agent will make $51800 in commission (740,000)x(.07) = 51800. Subtract the commission amount from the total sale (740,000)-(51800) = 688,200.

6. c. The agent makes $51,800 from the sale of this property. Find the commission amount: (740,000)x(.07) = 51,800.

7. d. The homeowner makes $88,800 after her agent's commission and paying off the outstanding mortgage. First figure out the amount the homeowner makes after the agent's commission on the sale: (740,000)x(.07)= 51,800. Subtract the commission from the total sale price to find what the owner makes from the sale: (740,000)-(51,800)= 688,200. Then subtract the outstanding mortgage from the seller's earnings: (688,200)-(534,00)= 88,800.

8. d. Helen's house is worth $305,000. To find the total worth of the house, add together all the mortgages and the accumulated equity: (213,500)+(35,000)+(14,400)+(42,500)= 305,000.

9. a. The agent made $43,430 in commissions off these sales. To calculate this, first determine the commission the agent made on each sale:

Sale 1: (425,000)x(.06) =25,500

Sale 2: (110,000)x(.04)= 4,400

Sale 3: (225,500)x(.06)= 13,530

Then add all three commissions to get the total: (25,500)+(4,400)+(13,530)= 43,430

10) c. Adam's tax rate, when rounded up, is 3.6%. To find this rate, calculate the percentage of the assessed value represented by $1500: (1500)/(42000)= .0357 = 3.57% = 3.6%
11) a. Lauren's property is assessed at $49,600. To calculate, first turn $$6.25 into a percentage: 6.25. Then convert to a decimal: 0.0625. Then calculate: (3100)/.0635 = $49,600.

12) d. The area of the pond is 314 square feet. To calculate, perform the calculation $A = \Pi r^2$. In this case, r = 10, so r^2 = 100. Π = 3.14. So A = (3.14)x(100) = 314 square feet.

13) b. The agent's commission is 7% of the total sale price. To calculate this, perform the calculation 222500x = 15715; x = (15715)/(222500)= .07. Convert to percentage = 7%.

14) d. The discount amount is $3450. Points are percentages, so a 3 point discount is 3% of the total loan amount. Calculate $x = (.03)(115000) = 3450$

15) a. The lot is 5100 square feet in area. For a triangle, A = bh [base * height]. Calculate the area by performing $A = (85)*(60) = 5100$

16) c. The total cost of the lot is $3315. First find the number of square feet in the lot by performing A = bh: $A = (85)*(60) = 5100$. Then find the total cost by calculating $x = (5100)*(.65) = \$3315$.

17) a. Sharon paid $62.50 per square foot for her duplex. To calculate, perform the calculation $\$200000 = 3200x = x = (200000)/(3200) = 62.5$.

18) b. Richard's tax rate is 3.69 percent. To calculate, perform $65000x = 3200$. $x = (3200)/(65000) = .0369$. Convert to a percentage: 3.69%.

19) c. The Lelands' mortgage amount, before interest, will be $123,500. First find the amount of their down payment: $x = (130000)* (.05) = \$6500$. Subtract the amount of the down payment from the total cost of the house: $x = (130000)-(6500) = 123,500$.

20) d. The Lelands will make a $6500 down payment. Calculate by performing: $x = (130000)* (.05) = \$6500$.

21) b. The Lelands' total mortgage amount will be $134615. First calculate the amount of the down payment: Calculate by performing: $x = (130000)* (.05) = \$6500$. Subtract the amount of the down payment from the total cost of the house: $x = (130000)-(6500) = 123,500$. They will need to ask to finance $123,500. Figure the amount of interest by calculating: $x = (123500)*(.09) = 11115$. Then add the interest to the loan amount: $x = (123500)+ (11115) = \$134,615$.

22) a. Sarah's total tax bill in Clay County is $273.10. First, total the number of square feet on which she pays tax: $x = (2000)+(3750) = 5750$. Then convert $4.75 per 100 square feet to a percentage: .0475. Calculate the tax bill: $x = (5750)*(.0475) = \$273.129$. Round to the nearest dime: $273.10.

23) c. Roland's total tax liability is $243.20. To calculate, first calculate the taxes owed on each piece of land. Convert the tax rate to percentage: $4.75 = .0475 and $3.80 = .038. Then calculate the taxes owed on Property 1: $x = (3200)*(.0475) = 152$. Then calculate the taxes owed on Property 2: $x = (2400)*(.038)= 91.20$. Add these two together for the total tax bill: $x = (152)+(91.20)= 243.20$

24) c. The agent makes $42,560. To calculate, perform: $x = (532000)*(.08) = 42560$.

25) d. The homeowner will make $73,000 on the sale if the house lists and sells for $200,000. To determine this, first calculate the expenses: x = (commission) + (mortgage debt), so x = (commission)+(115,000). Determine the commission: x = (.06)*(200000) = 12000. Then calculate expenses: x = (12000)+(115000) = 127000. Then subtract expenses from sale price: x = (200000)-(127000)=73000.

26) b. 73 feet. To find the length of a rectangular piece of land when you know the area and the width, calculate: l = A/w or l = 4400/60 = 73.33333. Rounding to the nearest foot, the length is 73 feet.

27) d. $135,000. For the homeowner to net at least $40,000 on the sale, the property cannot be listed and sold for less than $135,000. To calculate this price, you first need to determine the expenses for each option given: x = (commission) + (mortgage), then subtract that total from the asking price to see how much the seller would net. Figure the commission: x = (price)* (.06). If the property is listed for $135,000: x = (135000)*(.06) = 8100. Add this to the mortgage debt: x = (8100)+(85000)= 93,100. Subtract from the offering price: x = (135000)-(93100)= 41900. So the seller would make at least $40,000 without having to offer the property at a price higher than $135,000.

28) a. The homeowner owes $2200 for tax stamps. To calculate, first figure out how many $500s are in the home's sale price: x = 550000/500 = 1100. There are 1100 units of $500 in the price. Then multiply by the tax rate: x = (1100)*(2.00) = 2200.

29) c. The pool will be 176.6 square feet in area if it is built with a diameter (width) of 15 feet. To calculate area of a circle: A = Πr^2. In this case, we know the diameter, so to find r: r= d/2 or r = 15/2 =7.5. Thus, A = (3.14)*(7.5^2) = (3.14)*(56.25)= 176.625 square feet. Rounded to the nearest tenth, this is 176.6 square feet.

30) b. Two square feet of hardwood flooring cost $1.00. To figure this, first determine the cost per square foot of the flooring: x = (50)/(25.00) = 0.50. Then multiply the cost per square foot by the number of feet you desire: x (2)*(.50) =1.00.

31) c. The Allens' tax rate is 1.96. To figure this, calculate the tax rate based on the amount paid and the assessment amount: x = 1475/75000 = .0196. Convert the decimal to a percent: .0196 = 1.96%.

32) d. Leslie will need 54 feet of fencing to enclose her backyard. To calculate this, calculate the perimeter. Since the yard is a rectangle, you know that it has four sides, and the parallel sides are equal length. Add the length of all sides together to get the perimeter: x = (12)+(12)+(15)+(15) = (24) +(30)= 54 feet. Perimeter is measured in linear, not square, feet.

33) b. It will cost Leslie $70.20 to purchase the fencing. To calculate this, calculate the perimeter. Since the yard is a rectangle, you know that it has four sides, and the parallel sides are equal length. Add the length of all sides together to get the perimeter: x = (12)+(12)+(15)+(15) = (24) +(30)= 54 feet. Perimeter is measured in linear, not square, feet. Then multiple the feet of fencing needed by the cost per foot: x =

(54)*(1.30) = 70.2.

34) b. A pool with a diameter of 16 feet will be too large for Leslie's backyard. To determine this, you first need the area of the yard: A = lw = (12)*(15)= 180. Leslie's yard is 180 square feet in area. Then determine the area of the potential pools: A = Πr². Remember that r= d/2. So a pool with a 9 ft diameter would have a 4.5 ft radius: A = (3.14)(*4.5)(4.5) = 63.58 square feet. A pool with a 16 ft diameter would have an 8 ft radius: A = (3.14)*(8)(8) = 200.96 square feet (which will not fit in the yard). A pool with an 8 ft diameter would have a 4 ft radius: A = (3.14)*(4)(4) = 50.24. A pool with a 10 foot diameter would have a 5 ft radius: A = (3.14)*(5)(5)= 78.5. Only the 16 ft diameter pool is too large for the yard.

35) a. The new yards will each be 65 square feet. To calculate, first find the area of the entire yard: A = lw = (10)*(13) = 130. Then divide the area in half: x = 130/2 = 65.

36) c. The Jones' home is worth $176,233. T the loan amount ($155,500), is 75% of the home's total value. To calculate total value, perform (.75)x=155500) = x = 155500/.75 = 207333. Add this value to the loan value (20733)+(155500) = x = 176233.

37) d. Samuel's property is assessed at $46,784 (rounded to the nearest dollar). To calculate, perform: (.0513)x = 2400 = x= 2400/.0513 = 46783.6. When rounding to the nearest dollar, the value is $46,784.

38) a. Angela's yard is 750 square feet in area. For triangles, A =bh. Calculate A = (30)*(25) = 750. You do not need to know the measurement of the side of the yard opposite the right angle to calculate the area.

39) b. Richard will need to purchase 140 feet of fencing to enclose the yard. Because it is perfectly square, all the sides are the same length: 35 feet. To calculate the amount of fencing needed, find the perimeter of the yard: x = (35)+(35)+(35)+(35) = 140. Perimeter is measured in linear, not square, feet.

40) c. The total area of Richard's yard is 1225 square feet. The formula for the area of a rectangle is A = lw. Because squares are rectangles with sides of equal length, you can use this formula. Calculate: A = (35)*(35) = 1225 square feet.

41) d. Richard's property has a total area of 2450 square feet. First find the area of the yard. The formula for the area of a rectangle is A = lw. Because squares are rectangles with sides of equal length, you can use this formula. Calculate: A = (35)*(35) = 1225 square feet. Then find the area of the house using the same formula: A = (35)*(35) = 1225. Add the two areas together to find the total area: x = (1225)+(1225)= 2450.

42) a. Richard pays $30,502.50 for the property. First find the area of the yard. The formula for the area of a rectangle is A = lw. Because squares are rectangles with sides of equal length, you can use this formula. Calculate: A = (35)*(35) = 1225 square feet. Then find the area of the house using the same formula: A =

(35)*(35) = 1225. Add the two areas together to find the total area: x = (1225)+(1225)= 2450. To calculate total cost, perform x = (total area)*(price per sq ft) = x = (2450)*(12.45) = 30,502.50.

43) b. Marianne will have 4, 40-acre lots if she breaks up the quarter section in this way. A quarter section is 160 acres. To determine how many 40-acre lots a quarter section contains, calculate: 40(x)=160 = x= 160/40 = 4.

44) c. If she sells all the lots at $27 per acre, Marianne will make $4320. First, calculate the cost of each lot: x = (40)*(27) = 1080. There are 4, 40-acre sections on a quarter section. Take the cost of each lot (1080) and multiply by the total number of lots (4): x = (1080)*(4) = 4320.

45) d. Marianne will make $1080 for each 40-acre lot. Calculate the cost of each lot by taking the number of acres and multiplying it by the price per acre: x = (40)*(27) = 1080. Because you are looking for individual lot price, it is not necessary to multiply by the total number of acres in a quarter section.

46) a. Julie and Diane will make a down payment of $32,318 if they put 15% down on the house. To calculate this, find 15% of the total cost, $215,450: x = (.15)*(215450) = 32317.50. Rounded to the nearest dollar, this is $32,318.

47) b. Julie and Diane's total mortgage will be $183,132 after their down payment. First calculate their down payment: Find 15% of the total cost, $215,450: x = (.15)*(215450) = 32317.50. Rounded to the nearest dollar, this is $32,318. Subtract the down payment from the total cost of the house: x = (215450)-(32318) = 183132.

48) c. Julie and Diane's total mortgage will be $212,433. First calculate their down payment: Find 15% of the total cost, $215,450: x = (.15)*(215450) = 32317.50. Rounded to the nearest dollar, this is $32,318. Subtract the down payment from the total cost of the house: x = (215450)-(32318) = 183132. Then multiply the total mortgage amount by the interest rate to get the amount of interest charged: x = (183132)*(.16) = 29301.12. Add the interest to the base mortgage rate: x = (183132)+(29301.12)= 212433.12. Round to the nearest dollar: $212,433.

49) d. The seller will make $127,523 on the sale. To find this, first calculate the total expenses: x = (mortgage) + (commission). The agent's commission is calculated by x = (215250)*(.06) = 12927. Figure the total costs: x = (75000)+(12927) = 87927. Subtract expenses from the sale price: x = (215450)-(87927)= 127523.

50) a. The second house will cost $201,600 to build. First calculate the cost per square foot. Find the area of the first house: A = lw = (75)*(60) = 4500. Then find the cost per square foot of the first house: 4500x =157500 = x = 157500/4500 = 35. The cost per square foot is $35. Now find the area of the second house: A = lw = (80)*(72)= 5760. Then multiply the area by the cost per square foot: x = (5760)*(35)= 201600.

51) b. The cost per square foot for both houses is $35. Find the area of the first house: A = lw = (75)*(60) = 4500. Then find the cost per square foot of the first house: 4500x =157500 = x = 157500/4500 = 35. The cost per square foot is $35. Since the problem states that both houses cost the same per square foot, the cost of the second house is also $35 per square foot.

52) c. It costs Louis $195,000 to operate the property. To find operating costs, calculate: x = (gross)*(percentage) or x = (325000)*(.60) = 195000.

53) d. Louis earns $130,000 from the property each year. First calculate operating costs. To find operating costs, calculate: x = (gross)*(percentage) or x = (325000)*(.60) = 195000. Then subtract operating costs from gross income: x = (325000)-(195000)= 130000.

54) a. The most Louis can pay for the property is $650,000. First calculate operating costs. To find operating costs, calculate: x = (gross)*(percentage) or x = (325000)*(.60) = 195000. Then subtract operating costs from gross income: x = (325000)-(195000)= 130000. To find out what the total purchase price would be, calculate: 130000 = (.20)x = x = 130000/.20 = 650000.

55) b. The total value of the building is $54,300. To calculate total value, perform: x = (replacement value)-(depreciation) or x = (72,800)-(18,500) =54300.

56) b. The building's total depreciation is $123,000. To calculate, multiply the annual depreciation by the age of the building: x = (4100)*(30) = 123000.

57) c. The annual depreciation of the building is $3800. To calculate this, usual the straight line formula for depreciation: x = (years of life)*(replacement cost) = (35)*(95000) = 3800.

58) c. A building with a 5% depreciation rate has 20 years of useful life. To calculate, divide 100 by the depreciation rate: x = 100/5 = 20.

59) d. A building with 25 years of useful life has a 4% depreciation rate. To calculate, divide 100 (for 100% depreciation) by the number of years of useful life: x = 100/25 = 4.

60) b. If the Hendersons make a 3% down payment, their total mortgage will be $135,800. First calculate the down payment: x = (140000)*(.03) = 4200. Then subtract the down payment amount from the total sale price: x = (140000)-(4200) = 135800.

61) d. The Hendersons' total mortgage will be $154,812. First calculate the down payment: x =

(140000)*(.03) = 4200. Then subtract the down payment amount from the total sale price: x = (140000)-(4200) = 135800. Then calculate interest: x = (135800)*(.14) = 19012. Then add interest to principle: x = (135800) + (19012)= 154812.

62) a. Mariella's rent is $1575 per month. To calculate, first find the area of the apartment. A = lw or A = (35)*(30) = 1050. Then multiply the area by the price per square foot: x = (1050)*(1.50)= 1575.

63) b. The Smyths will need 51 feet of fencing to enclose their pool. To calculate, find the circumference of the pool: C = 2Πr. Remember that r = d/2 = 16/2 = 8. So C = 2(3.14)(8) = 50.24. To have enough fencing, the Smyths will need to round up and purchase 51 feet of material.

64) c. The Smyth's pool has an area of 201 feet. To calculate, find the area of the pool: A = Πr². Remember that r = d/2 = 16/2 = 8. So A = (3.14)* (8)(8) = (3.14)*(64) = 200.96. Rounding to the nearest foot, the area of the pool is 201 square feet.

65) d. The Lindos' new property is 1250 square feet in area. The formula for the area of a rectangle is A = lw. Find the area of each piece of property. For Property A: A = (30)(15) = 450. For Property B, A = (40)(20) = 800. Then add the areas together A = (450)+(800) = 1250.

66) a. The Lindos paid $6,275 for their property. First, find the cost of each lot. Find the area: The formula for the area of a rectangle is A = lw. Find the area of each piece of property. For Property A: A = (30)(15) = 450. For Property B, A = (40)(20) = 800. Then add the areas together A = (450)+(800) = 1250. Then find the cost for each lot. For Property A: x = (450)*(5.50) = 2475. For Property B, x = (800)*(4.75) = 3800. Then add the two costs together: x = (2475) +(3800) = 6275.

67) b. Harlen's tax liability for this property is $2125. To find, calculate: x = (50000)*(.0425)= 2125. You could also calculate by determining how many $100s are in $50000 (50000/100 = 500) and then calculating x = (500)*(4.25) = 2125.

68) c. The project will cost the Smyths $166. First calculate the circumference of the pool to determine how much fencing they will need. To calculate, find the circumference of the pool: C = 2Πr. Remember that r = d/2 = 16/2 = 8. So C = 2(3.14)(8) = 50.24. To have enough fencing, the Smyths will need to round up and purchase 51 feet of material. Then calculate the cost of the material: x = (51)*(3.25) = 166.

69) d. The broker's commission rate is 8%. To calculate this, perform the calculation 242000x = 19360; x = (19360)/(242000)= .08. Convert to percentage = 8%.

70) a. The broker's commission is $33,450. To calculate this, perform the calculation x = (557500)*(.06) = 33450.

71) b. The homeowner will make $109,368. To figure this, first calculate the agent's commission: x = (117,600)*(.07) = 8242. Then subtract the commission from the total sale price: x = (117600)-(8232) = $109,368.

72) c. Jesse and James' gross income is $295,273. To calculate this, perform: .55x = 162400 or x = 162400/.55 = 295272.72. Rounded to the nearest dollar, x = 295273.

73) d. The current value of the building is $114,900. To calculate, subtract the depreciation value from the replacement value: x = (150,600)-(35,700) = $114,900.

74) a. The building's total depreciation is $36,075. To calculate, multiply the annual rate by the age of the building: x = (2775)*(13) = $36,075.

75) b. The building's annual depreciation is $4,467. To find this, calculate the depreciation rate. You can do this by dividing the total replacement cost (100% depreciation) by the number of years left in the building: x = (67000)/(15) = 4466.66666. Rounded to the nearest dollar, the depreciation value is $4,467.

76) c. After 24 years of use, the building's total depreciation is $35,040. To find this, multiple the annual depreciation rate by the number of years of use: x = (1460)*(24) = $35,040.

77) d. It will take a building 25 years to reach 100% depreciation if it depreciates at 4% per year. To figure this, calculate: (.o4)x = (1.00) = x = 1.0/.04 = 25.

78) a. The agent's total commission is $32,975. Calculate the commission from each sale: x = (sale price)*(commission rate). For Property 1, x = (372,500)*(.07) = 26075. For Property 2, x = (115000)*(.06) = 6900. Then add the two commissions together: x = (26075) + (6900) = $32,975.

79) b. Kara's cottage has an area of 2917 square feet. To calculate, divide the total sale price by the cost per square foot: x = (70000)/(24.0) = 2917.

80) c. If William puts 10% down on the property, he will put down $32,670. To calculate, perform: x = (326,700)*(.10) = $32,670.

81) d. Each unit is 1600 square feet. To calculate, perform: A = (total area)/(number of units). So, A = 6400/4 = 1600.

82) a. The Nelsons make $4000 from each unit each month. To calculate, perform x = (Area)*(cost per sq ft) = (1600)*(2.50) = 4000.

83) b. The McGregors make $16,000 in rent from the property each month. To calculate, find the rent earned from each unit: perform x = (Area)*(cost per sq ft) = (1600)*(2.50) = 4000. Then multiply the per-unit rent by the total number of units: x = (4000)*(4) = 16000.

84) c. The Halsteads make $3500 per unit per month after operating costs. To calculate, find the rent earned from each unit: perform x = (Area)*(cost per sq ft) = (1600)*(2.50) = 4000. Then subtract operating costs from revenue: x = (4000)-(500) = 3500.

85) d. The Harrisons make a total of $14,000 from the property each month after operating expenses. To calculate, find the rent earned from each unit: perform x = (Area)*(cost per sq ft) = (1600)*(2.50) = 4000. Then multiply the per-unit rent by the total number of units: x = (4000)*(4) = 16000. Then calculate the total operating expenses: x = (500)*(4) = 2000. Subtract total expenses from total revenue: x = (16000)-(2000) = 14000.

86) a. Gregory makes $162,500 from the sale of his home. Because there is no agent commission to consider, calculate by subtracting outstanding debt from total sale price: x = (325000)-(162500) = 162500.

87) b. Gregory makes $139,750 from the sale. First, calculate the agent's commission: x = (325000)*(.07) = 22750. Add commission to the outstanding debt: x = (162500) + (22750) = 185250. Subtract the total expenses from the total sale price: x = (325000)-(185250) = 139750.
88) c. The agent makes $22,750 from this sale. Calculate by performing x = (325000)*(.07) = 22750.

89) d. Victor's tax liability is $1300. First, calculate how many 500s are in 325,000 = x = 325000/500 = 650. Then multiply by the tax rate: x = (650)*(2.00) = 1300.

90) a. Monica's property is 460 acres. To calculate, divide the total tax bill by the per-acre rate: x = (1150)/(2.50) = 460.

91) b. Each child will get 40 acres of land. There are 160 acres in a quarter section. Divide the total acreage by the number of children: x = (160)/(4) = 40.

92) c. Mr. Williamson's total tax liability is $360. First, figure the total acreage. There are 160 acres in a quarter section, so x = (160)*(3) = 480. Multiply the total acreage by the per-acre rate: x = (480)*(.75) = 360.

93) a. Mr. Hutchins makes $2608 from the sale. First, calculate the total number of acres sold. There are 160 acres in a quarter section so x = (160)*(2) = 320. Multiply the acres sold by the per acre price: x =

(320)*(8.15) = 2608.

94) b. The operating costs on the property are $363,450. To calculate, perform x = (total revenue) * (percent operating costs). So: x = (605750)*(.60) = $363,450.

95) d. Bertha's annual net income is $242,300. First, calculate operating costs: perform x = (total revenue) * (percent operating costs). So: x = (605750)*(.60) = $363,450. Subtract operating costs from gross annual income: x = (605750)-(363450) = 242300.

96) a. Sharla's operating cost rate is 55%. To determine, divide the total revenue by the operating costs: x = (435000)/(239250) = .55. Convert to a percent: 55%.

97) a. Tara must keep her operating costs below $195,750 to keep them at 45% or lower. To calculate, find 45% of the total revenue: x = (435000)*(.45) = 195750.

98) b. The land has an area of 4200 square feet. To find the area of a rectangle, calculate A = lw: A = (100)*(42) = 4200.

99) c. Daniel pays $21,000 for the property. First, find the area of the land: A = lw: A = (100)*(42) = 4200. Then multiply by the per-square-foot price: x = (4200)*(5.00) = 21000.

100) d. Alex's land is now worth $10 per square foot. First, find the area of the land: A = lw: A = (100)*(42) = 4200. Then divide the total assessed value by the area: x = (44000)/(4200) = 10.47. Round to the nearest dollar: $10.

Made in the USA
Lexington, KY
12 December 2014